Yankee Nomad

Yankee Nomad

a photographic odyssey

by

David Douglas Duncan

HOLT, RINEHART AND WINSTON · NEW YORK · CHICAGO · SAN FRANCISCO

Photography – Text – Design – Production
DAVID DOUGLAS DUNCAN

Printed in Holland by
JOH. ENSCHEDÉ EN ZONEN, HAARLEM

Coordination
H. CLEWITS/ENSCHEDÉ

Bound in Holland by
VAN RIJMENAM, THE HAGUE

Published simultaneously in Canada by Holt, Rinehart and Winston of
Canada, Limited.

Library of Congress Catalog Card Number: 66–10627.

Prologue quotation reprinted from THE PROPHET by Kahlil Gibran
with permission of the publishers, Alfred A. Knopf, Inc.
Copyright 1923 by Kahlil Gibran;
renewal copyright 1951 by Administrators C.T.A.
of Kahlil Gibran Estate and Mary G. Gibran.

81958–0116

First Edition: 1966

To

My Father and Mother
who started me on this journey

Jean
who gave me my first camera

Leila and Sheila
who have shared my life along the way

The Route

Introduction

New York City
12 June, 1966

Dear Reader:

My wife and I first met Dave Duncan in a Geisha house in Tokyo just before—or was it just after?—the Korean war began. That was in the early summer of 1950 as many young people in the United States—and even Japan—will not remember. From the first glimpse it was clear that this youthful photographer was a personality—at once frank, shy, and friendly. He carried a note of freshness, and somehow it was not a surprise to learn that he had never taken a drink or even had a cup of coffee in his life. But don't think he was effete. He had hands that looked as if he had spent the morning picking up fireplugs or tossing bulldozers around for fun.

A few years passed, like minutes, and then Dave, my wife Jane, and I found ourselves having dinner again one dulcet night in Stockholm. By this time he had become one of the best known photographers in the world, but he had not lost his simplicity no matter how tough, audacious and original his pictures were. We were en route to Moscow to do parallel assignments for *Colliers*. David had never been to Moscow before. I described fearfully some of the difficulties we would encounter there, if only because most Russians have skins like porcupines, and do not submit easily even to the wiles of a Duncan. I would call the first match between Duncan and the Soviet Union a draw. He won the second. Meantime we had a wonderful time together—crashing parties, meeting a wide variety of Soviet types, and eating caviar for breakfast.

Since those glowing (but slushy) days in Moscow Duncan and I have met all over the place. And two or three things about him have never ceased to impress me, like his gift for fellowship. This man is a nomad in name only. His passion for his work is continuous and undiluted, with the same target from first to last, taking creative photographs. The camera is his pony. Then too there is the matter of integrity. Read a couple of passages in this book wherein Mr. Duncan tangles with the boss.

Yankee Nomad is an adventure story. The author tells of his years from the time when he was a handy kid who "could play a tune on a Graflex" and got $3 a picture to the present, when he has about 25 cameras and his returns are a shade higher. Classic Duncans are here, from the gaunt, bristly faces of Marines trapped in Korean foxholes to prismatic fantasies of Paris and Picasso. And others will seize and enlarge the imagination too—sheep with blue wool in Ireland, monstrous sea animals off South America, a Greek peasant bandaged to the eyes, and a jamboree of horses in Afghanistan. One shot (Palestine) shows how close Duncan himself came to death fulfilling an assignment; another (South Pacific) was taken not by Duncan at all, but, incredibly enough, was made by the camera itself, jarred by enemy fire.

Anyway take a ride with *Yankee Nomad*. It will be an exciting as well as rewarding journey.

John Gunther

"...the breath of life is in the sunlight

and the hand of life is in the wind."

The Prophet

Prologue

"Dave . . . *please*—you goddamned idiot!
I can't get you out of here if you're hit. Keep your tail down."

Hill 106, Seoul, South Korea. 23 September, 1950 – precisely noon.

Ike Fenton, Captain, Baker Company, Fifth Marines swore at me through bearded, dust-caked, enraged lips. We were old friends.

Mid-autumn sunlight had filled our world. It still did. For all but one of us, that is. For him, the Marine beside me who had been opening his K-ration almost with anticipation—the sunshine made everything look better than it was that day—for him, night was already near. A North Korean sniper's bullet had just thudded into his chest, crumbling him sideways into our hilltop trench. The bold-face label on the waxed, half-open carton seemed ironic:

RATION, INDIVIDUAL, COMBAT

Ike Fenton ordered four other Marine riflemen out of their holes. Slinging the unconscious man in a poncho they suddenly, silently, stood erect, then disappeared over the edge of the hill headed back to where the helicopters could land. Now Ike Fenton's perimeter really was undermanned.

"The dead are dead. It's the wounded that wreck us."
Ike Fenton's bloodshot, angry eyes swept the four empty foxholes where the stretcher bearers had just been at work, then stopped on me.
"Okay. Get your pictures. But for Christ's sake don't get wounded!"
He tore open his K-ration.
"How about killed?"
Ike Fenton almost smiled.
We were old friends.

At dusk I found Leonard Hayworth. He was my reason for rejoining Ike Fenton's assault company after the Inchon landing for the attack upon Seoul. Corporal Leonard Hayworth stood six feet three and resembled actor Errol Flynn playing a Marine corporal in Korea.

Except Leonard Hayworth was small-town, shy and gentle, and a master machine gunner. I had photographed him in tears late one rain- and bullet-swept afternoon two weeks earlier on the Naktong River Perimeter when he had crawled back from his empty gun to plead for more ammunition from his captain, Ike Fenton—his captain who had neither ammo nor replacements for the wounded or the dead, nor aerial support nor radio contact with the rear. And the gooks were attacking. Leonard Hayworth wept his frustration. Ike Fenton's eyes were those of an apostle being crucified upon his own anguish and faith. Then in a shower of grenades, the final shower of grenades, the enemy attack had collapsed and that sodden, worthless hillock remained in Marine hands. My photograph of tear-cheeked, empty-handed Corporal Leonard Hayworth had opened a *Life* magazine story of the fight for the hill. It was called "This Is War."

Now, just before dark, surrounded by his buddies, I fished from my rucksack a copy of *Life*, his copy, which the magazine's editors in New York had rushed to me through their news bureau in Tokyo. One older, bristle-jawed Marine stood on tiptoe to peer over the machine gunner's shoulder. When he saw the opening photograph, he grunted, "Hell! We all cry sometime." Then it was night.

At dawn, the next morning, a North Korean machine gunner shot Marine machine gunner Corporal Leonard Hayworth between the eyes.

That same dawn, on another slope of the hill, the day's first sunlight warmed the friendly earth of nearby foxholes. Ike Fenton and I stretched. Leisurely. The night had seemed bitterly cold. The Marines were still fighting in lightweight summer gear. The gooks, too. But they had spent the night running around all over the lower slopes of the hill, attacking, so probably kept warm. The Marines, curled in their holes ignoring shrieking muscles, nearly froze. Except for those who had straightened into the mortar bursts and machine gun fire, and died. Still, as on each of the three preceding nights, Ike Fenton's skinny hilltop perimeter had held. So the sun felt good.

Lieutenant John Hancock, Baker Company adjutant, sat on the edge of Ike Fenton's commanding officer's double foxhole trying to raise battalion on his walkie-talkie. I turned my backside toward the warming sun. I still was half-embarrassed. The night before, Ike

Fenton had insisted that I share their hospitality. It meant not digging another hole, although crowding him and John Hancock to the edges of theirs. Again, as had happened down on the Naktong River Perimeter when the nearby gooks warmed up their tanks for a night's probe, and even earlier in the Pacific Islands campaigns of World War II, and all the way back during those pre-fight hours when I was boxing at college, my leg muscles and body had quivered and shaken as though I were feverish through most of the night's attack. In that cramped foxhole it was no secret.

Ike Fenton stood watching John Hancock work the radio at our feet. I turned toward the sun, scratching a chest muscle that suddenly tingled, slow to warm. Ike Fenton laughed. He leaned over into the foxhole, then held out his fist. A cleanly designed scrap of metal dropped into my hand. An enemy bullet, at the absolute end of its flight, had just struck me over the heart and fallen to the dirt below.

Later in the day I was a couple of miles and hills closer to the enemy-infested center of Seoul. Baker Company and Ike Fenton had been told to dig in and hold 106, so I was moving along with other Marines who were pointing an attack against the capital's railway station. I wondered a little about luck, and one's fate. And I pondered a bit over my profession.

It had started simply as fun.

* * *

A hot news flash broke into the day's first musical program. The biggest hotel in town was burning to the ground.

Tucson, Arizona. 24 January, 1934 – early morning.

Most of my friends ran out of the fraternity house. Poor guys, they were headed for school, not the blaze, for it was Exams Week on the University of Arizona campus. I was lucky—as

I was to learn later I always would be. I had no tests until later that day. Halfway to the street, starting for town and the fun of watching a really great fire, I stopped. I returned to the house for a glistening, Bakelite, thirty-nine-cent camera, a birthday gift from my younger sister, Jean. It was to become the most significant single move of my life. Even though I was studying archaeology, something deep inside me clicked on the simple combination of fire plus film, adding up to a special formula of adventure for an eighteen-year-old.

That fire did far more than just gut the old Congress Hotel. I ran more than a mile—fearing it would already be out before I arrived—to discover much of the roof in flames, firemen on ladders at the windows, and others at doorways helping the guests to escape. One knot of excitement intrigued me. A middle-aged, half-dressed, rather meek-appearing man kept sneaking around the firemen on guard, trying to re-enter the hotel. He argued that he had dropped his suitcase near his room, in a section not yet burning. I took a couple of shots with my new camera—the first photographs of my life—simply because the frantic little guy reflected the chaos all around. Even though typical, indistinguishable from other men in the crowd, he must have been persuasive. A fireman entered the smoking building to run back out moments later with the suitcase under his arm. I made another shot as he handed it to the grateful guest. Then, with glass and bricks starting to shower into the street, I moved away to "cover" other aspects of the fire.

The next day screaming headlines broke another story—of national interest. John Dillinger, America's most-hunted killer, had been captured right in Tucson. He and his gang had been fire-flushed at dawn from their hideout in the old Congress Hotel. A fireman had gone back into the blazing place for a lost suitcase which had burst open as he stumbled in the smoke, spilling pistols and money all over the corridor. Cramming the stuff back into the valise, the fireman had hauled it into the street where he gave it to its anxious owner. Then he tipped off the cops. My "grateful guest" was Dillinger himself—discovered *after* reading the story, with the film still undeveloped in my toy camera.

Later, I was to improve on hitting newsbreaks with pictures.

Mr. & Mrs. K. S. Duncan
629 West 57 St. Terrace
Kansas City, Missouri

David D. Duncan
University of Miami
Coral Gables, Florida
November 2, 1937

Dear Mother and Dad:

IT WON!

My picture of the Mexican netcaster fisherman won <u>Second Prize</u> of its class in Kodak's National Snapshot Contest.

And my prize?

Each of you sit down in a nice comfortable chair.

I won TWO HUNDERD AND FIFTY DOLLARS!

Two hundred and fifty bucks for one little snapshot. It's impossible. But it's true. *It really is true.* Maybe they'll announce the winners later in the Star there at home. The people at the Miami Daily News here, where I entered the picture in the competition, phoned me at school this afternoon.

Holy mackerel what a day!

I was working on an engraving in Richard Merrick's art class when I was called to the phone down in the hall. It was William Mathews, a reporter for the Daily News. He asked me what I was doing, so I said, as I told you, just working on an engraving. Then he asked if I remembered my old Mexican netcaster. When I said sure, he said, real casually, that it had won "two fifty" in the National Contest which was judged last night up at the National Geographic Magazine in Washington. I was crushed, for I had such hopes for that picture, ever since Bill Britton and I came back from Acapulco last summer. Anyway, I told Mr. Mathews thanks a lot, of course I was happy, but I sure did better in the local, Florida part of the contest where the shot had won twenty-five bucks. Mr. Mathews said, what do you mean better? You just won two fifty. *Two hundred and fifty dollars.* Richard Merrick and the others thought I had gone nuts the way I yelled, ran through the classroom, then dived out the door to tell everyone in the whole town.

Don't pinch me. I never want to wake up.

Dave

10

Yankee

So, it started simply as fun.

Acapulco, Mexico. 1937

Nomad

CHAPTER I

Finished!

Coral Gables, Florida. 7 March, 1938

Today, I graduated. Bachelor of Arts, University of Miami, mid-term, no formalities. Zoology and Spanish. They'll send the diploma later.

That's it ... except I intend to be a photographer.

Photographic Editor   1001 Coral Way
Scribners Magazine   Coral Gables, Fla.
New York, N.Y.   March 9, 1938

Dear Sir:

I have been closely following the photographic selections which you have presented each month, and have gained added pleasure from their quality. I also noted that some have been the work of little known amateur and professional photographers. It seems to be a chance to get started in a really fine publication so I am submitting these three prints in hopes that they prove both of interest and value to you.

"So Weary" is one of my favorite prints, and seems to me to express a mutual understanding between the dog and the old man. They are just "down" but not "out."

In "Wanted" I tried to capture the image of the criminal type, lurking in the shadows and protected by the night. The match was the main source of illumination.

"Bored" is another of my favorite pictures. It was a very lucky shot which turned into one of the most remarkable cat pictures I have ever been lucky enough to make. The very acme of laziness seems personified in that yawn.

Hoping to hear from you, I'll remain   Sincerely,
                                                       David D. Duncan

During those first years as an amateur my camera was rarely out of hand, which sometimes paid surprising rewards. The old timer with his dog was found wandering through Coral Gables—seemingly without money, baggage, plans, or the slightest desire to speak—which took care of my Christmas cards that year. The crook with his cigar was actually my closest boyhood friend, Hank Beardsley, who kept the portrait around for laughs—when he was an undercover agent for the FBI. During those later years, he also once kept me from being tossed into the Federal jail in Miami, when I tried to enter the United States from Honduras without a passport while accompanying a 2½ ton shipment of silver ingots to our own government. It was the first year of the war, all passports of military aged American men were being picked up at the frontiers upon entry, I had arrived at Miami airport before the telegram was received from Washington which was supposed to clarify my mission for the immigration authorities—and I was headed for the pokey, when Hank appeared, took me into overnight custody, and got me safely back on the plane the next morning for Honduras.

Then, there was "Bored", the big old Angora who lived with the Andersons—where I roomed in Coral Gables during college—just lolling around the screened back door awaiting dinner, trying not to fall asleep before the dish arrived. Dad later entered the shot—unbeknownest to me—in a national competition for cat portraits, while I was sailing the Caribbean aboard a 100-foot schooner. It won First Prize *and* $100. My future was silver-lined!

"Flirtation." Miami Beach. 1938. Margaret Wright and fighter Bill Britton, college pals.

Picture possibilities were everywhere in 1938. Picture "stories" were practically unknown. Picture markets were a joke. The guys and girls who used cameras to reflect and interpret this changing world created a new kind of nomadic life and their own professional caste: Photo-journalist.

My closest friends in Florida of 1938—that first year out of college—had two characteristics in common: toughness and an acutely developed sense of timing. Prize fighters, a racetrack bookie, deep-sea divers, a nightbeat cop who captained the national pistol champions—and men of the dark wilderness like Ross Allen, whose life was held in his left hand each time he caught another Everglades diamondback rattlesnake for his venom farm at Silver Springs.

That autumn of 1938,
Scott Harrison of Kansas City
extended an invitation coveted
by many mid-American
game bird shooters—
to join him for a week in
Missouri's quail-laden farmlands
bordering the Ozarks.
The coveys broke fast
for nearby hedgerows
but Harrison was even faster.
He never missed.

23

Life in America
was wondrously uncomplicated
for almost everyone—in 1938.
Hitler, Mussolini, Tojo
were just posturing foreigners
who failed to arouse much concern.
Our image as the open-handed,
atom-armed crusader
had yet to encompass
the entire world—
with its historic border conflicts,
pot-bellied starvation,
loves and hatreds and jealousies,
and the seeds
of convulsive social upheaval.
In all the land,
the whole isolated land,
there was perhaps no place
more remote from reality,
or happier,
than Kansas City, Missouri,
my hometown.

Mr. David D. Duncan
629 West 57th St. Terrace
Kansas City, Missouri

Donna Sutherland
Stevens Hotel
Chicago, Illinois
July 19, 1939

Dear David :–

I'm a few hundred miles nearer <u>home</u> but only to find we are starting off this afternoon to tour the north. When I arrived in Chicago Monday morning and was met by Bob and Mother, they informed me we were to meet Dad, and Clyde with the old open Pierce Arrow, and tour the north. You still know about as much about the trip as I do.

Bob keeps mumbling things about Lake Placid. I tell him you go there for winter sports. Mother has some idea of going up into Canada. Dad wants to go to Indianapolis. As for me, well I don't seem to count much, but if I could put my two cents in and have it hold much weight I'd say "let's go home." I don't believe I'll ever leave home again. Getting back home becomes too involved. I don't see that there is much I can do about it. In a large family you have to go where the flock goes.

I hope you really haven't been just waiting in K.C. for me. If you have I'm sorry to let you down so. You know I'd love to see you before you set out again on one of your long trips. Perhaps you'll find some photography work to keep you busy until I get back, perhaps in a week. Hope you keep busy in K.C. until I arrive. My tennis has probably gone all to pot, without our daily battles.

Best love always,
Donna

My pal Donna's family was exactly the same as ours in that there were five children, four boys and a girl. While my sister Jean was the baby of our family (being two years younger than I, and I was the youngest son—we were all two years apart), Donna was the next to oldest in her family. Both girls were treated and reared almost as fifth sons who could play baseball, basketball, tennis, run or fight like boys. They were as resilient as spring steel. Donna's father, like Dad, was in the lumber business. He was a pioneer around that part of the Middle West. Dad was a young Bostonian from California, who started his own business after he and Mother were married following their meeting at church in Salina, Kansas, two hundred miles west of Kansas City.

Even before the Wall Street Crash of '29 triggered the Great Depression of the thirties, the lumber business—among the first hit—was already in tragic shape, especially the producers who were just converting from mule power to trucks and tractors in the forests. Dad's stands of timber were in the Pacific Northwest and in northwest Arkansas, where thousands of mules were idle, could not be sold, and were almost literally eating his business into the ground. The Duncan Lumber Company failed. We nearly lost Dad when his health broke under the strain of trying to save his company and many of his friends' investments in it.

He next founded a theater corporation, consisting of three suburban movie houses in Kansas

City. On Saturday afternoons as a kid I used to fill entire streetcars with schoolmates and, by running between performances, hit all three shows starting with the two o'clock matinee at the first, ending with the seven o'clock serial at the last. Initially, this movie business went beautifully for Dad, then started into a decline: sound, the "talkies," had arrived and the period of transition was one of disaster for film exhibitors while public taste readjusted.

Of course, Dad and I contributed to the increasing losses at the box office, I with my hordes of free-ticket buddies (my entire school class, time after time, yet Dad never objected; he loved it), to each of whom I grandiosely handed out boxes of pop corn as we climbed into our tiers of seats. But then Dad, perhaps first among the nation's exhibitors, got really enthusiastic and started Bonus Nights for the audiences, too—anything to fill the yawning banks of seats. Thanksgiving and Christmas he gave away dozens of prime turkeys. Between holidays it was Oriental rugs (which he loved) and porcelain dinner services (he was an expert on china, early American furniture, and English silver). The trouble was he admired and believed in the best, so felt that his gifts should reflect this taste. They often cost more than they earned. From a business viewpoint even that might have been tolerable. What probably accelerated the downfall of his cinema empire was his tender-heartedness.

He would stand at the rear exits—in what he assumed was total incognito; ridiculous, because of his Navajo knitted neckties, Harris tweed jackets, silver hair, and Santa Claus smile —trying to spot the most dejected-looking young couples, or the very old patrons, who looked as though they had come to the film because they *had* to win a turkey for their holiday dinner, or not have one at all. So Dad always had a generous extra supply of fat gobblers which he proceeded to hand out in what he hoped was a completely surreptitious way.

After the movie chain went the way of lumber, Dad got deeply involved in the then embryonic airline business of the country. He was too visionary. He bet on planes for hauling special cargo such as flowers, exotic fruit and vegetables, and even Rocky Mountain trout and Maine lobsters into areas of the United States, like the Mid-West, where the residents were almost entirely dependent upon the seasons for changes in their menu since the railroads could not carry such perishables quickly enough to the distant inland markets. Later, he went into life insurance, then finally real estate management with two of my older brothers.

Pauline, Mrs. Alfred Fowler, lived with her husband on the third floor of our home in Kansas City. They had come as a young couple from their homes in Mississippi, Pauline to help my mother with the house and five children while Alfred worked in a home near ours. Tall, slender, speechlessly shy and gentle, Alfred was one of the closest of all friends during my childhood. Having lived through his childhood near some of the great plantations of the South, where wild game abound, it was he who taught me how to handle firearms, and a fraction of his knowledge of the woods. By the time I was twelve I hunted rabbits only with a .22 rifle, and then only when they were running full speed. Later, when I graduated to hunting quail, I matriculated to a 12-gauge shotgun but, I remember, with some regret.

Thanks to Alfred, my autumns during the final two years of primary school were joyous. I was between ten and twelve. He would call at Bryant School, explaining that I was being asked to come home for some family reason, then, after swinging by the house to get our guns, we would head for the great river bottoms south of Kansas City in his Model-T Ford to spend the rest of the day hunting. It was on one of these special holidays that we saw a great barn owl floating away ahead of us through the leafless trees. Alfred posted me at the base of an ancient oak, telling me to watch the lightning-shattered trunk of a nearby giant sycamore—then he disappeared on soundless feet in the direction of the owl. I'd about given up, but was afraid of losing his respect by moving, when that old owl landed right in front of my gun sights. For years thereafter he sat, stuffed, on the piano in our living room, having fallen at my first shot, November 25, 1928. That was also the day I first became bluntly aware of any difference between Alfred and myself—except for his age and wisdom in the woods. We were stopped by the overseer of the farm, who looked at me and said. "Whose boy is *he*?"

Pauline was as robust as her husband was so seemingly frail. She needed both her strength and sense of humor around our home. She suffered with our family as the family when my sister Jean caught fire while playing with matches as a child in the backyard; she worked with her on her exercises for many years afterward until she regained full use of her arms. Pauline was in the midst of the wreckage when the basement furnace of the house exploded; and she was the first to phone the firemen, a short time later, when the roof burned.

She caught hell like all of us when my father stepped into a 50-pound tub of lard while chasing my eldest brother Ken, who was trying to escape a razorstrop thrashing being administered for some probably good reason. She calmly swept up the plaster after the living room ceiling fell, almost upon Ken, one Christmas morning, plus the debris from another corner of the maltreated room after Ken's unloaded 12-gauge shotgun went off through the ceiling, plus the fragments of the second-floor bathroom mirror door when, again, Ken let go a .22 rifle from where he was oiling it in his own room. She dug the slug out of my right leg after my next-to-eldest brother Bob made a mistake regarding the safety on his rifle. I also went to Pauline to be patched up after being thoroughly whipped by brother John, two years older, who had made no mistake in determining which of us had broken his favorite tennis racket. She continued the repairs, shortly thereafter, when Dad caught me hard at work chopping down the third tree of a matched line of poplars which bordered our tennis court. I resented not being included with others of the family whom he had invited to a Sunday afternoon movie. I had been left at home to clean up the mess around my guinea pigs.

Pauline only once drew the line on my greatest hobby, but that was Mother's fault. Late one autumn I moved my collection of non-poisonous snakes into my room, into a converted bookcase with glass doors, so that I could enjoy them while ignoring my homework. The timber rattlesnakes and copperheads, as usual, were still in their double-meshed cage in the backyard. Mother had been taking her afternoon nap. Upon awakening, she was poking around with her bare toes trying to hit the floor—being only five feet tall—and line up her bedroom slippers. She nudged an escaped blueracer that had curled on one slipper to take his siesta, too. Mother eased down to the floor, picked up the drowsy snake by the tail, and walked through the house to my room. She simply handed him to me and turned away with, "Now—they go!" Pauline had always dusted my room only after hanging a bed sheet over the windows of the bookcase. Pauline *offered* to help carry them out of the house.

Pauline burned sugar in the kitchen to kill the smell after catching Hank Beardsley and me smoking our first-ever cigarette in the back pantry. Many autumns she just ducked her head carefully when walking on the front sidewalk, because Hank and I were straddling the gabled roof of the house, blasting with our 12-gauge shotguns the blackbirds that came in at dusk to perch among the tops of the elm trees, which line all of the residential streets of that section of Kansas City. No one ever really complained about our shooting inside the city limits. Not even the cops. They, and Wally the iceman—who tied up his horse and wagon to join the competitions—always got extra exercise playing tennis on our sideyard court.

Nor did Pauline complain when as many as a dozen friends appeared for Saturday morning pancake breakfasts—friends of all five of us—even though she and Alfred had lost hours of sleep making sure it was only Hank, or Chet, or Duncan, or others of our closest pals who were casually climbing up the back—or front—of the house to sleep in the extra room on top.

It was Pauline who seemed to know just what emergency treatment would revive Dad after Ken came home from college, where he had been taught to box, and knocked Pop into an astonished, then unconscious heap in the living room. Ken worked summers on the ice route with Wally, so his slight build was dangerously deceptive. He could handle 100-pounds blocks of ice all day, then still be fresh enough when he got off work in mid-afternoon for as much tennis as anyone wanted to play.

Pauline was the first to appear with a butcher knife the afternoon my foot got entangled in a loop of rope that had fallen from the car door when Ken took off in our Chalmers for a date with his girl. My head had been bouncing on the driveway next to the car's rear wheel, until Pauline's screams and knife set me free. Of course, it was Pauline who first threw water on the blazing table spread I had set afire in protest over being locked in the west sleeping porch after again being caught stealing from the local drugstore; Hank Beardsley, Sam Pearson and Knox Brookfield and Buford Jones never got caught, yet they lifted far more candy and magazines than I ever took and their parents never even knew it. Throughout childhood it was always I who was caught, especially at Bryant School where I was expelled so often that my presence in class for a full unbroken month was considered rather unusual. Naturally, on those autumn days when I was expelled and Alfred had his day off, we slipped up the backstairs at home, got our guns, and went hunting.

Pauline and Alfred Fowler endured the wildest growing years of five Duncan childhoods —and would be willing to do it again, I think.

Kansas City, Missouri,
was "The City" to everyone
who farmed the rolling
alluvial hills nearby,
or fought summer's blasts
and winter's blizzards
on the flattening wheatlands
and cattle ranches
that started just beyond
the city's western limits.
Of course, Chicagoans and
New Yorkers—all Easterners,
saw good old K.C. as just
Hick Town, U.S.A.,
as a gag in musical comedies,
the source of corny jokes
and "K.C. steaks"—
also silence when
chancing upon her bejeweled
Country Club Plaza,
Christmas Eve.

Plowsmen of central Mexico, in the late thirties, had much in common with
mid-western American farmers, and townsfolk, too: black soil,
ingrained religious convictions, insulation in depth from the outer world.
Even erupting Axis conquests were viewed as from another earth and time.

Little more than language, tempo, and the majesty of an eternal land
separated Mexicans from many rural Missourians, in their pursuit of daily life.

Alone on their high mountain lake,
Pátzcuaro's fishermen
also lived tranquil, aloof-from-change lives,
in 1938.
There,
another Mexican,
before Cortez or even Columbus,
fashioned the butterfly nets
as still used by this Tarascan Indian
whose hand
might have been carved
of oak,
for the Madonna
mourning her Son
above the village altar.

My own life in the late thirties
was a tumbleweed,
the least complicated of all—
as when I wrote home
from the fastest schooner
in the Caribbean,
while hunting giant sea turtles
with Cayman Islanders.

Schooner Adams
℅ Captain Allie Ebanks
Cabo Gracias a Dios, Nicaragua.
24 February, 1939

Dear Folks:

Pardon the worse-than-usual scrawl but there are a couple of reasons for it. First, I'm sitting on the afterdeck dodging the mainsail boom, hoping I don't get knocked overboard. We're anchored between two little islands twenty miles off the coast of Honduras while the crew gathers coconuts ashore.

Left Georgetown, Grand Cayman, Tuesday morning and yesterday, after two days sailing, arrived at the Swan Islands to unload a family. They stay on Big Swan growing bananas for the United Fruit Company. I spent the day on Little Swan catching huge iguanas (two are in a sack under my bunk right now) which really look prehistoric. Leathery frills run down their spines. They have beaded old hides of dusty gray or green or even faded rose, piercing eyes, and claws as sharp and long as eagles' talons. They're about six feet from snout to tail— creatures surviving from the beginning of time.

Albert Ebanks
Second Mate

Rudy Ebanks
Seaman

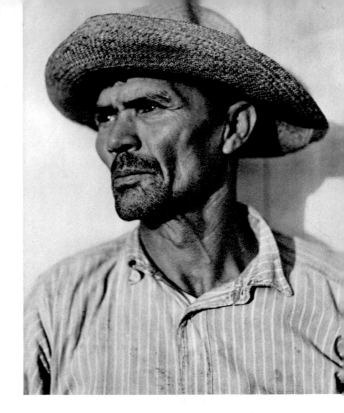

Henry Ebanks
First Mate

As the islands are made of coral which has been eroded
by rain and surf into razor-edged fissures, I managed
to fall down a cliff about fifty feet high. Didn't hurt
my camera but tore up my right arm between elbow and
wrist. Captain Ebanks wasn't prepared for that kind
of repair job so I had the first mate file the barb off a
small fish hook and tighten the eyelet. Then I sewed
everything together again with sail thread that had been
stuck in boiling water. Being right handed made it tough
because everything seemed backwards, but it worked
okay. Captain Ebanks poured iodine on it so it's well
cared for. Should be fine by the time I get home. But I
must look like an old Chinese patched shirt.

Allie Ebanks
Captain

After taking pictures on the little islands this morning,
we soon were cutting coconuts for their milk. Got dirty
chasing another iguana so went right into the surf,
clothes and all. This is the life I've dreamed of. My
shipmates—all cousins—are quiet, proud, hard men.
What more could I ever desire!

Lookouts sought shoals—fifty feet down—to which the great green turtles would return at dusk. Deckmen tossed weighted floats marking every lair. With sunset, Captain Ebanks and his crew sailed dugouts back into those buoy-flecked waters, spreading meshes above rocks where their quarry would awaken during the night to rise and breathe and—if the trap was perfect—be snared. Away from the schooner at dawn—racing sharks to the catch—each Cayman Islander cleared his nets grateful for even an average two-hundred pound turtle. For theirs was an ancient profession, where a boy earned manhood upon an often empty sea.

Only hurricanes drove the Cayman Islanders from the reefs off Nicaragua's Mosquito Coast. Then, with an eye for the sky and another for the sea, they recaptured their turtles in kraals where each week's catch had been herded since the voyage began . . . a rodeo, mostly under water, as wild as any of the bronco-busting West. Noah perhaps captained creatures more varied, but never more bizarre, than those upon our deck when Captain Ebanks ran his loaded schooner north through the Caribbean, toward the waters of home.

Richard L. Sutton, M.D.
Suite 1308 Bryant Building
Kansas City, Missouri
June 24, 1939

Mr. and Mrs. Michael Lerner
c/o The Lerner Shops, Inc.
354 Fourth Avenue
New York City

Dear Mr. and Mrs. Lerner:

Mrs. Sutton was greatly pleased with your kind letter. She told me she would write you, but knowing her as I do, after nearly forty years, I doubt if she does. She seldom writes to anybody except the children.

Your plans for the Summer sound interesting. We did not have very good fishing at Guaymas this season, but the tarpon at Port Aransas did their stuff, and we caught a lot of them. In addition, I taught my grandson how to fish for perch and catfish. He certainly got results! He once caught twenty-two in one morning. Here is a picture of the young gentleman.

We have a fine young photographer here whom I should like for you to try out sometime. His name is David Duncan, and he lives at 629 West 57th Street Terrace, Kansas City, Mo. He is a "natural" with a camera, and he can play a tune on a Graflex. He is a fine, clean young chap of about 23, of good family, and has sold a number of pictures to "Life" and other national publications. Recently, he made a series of turtle pictures off an island south of Cuba. He is anxious to see the world, and I think you could make very satisfactory arrangements with him without going to very great expense. He is a dandy young chap, sensible, well balanced and reliable. If I could afford to do so, I should like to take him North with me for polar bear this Summer. All he asks is a chance. I have the greatest confidence that he will make good.

With all good wishes, I am

Your old friend,
R. L. Sutton

44

My first memory of Dr. Richard L. Sutton dates back to 1923, when I was seven years old and in the first grade of W. C. Bryant primary school in Kansas City.

I had heard that the guest speaker during the following Friday's assembly was to be "Doc" Sutton, Kansas City's famed dermatologist (his textbooks were recognized as nearly classics —required sources—in their specialized field) who was also *our* big-game hunter. He had just returned from an African safari and was scheduled to lecture, supported by lantern slides, elephants' tusks and python skins. There was only one hitch. Attendance was limited to the very old students of the school—the sixth and seventh graders. I clearly remember peeking at Doc Suttons' exhibits the morning of the lecture: the python skin looked as long as a city block—and that did it!

I went to Mr. W. W. Clements, the incredibly severe principal of Bryant who during later years expelled me time after time for such terrible misdemeanors as riding two on a bike, punching Knox Brookfield, or peddling guaranteed *freshly caught* 12-inch ringneck snakes to my classmates for twenty-five cents, money that was intended for their lunch. My mission and message were apparently short and clear: either I be permitted to attend Doc Sutton's lecture —in the front row because I was too small to see over the big guys—or else I was quitting school, forever. Dr. Sutton was told of the ultimatum. Perhaps Mr. Clements also found something appealing in me at that age which he tended to overlook later. I was released from class to attend the lecture: front row center.

The Doctor was almost as much a landmark around Kansas City as was the bronze sculpture of the "Indian Scout" astride his pony which stood in silhouette atop a Parkway hillock. He was a truly elephantine man, standing well over six feet tall, massively framed, slowly shuffling, toes out, and gregarious to the point of being tireless in his quest for friends. Some of them, even he admitted, were "weaselly—hell—even worse than polka-dotted pole-cats" … and he found a place in his affection for them all. He almost always *backed* into the elevators of his medical building until he heard squeals of anguish; he would then reach deeply into his pocket, pull out a fistful of sharks' teeth and Chinese coins, semi-turn to the rear, and beam, "Here! Bless you young ones—take *these* home, Well, take your pick!" Everyone was a "young one", even other grandfathers and grandmothers, and all were treated to the same rumbling, volcanic humor and affection—and to his love of life itself.

He swore brilliantly, yet always reproached Mrs. Sutton: "Mama. Who'n hell is teachin' the young ones *those* words?"

Doc Sutton was unique, maybe my patron saint.

Helen Johnson, my luminously beautiful neighbor who spurned Hollywood, seemed born to fly. According to Joe Jacobson, she could have soloed after that first day's lesson. The story hit most Mid-West roto-pages in my widening picture market. Everyone was thrilled. Especially DDD. It was my first flight, too.

46

Harbor Master
Boston Harbor
Boston, Mass.

David D. Duncan
629 W 57th St. Terrace
Kansas City, Missouri
July 14, 1939

Dear Sir:

I am writing, hoping you might be able to give me some much desired information.
I would like very much to get in touch with a firm operating four-masted schooners to
South America. While recently in Belize, British Honduras, I understood that there was
a firm of Crowe & Thurlowe operating out of Boston, but so far I have been unable to
contact them.
The reason for this interest is that I am a travelling photographer for several of the nation's biggest newspapers, and want very much to film life aboard one of the old-time
vessels. Would like if possible to sail to Buenos Aires, on to Sydney, up to Oslo or
Liverpool, and back to Boston. It won't matter much how long I am away, just so I bring
back the pictures.
The idea is though, that I sail aboard one of the four-masters, preferably as nearly around
the world as possible, and then glorify the life aboard this vessel so as to give the readers
the feeling of having made the voyage themselves.
Perhaps you might have some suggestions as to the features of such a job, which will
make the pictures even more interesting. If so I sure would appreciate any suggestions
you might have to offer.
In hopes that you are able to give me the desired information, I'll remain

Sincerely,
David D. Duncan

David D. Duncan
629 W. 57th Street Terrace
Kansas City, Mo.

LETTER
RETURNED

Boston Police Department
Station #8
Boston Harbor, Mass.
July 17, 1939

Contact
Crowell & Thurlow
131 State Street
Boston, Mass.

Also Contact
Admiral Byrd

%"Bear Of Oakland"

Boston Harbor

Boston, Mass.

For A Trip
To The

North Pole

Dear Mother and Dad:

Shirley Courts, Mexico City. 4 September, 1939

You know, that's just about the most gratifying line a fellow can ever write. I'm so doubly grateful, when I realize that this very evening there are several million other young men in another quarter of the world who may never see home again. May the conflict be kept over there and not entangle the homes we know.

So far I've run into a series of setbacks which completely changed my plans. First, due to torrential rains, I failed in my attempt to drive down the west coast of Mexico and on through to Guatemala.

From all reports I had every reason to believe that the rains were finished, yet I learned soon after crossing the border at Nogales, Arizona, that they were in full swing. Managed to get south of Guaymas, where the trail disappeared into a slough of water. This was after I'd spent a day and night digging the car out of the sandy bottom of an *arroya* where a cloudburst caught me. But it was all well worthwhile because of two unforgettable phenomena, unlike anything seen during my entire experience in the desert. And Sonora is *real* desert, despite the rains. Anyway, each time a downpour stopped, dozens of great Gila monsters—venomous, black-and-orange, bulldog-jawed, two-foot-long lizards—appeared from under the mesquite bushes and started crawling across the trail. All were headed in the same direction—west. I caught the first several, of course, then got bored and released them. It happened for two days, after which I never saw another.

The other incident was as beautiful as that of the Gila monsters was eerie, rather terrible, really. It was a phenomenon of butterflies. Butterflies by the thousands and of every color gathered *on the ground* to watch each pool of rain water sink into the sand. Quivering, multihued choruses of tiny angels clustered in Solemn High Mass—until I had to shoo them heavenward to keep moving back along the trail toward the border.

I returned to Nogales, then drove to Laredo, Texas, and came down the Pan-American highway. Am basing in a sprawling place—once the *hacienda* of Cortez; now run for guests—with a great guy, my age, Jim Shirely and his family. It's home. I've given up all plans for Guatemala and El Salvador, instead am concentrating on what seem to be good pictures within the heart of Mexico—stories on jaguar hunting; Indians who *spear* ducks from canoes; wild orchids near Jalapa; climbing Mexico's towering volcanoes; and a feature on other Indians who *dance* on a whirling disc atop a hundred-foot pole.

All of this is another world from Warsaw—and dive-bombing Stukas . . .

```
TO: MR. DAVID D. DUNCAN          CONSOLIDATED NEWS FEATURES, INC.
    629 WEST 57TH STREET         AUTHOR STATEMENT
    KANSAS CITY, MO.                            OCTOBER 15, 1939

SALES ON: "DAVID DUNCAN PICTURES" FOR SEPTEMBER 1939

SALES:              MILWAUKEE JOURNAL . . . . . . . $6.00 – 2 PICTURES
                    TOTAL SALES  . . . . . . . . . . $6.00
                    50% DUE DAVID D. DUNCAN . . . $3.00
```

There were days when "photo-journalism" as a profession seemed futile. I resolved for the future to seek out markets myself—from start to finish to go it alone.

Mr. David D. Duncan   THE SUN
629 West 57 St. Terrace   Morning Evening Sunday
Kansas City, Missouri   Baltimore, Maryland
                                            November 21, 1939

Dear Mr. Duncan:

I have found three of your Miami Flirtation reflection photographs and five of the Iguana Hunting photographs suitable so far, and am remitting to you our standard rate of $3 per print for those pictures. I have no need for the rattlesnake trapper, nor the aerial co-ed pictures.

I am retaining the pictures on Shark Fishing and Turtling for very likely use in the near future. As soon as I have made selections from those offerings I will return the unused ones to you and remit for those published.

When next you are in Baltimore please give me the pleasure of talking further with you. The last visit was all too brief.

                                            Sincerely yours,
                                            H. Lowrey Cooling
                                            Sunday Editor

Harry Cooling, Sunday Editor of the *Baltimore Sun*, represented a very special breed of men whom it was my privilege and pleasure to meet and "work" with shortly before the war. These were the managing editors and picture editors of many of America's greatest newspapers east of the Rocky Mountains: Cal Eby, of the *Kansas City Star;* Mike Kennedy, of the *Chicago Sunday Tribune;* Thomas B. Sherman, of the *St. Louis Post-Dispatch;* Earl Heap, of the *Washington Star;* Ralph Peters, of the *Detroit News;* Allan Cass, of the *Miami News* (who gave me my first full roto-page, with by-line for payment, then a second one, for which he paid $25 cash when I asked whether he would at least pay for my print costs—and he *still* gave me a by-line, so I chose my life's profession that day); Clyde C. Caldwell, of the *Cleveland Plain Dealer* (who roared in mock indignation when I wrote my name on the backs of some prints and included my middle "D." He claimed I was stealing his line with his middle "C." Finally, there was an erudite Harvard visionary who was at the same time a practical, *total* editor: six-foot-six, two-hundred-and-fifty-pound Robert Endicott, of *Family Circle*, whose genial bulk was an ambling cross-index that spanned the editorial, managerial, and advertising spectrum of American journalism—knowledge which he matter-of-factly shared with me.

For some reason, the West never became an outlet for a single photograph of mine; no interest was ever expressed in them—perhaps because, as one editor told me, "We and our readers really only care about ourselves."

Most of these men were shirt-sleeve editors who had learned and earned their professions in newspaper city rooms, having started there quite often as youngsters. Not one (to my knowledge) had been a reporter or foreign correspondent. Almost all were twenty to thirty years my senior. Yet each treated me as a professional with seemingly equal experience behind me when I called at his desk. Never, that I can remember, did one offer suggestions for making my work more suitable to his paper's needs in anything other than a spirit of two old pros discussing a mutual problem—even though I was young enough to be dating his daughter. Many times, after making selections (or rejections) of my work, they would explain that their schedules were too loaded to take more of my stuff, so why didn't I call on "X" down the street. In fact, sometimes a phone call would even be made on my behalf straight to "X" even though he was editor of the newspaper in direct competition with "my" editor's paper.

Each of these editors seemed to take a deep personal interest in making my break-through successful in the then tepid (except for *Life* magazine) photo-journalistic world. They always gave me full by-lines. If a page appeared without one, it was a makeup room error. Management gave them almost nothing as a picture budget for their roto-pages, usually $3 per photo. Thomas B. Sherman's *St. Louis Post-Dispatch* was the one great exception: his $10 per black-and-white shot and $25 for color seemed like tapping the U.S. Treasury itself. Sometimes efforts were made to crack that ceiling; Mike Kennedy, of the *Chicago Tribune*, for instance, would call in a reporter to ask me a couple of questions about the trip for a textblock, then I could get paid extra. That meant overnighting in a hotel instead of turning my old Ford phaeton—the Dreamwagon—off the highway to the next city and sleeping in the front seat wrapped around the gear-shift knob. It was a fabulous time of meeting rare men. I feel the loss for the younger photographers. Like the roto-page, these men are mostly retired, or gone.

MR. GERALD O'BEIRN   **WESTERN**   JANUARY 8, 1940
HALL BROTHERS, INC.   **UNION**
EMPIRE STATE BUILDING
NEW YORK, NEW YORK

> DAVID DUNCAN FLYING TONIGHT TO TAKE PHOTOGRAPHS
> FOR US IN NEW ENGLAND. WANT HIM TO USE OLDSMOBILE.
> HE WILL CALL FOR IT TUESDAY MORNING
>
>   J. C.

Just . . . "J.C." But that was plenty! Those two initials, when seen by the recipients of telegrams, letters, office requests, project analyses, or simple sheets of pseudo-antique parchment stationery, were enough to conjure up visions of economic Shangri-La—or oblivion; to ram every machine into fullspeed production, or to reverse all whirling wheels and bring the entire plant to an awful, cog-shattering, irrevocable stop. For they were the heraldic seal stamping each decision made by the muscle-jawed, chrome-tempered but folksy Mid-Westerner who was building his cow-town Christmas card factory into a world empire with himself on its throne . . . J. C. Hall of Hallmark. Sir Winston Churchill was later to see *his* work decorate Hallmark greeting cards, but for three weeks of that pre-war American winter of 1940 I had the empire and J.C. to myself.

Cal Eby, the *Kansas City Star's* extraordinarily resourceful and cheerful picture editor, who several times saved my "career" from total financial insolvency by creating assignments in his news area, finally had to admit that he was, for the moment, utterly without roto-page ideas—and so was I. Then one freezing afternoon, as he was weeding out for return my latest published Mexican shots from a pile of other prints on his desk, he shoved his glasses back on his gray crew-cut head and looked up at me.

"Take 'em over to J.C. He might be able to use 'em."

"J.C. Who?", I asked. Cal Eby only glanced at me quizzically, telephone already in his hand, as though I didn't deserve to be in business. Dropping the phone, handing me my prints, reaching for another phone and another stack of pictures which the floor runner had tossed into his basket, he took the time to add, "Not J. C. *WHO*! *J. C. Hall.* Joyce Hall, up at 25th and Grand. He's waiting for you. And say! As you go in, take a good look around—it's filled with the prettiest gals of this town."

Cal Eby was right on both counts: Hall Brothers was loaded. A Hollywood scout would have ended in leg-irons. Talent was perched on stools, at desks, draped over drawing boards, running around as messengers, and even ushering me in to see J.C., who *was* waiting for me. Afterwards I felt that he had bested me on the financial arrangements of our picture deal —something darned hard to do—so I figured there was a lethal logic behind the tactical defenses surrounding his GHQ command post.

The phone rang.

Long distance calling David Duncan.

Kansas City, Missouri. 24 February, 1940

A stranger, a man, came on the line. At first, I thought it was an editor of the *National Geographic Magazine,* which had just bought my turtle fishing story. But this was no one I knew. The operator had not told me where the call originated, and the character didn't offer his name. Then I figured it was my old fighter friend, hammerhead Bill Britton disguising his voice, splurging and phoning me from Miami as a delayed birthday present. Then I *knew* it wasn't Bill, yet refused to let this guy blast me off my feet with his seeming indifference to the mounting time charges on the call, his cheery, almost hillbilly, Missouri drawl (I was sure he was just having fun with me), and his refusal to identify himself or explain his reason for phoning.

"You say it's freezing up theaah?"
Terribly cold.
"And you enjoy taking picteaahs?"
It's my profession.
"Do you keep a camera handy—so's you can use it right awaay?"
Always.
"And you like to travel?"
Just came back from one trip. Hope soon to be off on another.
"Have you got a passport?"
No.
"Can you heaah me okay—nice and cleaah?"
Yes, perfectly.
"Saay. Aren't you curious who I am?"
Maybe you'll tell me.
Laughter.
"Well, can you still *play a tune on a Graflex?*"

"Can you heaah me? I said, 'Can you still pl—'"

Juuudas priest! Are *you* Michael Lerner?
"Yeaaah."
Look! Only Doc Sutton ever used that line about my Graflex. Are you *really* Michael Lerner? And where are you?
"Yeaah. I'm Mike Lerner . . . and I'm glad you can heaah me and *finally* got a bit curious. I'm on a yacht in the Bahamas. How would you like to go big-game fishing with me in a couple weeks? For maybe half a yeaah—off the coast of Peru and Chile."

Today I met a *man!*

The Compleat Angler,
Bimini, Bahama Islands.
9 March, 1940

After flying across the Gulf Stream from Miami—about fifty miles—Chalk landed our little seaplane in the leeward lagoon at Bimini and taxied to the docks where a couple of yachts were tied up. A lone figure stood at the end of the pier leaning against the wind and the prop-wash of our plane as Chalk gunned around to hit his anchor buoy.

No hat. Thick, wild, wind-blown hair swirling around a massive head. Deep-lobed ears flattened against a tree-trunk wrestler's neck. No sunglasses against the glare. Gem-blue, friendly eyes, dark in the wrinkled corners under a broad, heavily furrowed brow. No jacket. Plain cotton long-sleeved sports shirt, impossible to button at the top across the chest and shoulders of the powerhouse below. No belt. Gray slacks, into which his shirt was tucked, yet there were no wrinkles at the waist where those shoulders slanted into pile-driver legs seemingly rooted in the dock. No jewelry. Not even a wristwatch. And no pretense—just a guy who shoved out a gentle, steamfitter's vise of a hand and said, "Hello, David. I'm Mike Lerner."

So, here I am in Bimini.

A moment ago I left Mr. Lerner, after having talked for several hours. He has seen my set of pictures, and I'm quite sure that he likes the work. Of course, it is a different type of picture than I'll be taking on the expedition, but even so he enjoyed the pictorial nature of my work.

An order has just gone to New York for both a Speed Graphic and a Leica. Each will be equipped with a telephoto lens. Film, paper, chemicals—everything is being shipped from New York. So, as an outfit, I could ask for little more. Hope my efforts will justify his and Doc Sutton's confidence.

54

Mrs. Lerner is amazing! She's a world champion fisherwoman, so I expected someone between Barnum & Bailey's "Strong Woman" and Olympic track star, sinewy Babe Didrikson. Boy, how wrong could I be! Mrs. Lerner is tiny! Maybe only five feet two. Whereas Mr. Lerner is about fifty, she's probably ten years or more his junior. He looks as though he was put together with a crow-bar and sledge hammer, and handles himself with the casual ease of men of enormous physical strength. She is finely drawn, instant in her opinions and reactions, and dresses with impeccable simplicity. Her direct dark eyes seem to *see* things the first time, and she truly adores Mr. Lerner, whom she looks at, in flashes, all the time. An intense, lovely—and I'll bet fearless—wren of a person. I already have the feeling of having known Mr. Lerner for years. Now I really look forward to knowing her better while fishing for the giants down in the Humbolt Current.

One aspect of this trip I guess I haven't made clear. It will be an expedition seeking broadbill swordfish, for the American Museum of Natural History in New York. Because the American Museum, like most publicly endowed educational institutions, is always hard pressed for funds sufficient to maintain even minimum professional staffs and daily operational costs, expeditions such as ours are rare indeed. They are paid for by "angels", usually men of considerable means whose personal desires for adventure, exploration, or research coincide with the museum's desire to put an expedition in the field. The two get together. The museum puts up its prestige, influence, advice, and expert members of its staff, while the "angel" puts up his enthusiasm, drive, interest, and *money*. There is no profit motive on the part of the "angel", yet he sometimes gains access to remote corners of the world that no amount of money could ever make possible without museum endorsement.

The museums have nothing to sell and are so broke, generally, they really have a tough time. People who work there are very special in the world today—they work for love, and few ever gain fame wider than the circle of other experts in their field. Now, although not as a zoologist or archaeologist—after all those years at the universities of Miami and Arizona—I am thrilled to be going on an expedition with American Museum people . . . at last. I'll be using my Spanish, too, as the expedition interpreter, so everything that I struggled through in school is beginning to add up.

CHAPTER II

Each day drifting out over the Pacific on balsa rafts, Peruvian fishermen handline the depths as they have been baited since Man first appeared on that arid shore. They hope, as surely did those earlier voyagers, to beat sentinel, satchel-beaked pelicans to the catch. For in these waters, birds are the best fishermen of all.

Lima, Peru. 25 April, 1940

. . . yesterday I visited the Guano Islands of San Lorenzo, directly off Callao. Was about two months too late. The nesting season is finished. Except for one exciting panorama, all I got was a bunch of mediocre shots and a shower bath unique in the entire world. There still were hundreds of thousands of timid cormorants on the rocks. They rose in clouds at my approach. I was downwind.

Flowing north out of Antarctica,
the icy Humboldt Current
passes close to the desert shores
of Chile and Peru,
then swings west
to engulf the Galapagos Islands
before losing itself in the final
vastness
of the outer Pacific.
Somewhere
in that ocean river of frigid water
cruised the object of our search,
an aristocratic wanderer of all seas—
the broadbill swordfish.

Back in early today because of very high seas.

Tocopilla, Chile. 24 May, 1940

When the seas run like that it is all but impossible to sight fish. The tips of the bamboo out-rigger poles on each launch are at least thirty feet long, yet they and the second boat were disappearing between the waves as soon as we cleared port. Broadbill, like submarine captains, submerge to lower levels in such wild weather to where the water is calm. *Sometimes,* however, one will travel with only the points of his fins cutting the surface. This is known as "tipping" and is the hardest of all conditions under which to spot a fish—yet it can be done. So out we went. Mrs. Lerner, sensibly, came back in fairly soon. But Mike Lerner and Captain Doug Osborne are stubborn critters, bless them, and figured they'd come a long way for the "little finny beauties," as Doug calls them. So we stayed out until we started knocking rigging off that poor old boat. Then Mike, shouting over the wind and engine and waves crashing past us, told Doug to head back in toward Tocopilla. "If you can find it. . . I just remembered . . . somebody invited us to a tea party."

62

We have been here for a couple of days, since returning from Iquique on the Peruvian border. No broadbill at all up there, so we sent the launches back again, climbed into some old touring cars, and drove down over the salt and nitrate fields which skirt the whole coast. Anyone thinking that our western deserts are bleak should take a look at this place. *Nothing* grows up there at all and it *never* rains. It is totally bare. Makes Death Valley look like the Garden of Eden.

Tomorrow I get to start fishing with Mrs. Lerner and Captain Bill Hatch—white-haired, hawk-beaked, icy-blue-eyed, and silent—the veteran captain of all big-game fishing captains. Tough? Leaner and stronger than a harpoon pole! I saw him hold, bare-handed, a nearly boated, but plunging, 600-pound swordfish, with the steel wire leader cutting his fingers to the bone, but he wouldn't release his grip until the line itself ran out again, which would have disqualified the fish had he touched it. He was in a seething, wordless fury when he let go. The fish was later boated. But Bill was still mad that night while bandaging his butchered hand; said the deck had been too wet for a good tug-of-war. Bill Hatch is over seventy years old.

63

Don't think for a second that Mrs. Lerner can't match courage and stamina with anyone aboard. Just before we went to Iquique we were many miles offshore—couldn't even see the mountains right behind Tocopilla—when Mike made our regular noon radio-phone call to her launch and learned that she and Bill had spotted broadbills finning. They were hopeful of hitting a fish—her first since arriving in South America almost two months ago. She's had tough breaks ever since we started. Anyway, when we called at 2 o'clock Bill reported that she was hooked into a "nice fish." Coming from super-conservative old Bill we immediately knew there was nothing *nice* about her fish.

Mike ordered in all lines (we usually troll for marlin even though hunting for broadbills) and told Doug to kick it up to full throttle. We found their boat about half an hour later and cruised, at first, in wide circles around them until we could see that her broadbill was a deep fighter. The line was running straight down from her rod tip. As their launch caught the slight swells—luckily almost a calm sea that afternoon—the rod itself bent dangerously. She refused to give him an inch of line unearned, although the brake tension on her reel arced the rod to where we started praying it wouldn't snap.

Sometime after 3 o'clock she had him coming up and Bill reached for the 30-foot steel airplane control cable which served as a leader. At that moment the fish saw the hull of their boat and sounded, straight down. He stopped somewhere around a thousand feet. Mrs. Lerner had fought him, as he plunged, for every foot. That meant taking the full beating weight of the broadbill against her back and shoulders which were in a special harness and buckled to the reel. Remember, Mrs. Lerner is about five feet two and weighs a hundred and ten pounds, maybe less.

Mike asked Doug to put him aboard her boat. We came in prow to prow, without danger to her line or fish. Mike probably would have swum over had he been unable to get there any other way. Then Doug took our launch off a couple of hundred yards in case that spike-nosed submarine suddenly breached or started fighting on the surface. No one was taking the slightest chance. Bill Hatch's eyes never left her rod tip, that barometer of everything happening down in the blackness of the deep ocean where the broadbill, although discovering that he couldn't swim freely, was apparently not even slightly tired.

No one had yet seen him. But from every sign he was a brute. Just before 5 o'clock she had him again rising to the surface. Bill (and Mike, on the little cabinhouse roof) could see the leader ferrule in the gloom below. At that moment the line swung in a tight circle then ripped out and out and out with Mrs. Lerner giving the fish slightly less brake tension to help him run, without fouling the line. By the line's action all aboard were instinctively on the side of the broadbill and knew what had happened. Picking up a blood trail from the hook in its jaws, or somehow sensing its semi-captive condition, a shark must have swept in upon our swordfish. He escaped, perhaps after using his own great weapon in self-defense, for he stopped and lay perfectly motionless—again at one thousand feet, straight down.

64

By 7:15 it was nearly dark and Mrs. Lerner had again pulled that terrible fish up from the ocean bed. He was beaten, thoroughly beaten, this time.

We had been watching through binoculars. When the fight was over, Doug slow-throttled us ever so gently nearer the other boat so that I could get pictures if the light held for the few minutes needed to gaff the giant and hoist it aboard. Bill Hatch had the leader wire safely in hand and was easing the fish alongside to be gaffed. Mike stayed clear. It was his wife's and Bill Hatch's broadbill. Mike was making sure they would get all of the glory. By this time the fish had been clearly seen. Bill and Doug and Mike Lerner are as professional as fishermen come. They estimated that broadbill swordfish to weigh over one thousand pounds, the world's record for women, *and* men.

Daylight was gone. Bill held the fish parallel to the launch. The local boatman on the gaff lunged to sink the barb—and triggered a slow-motion disaster. Instead of going over the broadbill he went *under:* the weight of the gaff pole carried the hook far below the belly level of that huge fish. Its point only grazed him, spurring one last, almost dying effort. With a swish of his mighty scimitar tail, he rolled over and again sank from sight. Unnoticed in the night, the leader cable caught on a gunwale cleat, drew taut, and—snapped.

Tears were on every face. Except Helen Lerner's.

She didn't say one word.

Broadbill swordfish love to travel, or sun bathe, just below the ocean waves. They dive for the depths, fight for the bottom, when hooked. It is an event so rare even they appear astonished that such impertinence could shatter their majestic lives. The great Pacific striped marlin, by contrast, spear the sky when hooked, as though beseeching their God in a far-above heaven, but they rarely throw the barb. Arcing wild-eyed in ever-tighter circles, barely under the surface, martyred upon a slender thread: it is futile. They perish.

By day we hunted broadbill swordfish, each a handful for every man aboard, although the *big* ones, naturally, got away. At night, drifting beyond all shipping lanes, on the far edge of the Humboldt Current, seventy miles offshore, we hooked cannibals: giant Pacific squid.

Again we cut the motor to drift in over our favorite spot.

The Humboldt Current. Northern Peru. Midnight – any night.

Hurrying to the rail we looked down. We drew back reassured. Long phosphorescent tracers were igniting submarine blasts of freezing light. There was no sound. The giant squid were still there. Beaming, Mike Lerner appeared from the cabin carrying the two parcels he had slipped aboard back in Cabo Blanco, our home port. "Now for a little surprise party for these refugees from a nightmare." He opened one package, pulling out a handful of pillow cases. Then, gleefully, "Happy Birthday, me little beauties!" He unwrapped and laid on the deck the most murderous looking fishing rigs any of us had ever seen.

"That's right!" Answering our surprise. "We'll use these pillow cases for squidding. You follow me? No? Well, we'll use them as helmets. Breathe through the bottom, and with little eye-holes cut in front we'll be able to see but the ink from those devils won't get on our faces. With sun goggles underneath it won't get in our eyes, either."

The night before, Doug Osborne had been reluctant to gaff another squid after a firehose blast had struck me at chest level, twisting the camera from my surprised hands and drenching everyone else with ink-saturated water. Used either offensively or defensively, the sepia ink is stored in the squid's body, ready to be shot into the surrounding water. When hooked and lashing on the surface, a giant squid could eject its ink over the gunwale and into the cabin of the fishing cruiser, soaking everything in the way. We had no idea what would happen if it hit our eyes.

"Sure. The helmets are a great idea—if I admit it myself. But these are even better." Mike dangled one of the rigs he had just invented.

"We couldn't snag 'em last night on our twin-hook gear for broadbill. Well, this should work!" His squid-rig hung in a barbed tassel—dozens of small hooks lashed end to end and tied to a 30-foot section of the toughest steel leader cable obtainable.

Two of the rigs soon lay again upon the cockpit floor . . . bitten in half.

"Now when a squid takes one of the hooks into his beak, if only to snap it off, we'll still have a chance of boating him because the other hooks should get tangled in at least one of his ten arms. But come on, me merry spooks. If we don't hurry it'll soon be daylight and they'll all be gone again, down so deep we'll never catch one."

70

Unlike anything experienced by anyone aboard, fishing for giant squid was in a class by itself. There was no waiting while one sat wondering what was happening below. Instead, the problem was to drop baited hooks into the ocean fast enough to sink through upper layers of squid, which attacked in schools, to reach the depths where gigantic horrors prowled alone. No sooner did the hooks fall amid showers of phosphorescence than the rod whipped and snapped. Line faded from Mike's reel, slicing one way, then back, finally straight down—only to lie limp and still. It was impossible to interpret what went on below. As Mike began to reel, the line shot back up. The hooked squid was fleeing cannibalistic hordes of its own kind. On the surface, unable to leap or escape, it sizzled around in hysterical circles for a moment—then streaks of fire closed in from all sides. An incandescent voiceless bomb lit the night-sea around us. Once again the line lay slack. Mike reeled it in. His steel leader wire had been bitten off cleanly just above the hooks.

"Whew!" Doug's exclamation was eloquent. It spoke for us all.

Mike doubled his leader wire. With the new rig overside, his rod arced as the line was yanked in circles. His reel howled; full, then empty, then full—then empty again. The snared squid was eluding one gang of fiends only to hit another. Then, somehow, it got to the surface unnoticed by the hunting swarms below. For seconds it lay resting, shimmering at the center of a widening and inescapable pool of phosphorescence. Betrayed, off it fled. The end came unexpectedly.

Following the pressure of Mike's rod, the squid plummeted straight toward the boat. In that fraction of a second when a crash seemed inevitable, it saw the barrier and reversed to shoot away. Too late. Doug lunged with the gaff, heaved back, and we had a giant squid in the boat with us. It lay immobile at our feet totally helpless out of water. Only then did we see, how truly grotesque was the thing Mike had been fighting.

It was a foul creature.

Drooped across the stern, it measured nine feet. A day later, it still weighed more than one hundred pounds. One end supported ten snakelike tentacles. Each was three inches in diameter at its base. Every tentacle was edged with hundreds of disc-shaped sucker cups, at first glance similar to those of an octopus, but they were even worse. Each cup was lined with calcareous saw teeth, giving the squid a deep-cutting death grip on its prey. Nestled at the confluence of its tentacles glistened a muscle-cushioned black beak sharp enough to sever steel cable. Two baleful, unblinking eyes resembled a pair of fried eggs—with grisly green yolks. That was its head.

A strangulated neck, of solid muscle, joined head to body, which was heavy and round, an over-size rubbery bag, now deflated and changing from brick-red to splotchy mushroom white as the animal died. At its extremity, the body flattened into a pair of caudal flukes used for steering during submarine attack or flight.

An elongated chamber ran the full length and circumference of the body, separating its outer surface from the inner organs. It was a water tank with intakes and a nozzlelike outlet near the beak. When a squid swam, pulsating muscles pumped water inside, then ejected it to rocket the beast through the depths. Its sepia sac squirted stain into the water during stress or attack. But once out of the ocean a squid was harmless except for its beak, which was lethal until the creature was dead—a condition difficult to determine. Local fishermen—and our boat captain—bore maimed hands, witness to the slashing beaks of "dead" squid.

Once again morning sunlight brought reality into what had been a ghostly world. We boated a dozen squirting, thrashing terrors during the night, the biggest fifteen feet long—the first giant Pacific squid ever taken on rod and reel. Others, vastly larger, had been hit in deep water—at over five hundred feet—but were cannibalized alive off the hooks before we got them to the surface and saw them. Their tentacle discs, all that remained, dwarfed anything found on those that were caught. Perhaps even still deeper lived those monsters whose coffee-cup-size disc impressions have been recorded upon the heads of battered whales.

We had been fishing among primordial shadows, probing the unknown.

After basking for a moment in the sun's first warmth, we reeled in our lines. The launch was an ink-splattered mess when we pulled alongside the Cabo Blanco wharf. Our gruesome catch—tentacles dangling—was hoisted ashore. Doug and Bill painted each giant squid with oil, then made plaster casts for the American Museum of Natural History in New York. Mike and Helen Lerner flew away to roam the Incan ruins of Machu Picchu. The rest of us sailed north with an old friend—the Humboldt Current.

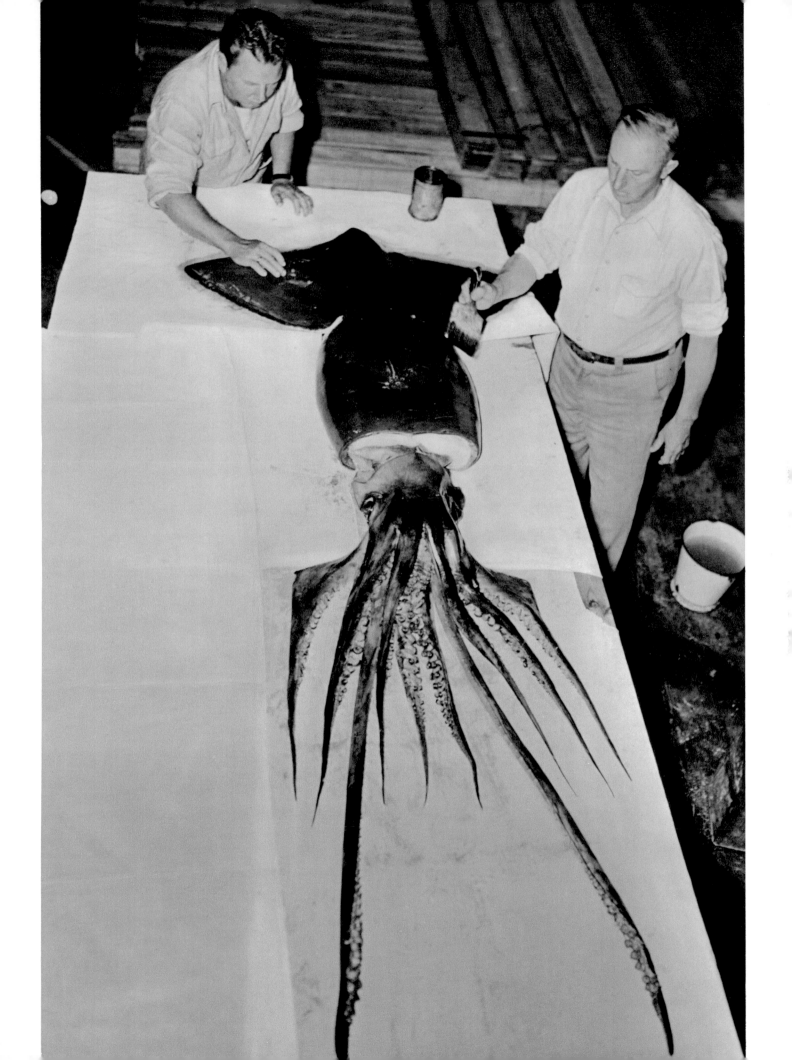

Shortly after returning from South America with a suitcase full of fishing negatives, I received an airmail letter from Washington. All of the promises and dreams of a Utopian picture career seemed to be mine:

National Geographic Magazine
Washington, D. C.
J. R. Hildebrand
Assistant Editor
October 9, 1940

Mr. David D. Duncan
% Public Relations
Pan American Airways
Miami, Florida

Dear Mr. Duncan:

You will be gratified to know that your photographs were so good that you have upset a precedent around here. I take pleasure in enclosing a check as a supplementary honorarium for your two articles; turtles: Capturing The King Of The Mosquito Coast, and swordfishing: Fighting Giants Of The Humboldt. Dr. Grosvenor, the President of the National Geographic Society, has authorized this payment after seeing your photographs, about which he is most enthusiastic.

We are glad to have your assurance of the first and exclusive publication rights to this material, and this honorarium also is sent because it may be some months before we can use either of the articles and release to you after publication the photographs for further distribution.

When you get through Washington again, drop in and see us. We should like to know of other projects you have in mind.

With best personal regards, I am

Very sincerely yours,
J. R. Hildebrand

Then another letter arrived—from just around the corner at home in Kansas City. It cast a sinister shadow across the path and plans of a young gypsy photographer, for behind its permission to leave the country lay the grim specter of what lurked ahead of everyone in the entire happy-go-lucky land.

76

SELECTIVE SERVICE SYSTEM

LOCAL BOARD No. 8
6247 BROOKSIDE ROAD
KANSAS CITY, MO

November 20, 1940

PERMIT OF LOCAL BOARD FOR REGISTRANT TO DEPART
FROM THE UNITED STATES

This is to certify that **David** **D.** **Duncan**

(First name)   (Middle name)   (Last name)

Order No. **1037** , Serial No. **948** , Class _____ , Division _____

(Number)   (Letter)

a registrant of this Local Board has applied for a permit to depart from the United States, and this Local Board, being convinced that said registrant is not likely to be called for military service during the proposed absence and that the granting of such permit will not result in the evasion of or interference with the execution of the Selective Service Law, hereby authorizes the said registrant to depart from the United States and to remain

absent therefrom for **Unknown exactly—probably six months**

(Designate period of absence)

In his application the registrant gave this information:

1. Countries to be visited **South American Countries**
2. Individuals or organizations represented **Pan American Airways**
3. Nature of business **Advertising photography**

Description of registrant:

	Race	**Height** (Approx.)		**Weight** (Approx.)	**Complexion**
White	x	6 Ft.		160 Lbs	Sallow
		Eyes		**Hair**	Light
Negro		Blue		Blonde	Ruddy
		Gray		Red	Dark x
Oriental		Hazel x		Brown x	Freckled
		Brown		Black	Light brown
Indian		Black		Gray	Dark brown
				Bald	Black
Filipino					

Other obvious physical characteristics that will aid in identification _____

Date of birth **Jan 23, 1916**   **Geo W. Catts**

Member of Local Board

The whole Persian carpet of map names in the West Indies became reality when Pan American Airways turned me loose along their routes—with the biggest surprise Trinidad, where I discovered *East Indian* Hindu priests wandering around the back-country, one even carrying his evil-eyed macaw. But for sheer romance, the best of all was that lost land—Yucatán.

Yucatán is even more than I dreamed.

Chichén-Itzá, Yucatán,
Mexico.
9 April, 1941

Carlos, a Mayan Indian of about my age, and I have been going by foot to
many of the ruins, cutting our way in with *machetes*. Usually we see no
other persons than local Indians, who are gentle and handsome and look
amazingly like the stone profiles of their ancient ancestors which we find
carved on the monoliths and temple columns. This is low, slightly rolling,
tree-covered country with lots of wild game, especially a type of jungle
turkey. Many nights have been spent at ruins, others in the colorful inn at
Chichén itself, where the turkeys often end up in the center of our dinner
table. Sometime, I'd like to walk from here to Guatemala with Carlos—ruins
to ruins to ruins—through the forests.

If only I could see a shaggy old
Rocky Mountain billy goat—said to be the
shyest creature in the Canadian wilds...

Edmonton, Alberta. 4 October, 1941

Uneventful, long train trip up, but now I really have seen
the American and Canadian wheat belt, horizon to endless
horizon. The Lerners are grunting and groaning, trying
to make their gear fit into packsacks and duffle bags which
seem to be absolutely full already. My old cameras are
much easier.

We leave early tomorrow morning for a lake back in the
Rockies, east of Jaspar, where we'll pick up the horse-train
and wranglers. Plane's a dual-engined job so we should
make it in one flight, two at most for the equipment.
Be in until November, praying for a break in the
weather—has been rainy and cold thus far, yet it all looks
plenty good to me, after the jungle.

Charlie, the old guide had told me that no one just walked up to a billy. A guy was lucky even to see one—a fleck of white among the peaks. So, the last day, the Lerners said, sure, go try and see one, then they took off for a final crack at big horn rams. At midday I rested slightly below the rim, looking around, wondering if I should find a mountain even higher, when old Mr. Billy Goat popped over the skyline almost on top of me, maybe a hundred feet away. He stood quietly watching something in the meadow far below. He looked so *pure*, and so alone, and so gosh darned big! Probably weighed three hundred pounds. While watching him watch something I couldn't see, I'd been easing up my camera, slower than melting ice, until I had my shots. Then, simply for the hell of it, I called to him, expecting to see some fancy foot-work on the rocks. He only glanced at me, as if to say, "Howdy, son. Saw you all the time. It's those folks down there with guns who interest me most right now. So, if you'll 'scuse me." And he turned his head to look far away.

CHAPTER III

"... *struck just after dawn. Almost all of our war planes were destroyed on the ground at nearby Hickam Field. Our battleships and heavy cruisers were caught at anchor by the first waves of bombers and sunk, trapping many of their crews below decks. Loss of life is still uncalculated, but it is feared to be extremely high. Eye-witness reports from Honolulu describe the entire Pearl Harbor area in flames and covered by heavy oil smoke as more ships, planes, and hangars catch fire and explode. Enemy planes are still overhead. We are now standing by to hear from our Washington correspondent in the press room of the White House, who has already reported Secretary of State Cordell Hull as having been in conference with the Japanese ambassador when the attack began, All further programs originally scheduled for today will be interrupted for any additional accounts of the situation in Honolulu. Keep tuned to this station also for the expected broadcast to the nation by President Roosevelt. We repeat the newsflash: Japanese bombers flying from still undetermined bases this morning are attacking the United States Pacific Fleet base at Pearl Harbor. Hundreds of enemy bombers and fighters swept in over the Hawaiian Islands, seemingly unchallenged, and struck ..."*

Coral Gables, Florida. George Rawlins' Service Station radio.
Sunday, 7 December, 1941 – 1:37 P.M.

88

WESTERN
UNION

MR AND MRS K. S. DUNCAN
629 WEST 57 ST TERRACE
KANSAS CITY MISSOURI

CORAL GABLES FLORIDA
DECEMBER 8, 1941
4 14 PM

JUST PHONED OFFICIALS IN ROCKEFELLERS COORDINATORS OFFICE
AND LAVARRE WONDERING WHETHER I SHOULD FORGET ALL LATIN
AMERICAN PROJECTS AND ENLIST BUT THEY SEEM CONVINCED MY WORK
IS IMPORTANT ENOUGH TO CONTINUE AS PLANNED BESIDES THERE
IS SUCH CONFUSION AT MOMENT IN WASHINGTON AND MORE GUYS
ARE IN UNIFORM THAN CAN BE USED IMMEDIATELY SO THEY ADVISE
ME PROCEED AS SCHEDULED LOVE =   DAVE

* * *

DEPARTMENT OF COMMERCE
Bureau of Foreign and Domestic Commerce
WASHINGTON

December 9, 1941

The bearer, Mr. David Duncan, is traveling in Mexico, Central America, Panama, and Colombia on an important assignment from the Office of Emergency Management...

Any assistance or advice which can be given to Mr. Duncan, especially by Commercial Attachés, Consuls, and Vice-Consuls will be appreciated and will make it possible for him to send back from the field material not only useful in our files but which can be published and featured in the Department of Commerce's weekly magazine, FOREIGN COMMERCE. We are, from the Latin American Republics, especially anxious to secure sets of photographs showing...

We are also anxious to secure photographic records which visualize mines and other developments from which the Defense Supplies Corporation, the Metals Reserve Company, or other companies of the Federal Loan Agency are securing or will secure vital war supplies.

Mr. Duncan's abilities are well-known to me...

The Embassies and Legations of Mexico, Central America, Panama, and Colombia have, at our request, endorsed his passport with special visas...

William LaVarre,
Chief, American Republics Unit.

During the late 1920s and early thirties, America's favorite adventure author was Richard Halliburton with his tales of the romance and risks of swimming at midnight in the foot-deep reflection pool fronting the Taj Mahal. At the same time, a young Virginian was camping along Latin America's steaming jungle rivers, scaling Andean heights to poke among long-forgotten ruins, calmly bartering passage through the Jivaro head-shrinking Indian country, and sipping frosted drinks as a welcome guest of Yankee-hating land barons and banana generals who owned or controlled empires within empires. And always, at the side of the sophisticated, articulate, colonial planter-type wanderer one would see his petite, chestnut-eyed, devastatingly beautiful wife, often in sun helmet, khaki shirt and pants, high laced anti-snake boots, and a revolver at her hip. No one who met them, from the Rio Grande to the Tierra del Fuego, ever fully recovered.

William and Alice LaVarre were the first, and the last, of their kind: individually unforgetable, collectively a fusion of Richard Harding Davis' on-the-spot reporting, Jules Verne's fantasy, *Vanity Fair*'s chic, Cecil B. DeMille's pageant extravaganza, and America's first Good Neighbor Policy ambassadors—a decade before President Franklin D. Roosevelt inaugurated such a program as a national objective. Alice and Bill LaVarre were also great fun, and great friends.

I met them first in the late thirties. Ralph Peters, Sunday editor of the *Detroit News*, sent me to see Bill LaVarre in New York for guidance in selling my roto-page layouts. Peters said LaVarre had had more such experience than anyone else in the United States.

On all of his trips LaVarre had carried a Graflex. With an infallible sense of roto-editors' needs he sent back, or brought in, pre-fab picture pages of everything from Guatemalan tribesmen whose costumes seemed to be copied from Uncle Sam himself—complete with stovepipe hat, star-spangled vest, and striped pants—to illustrated stories of San Blas Indians of Darién hunting alligators for the hides, and the gold nuggets often found in their stomachs—the treasure being scooped up in river clays which the great reptiles apparently ate as digestive aids along with their regular diet of fish, wallowing wild pigs, unwary wading birds, and an occasional San Blas Indian.

Unfailingly in the layouts there were shots of Alice. In one gem she was reclining in a log canoe—shielded from the withering tropical sun by an arched palm frond as she was swept along a jungle-embraced river by stripped-to-the-waist savages with muscles gleaming.

90

Other shots found Alice wading a frothing cascade—water just touching the chin of her heart-shaped, wide-eyed face (closeup)—holding her revolver high and dry atop her sun helmet. She made the cataract look like Cleopatra's bubble bath.

By the time I met him, Bill LaVarre had roto editors churning around him thicker than piranhas at the kill. He had his own nationally syndicated newspaper feature of astonishing facts from Latin America. His books reflected a deep affection for tropical America, where adventure still awaited the twentieth-century explorer. During one expedition into the Colombian jungles he was threatened by a starved, half-mad French escapee from Devil's Island who was shielding a massive diary of that penal colony's horrors. Bill LaVarre helped the human wreck find refuge in the United States, placed the manuscript with competent publishers, and guided its promotion until the book, *Dry Guillotine*, hit the best-seller lists. He did it for nothing.

I walked into his New York office one morning without even phoning. By the time we had finished lunch (I was his guest), he had given me his complete file of American editors who might be interested in my work. Then he phoned two Manhattan editors on my behalf. After looking over my folio of features and offering some humorously critical but easy-to-accept advice about editing for impact, he began wondering aloud where I might dig out new features down in the republics he knew so well.

In one afternoon, Bill LaVarre became a major force in my life.

Just before America's entrance into World War II, Secretary of Commerce Jesse Jones asked LaVarre to join him in Washington to take over the top desk for Latin America at Commerce. Had it not been for their daughter, Yvette, who was still in school, and the fact that both he and Alice periodically suffered relapses of fevers and maladies—some unidentified—contracted during earlier years in the tropics, the LaVarres probably already would have been headed south to aid the war effort in areas which they knew well. Instead, as our friendship grew deeper, they sent me down to take over, as best I could, in a field where they had been the first pioneers. I could easily match Bill's old Graflex with one nearly as battered, but I never touched him for sheer genius in unearthing romantic or hilarious stories in the least likely places. Anyone can do it when world-shattering news is breaking.

And no one ever replaced Alice LaVarre.

That trip to Durango really was something!

Monterrey, Mexico. 27 January, 1942

My purpose for the journey into that wild region was to photograph *guayule*, an astonishing desert shrub, the juices of which are being refined into rubber for the U.S. Army and our war effort, now that the Japs have overrun most sources of natural tree rubber in Southeast Asia and Java.

A few hours before leaving Monterrey I decided to take my Mercury and do my own driving —thank God! The road from Monterrey to Torreón is hard-top and good all the way. From Torreón to Durango I went over a goat trail which was really incredible. Nothing could exaggerate the horrible condition of that little path. No rain had fallen there for months. Deep pools of unbelievably fine dust filled every bump-hollow. Even though scarcely moving forward, I *plowed* into those holes, which when hit by the front tires exploded into fountains of dust higher than the top of the car. The windows were of course kept rolled up, but dust still filled the inside of the car, blinding and choking us simultaneously. Torreón to Durango is only about 175 miles, yet it took 15 hours and I did it without any damage to the car. Even the local people never drive that route between the towns. They catch the train. Now I know why.

I took Ashman Salley from Monterrey. He is the Kodak man here. Very boyishly and not wisely he asked to take his wife, Emma. Very unwisely—and maybe boyishly, too, not to refuse a request which could prove foreseeably difficult—I agreed. So she was with us on that road, at first reading aloud from *How Green Was My Valley*, which I was in no mood to appreciate since I am accustomed to driving by myself, in total silence. Anyway, after Torreón we hit the dust and roughness and discomfort, which were not for a girl—and neither was the country.

You see, for the first time in my life, I ran smack into bandits.

We were high in the wildest mountain plateaus, having just lost even our goat path. It was cloudy and about ten o'clock at night. I was following *a* trail, but not *our* path, through the *mesquite* when I saw a momentary flash of something in the headlights. Then between twelve and fifteen men rose up in front of and around us, all wearing *serapes*, *sombreros*, and with enough rifles, pistols, and knives to scare Pancho Villa himself.

They had the car surrounded in an instant. We were moving just a few miles an hour, as I have mentioned. I had put my window down to ask directions in that moment before realizing what we were facing. The men on my side pointed their armament right at my poor ole heart. It seemed that their chief, a really super character for the part—for he was stocky, swarthy, and his belligerence was equalled only by his shooting equipment—wanted to take the car first, then whatever else we might have. How any of them would have driven my car I'll never know but will always wonder. Anyway, realizing that the setup could get nasty very quickly, I immediately started speaking English just as normally and quietly as possible—yet loud enough for them all to hear.

I felt sure that English would leave them confused and not so sure of their own situation, rather than if we all had been speaking Spanish, which Ashman and Emma handle fluently. I'd already told them to sit absolutely quietly, without speaking, and for Ashman to lock his door, as I had mine.

It worked. One of their gang knew just enough English to want to show off by taking over his chief's position. Even though he didn't get things at all straight as he spoke, or know what he was saying, he at least gave me a second person with whom to speak English and the word *Americanos* keep on the rest of their ears. I also tossed in the name of the governor of Durango, trying to make it sound very familiar. Emma was sitting between Ashman and myself in the front seat, and I could feel her leg muscles quivering and jumping but she didn't utter one peep. Both could understand every word being muttered by the cut-throats outside, yet both sat silently, giving me a chance.

It went on for about fifteen minutes with that half-drunk highwayman leaning on the car with his head poked in my face. He was dragging out the stupid discussion—and so was I. None of them seemed to realize that by standing in front of the car they could stop me for sure. Also, their curiosity and desire to hear and see us better pulled them to the sides of the car. So when all of them were on each side of the car, momentarily discussing among themselves what to do next, I hit the gas and let out the clutch . . . and darned near keeled over with surprise. Instead of shooting away, that great Mercury engine just roared and the car *stood still.* Emma's knee had pushed the gear shift into neutral!

Funnily, not one of them realized what I had done. Fifteen minutes later I had another chance to hit the throttle again—clear to the floor. I flicked off the headlights, and with my left arm held my "friend" by the neck with his body dangling out of the window, then shoved him under the chin. He went sailing into the night, dust, and *mesquite.* His body smashed into the chief. Then we were lost in dust and there were no tail lights to shoot at. Thank God for the dust!

Amazingly, we ran straight into our old goat track after tearing across that plateau for only about a quarter of a mile. Emma was still shaking when we finally pulled into Durango early the next morning. And with good reason! Just wish that I could have heard what the bandits had to say about that night when they got back to their camp fire. Of course, one thing the guy in the window—or his chief—never knew was that I had a Colt .38 pistol on the seat between Emma's leg and mine. A good place to leave it, with so many against us, except in a final emergency.

I felt that the Salleys shouldn't be with me when I tried to return to Torreón by another route. Luckily, he had business there. I drove back alone. They came by train. We reported the incident to the governor, who was familiar with the gang's raids, but by the time the soldiers got back to where we figured we were stopped, there was nothing to be seen but *mesquite* and boot tracks in the dust.

* * *

How would you like a matador for a daughter-in-law?

Monterrey, Mexico. 4 March, 1942

Flew back up here last Sunday and am returning this afternoon to Mexico City for dinner. A short trip that turned into one of the most colorful adventures of all—photographing Conchita Cintrón, the greatest woman bullfighter in the world.

I arrived at noon Sunday. She phoned the *plaza* (bull ring) to make all necessary pass arrangements. We went to the fights escorted by her tough old *banderilleros* (men who help her in the ring), each a tinsled Christmas tree in his sequin-embroidered "suit of lights." While the other matadors on the program fought, Conchita returned to my shoulder, just behind the barricade of the ring where I saw the fights with the world's most exotic narrator.

Monday and Tuesday were fabulous! We shot a story on how she trains to be a top-flight bullfighter. Actually, she is called a *rejoneadora*, a woman who battles bulls from horseback. Not to be confused in any way with a *picador*, who weakens the bulls with a pike for regular foot-bound matadors. The amazing thing is that she never before has given such cooperation or anything like so much of her time to anyone, much less to a total stranger.

Then, besides the pictures, I've had the fun of taking her to dinner and lunch each day, always in true Castilian style—accompanied by her aunt. Same with the movie, last night—with Señora da Cámara. Ruy da Cámara, her trainer, is also her uncle and the Portuguese consul in Peru, where Conchita first learned to fight bulls just for fun.

94

Forgot to mention that Conchita is only nineteen, slender, fair, about five feet eight, smart as any girl I've ever known and good looking to the point of being classic. In fact, regardless of all obstacles, if it weren't for my own work requiring solo trips, I would really join her league—but permanently. I can just see Kansas City if I came home with the lady of my heart . . . a bullfighter.

Another two days would have finished me, for sure. Now I'm hoping to be here when she returns from fighting in Chihuahua. If smart, I would leave right now. She probably wouldn't and doesn't want a wanderer as more than a friend—because she's a very wise little girl.

* * *

I've just knocked off a story after waiting for it seven years.

Mexico City. 13 March, 1942

It was the dance of the *voladores*—flyers—a ceremony performed by six Mexican Indians from Vera Cruz atop a *one-hundred-foot pole*—on a spinning platform smaller than a card table. Feathers cover their bodies and heads to resemble birds. Each, in turn, dances upright on the whirling disc while the others perch around its rim balancing themselves and the dancer. As each performer twists and weaves and stamps his feet in a pagan rhythm, the pole itself bows and weaves almost in a rhythm of its own under the weight of all those men at its tip. From the ground they appear to be enormous fledging eaglets taking turns stretching their wings in a flat and barren nest.

Tying to their waists the ends of ropes that entwine the pole, they crouch for a moment at the edge of the platform—then dive straight out into space. Flapping their feather-covered arms like wings, they spin down in ever-faster and wider circles while the ropes untwine from around the great pole. One dancer, the chief, plays a wailing, high-pitched flute during the entire descent, which is head down until just before crashing to earth. In that final instant each man swings upright and lands running at full speed around the base of the shaft. Terrific! Apparently the dance originated with the Aztecs, who performed it at their Thanksgiving feasts. Rather different from sitting down around a family turkey dinner, today.

* * * 95

Yesterday worked—if you could call it that—taking more pictures of Conchita.

Mérida, Yucatán. 29 April, 1942

I had already completed the story without showing her killing the bull (figured the humane societies would holler if I showed her actually finishing a bull). Then Washington decided the fight pictures were necessary, even though knowing I was scheduled to start for Guatemala today. Luckily, she had a fight scheduled right in Mexico City, which was an incredible break. Getting permission from the bullfight photographers' syndicate for use of my camera in the ring was something else. However, having kept in contact with her since Monterrey, I felt free to explain my predicament. Had buzzed her hotel with our Embassy plane at Guadalajara, and again in Mazatlán, which delighted us both. Then, too, last week at her request, I took some portraits of one of her favorite fighting horses, Recuerdo, given to her by the brother of President Camacho.

Anyway, she tried to obtain permission from the photographers' syndicate for me to work above the *barrera* (barricade lining the edge of the ring, which keeps the bulls out of the audience and supposedly vice versa) from a special basketlike seat clamped on the boards. Several of these seats are assigned to syndicate photographers covering each fight. They refused. There wasn't enough time. Not defeated, Conchita told me to try to get a front-row seat in the shade. She would look for me, then see what might be done.

The ring is the largest in the world. It was festooned with more than 30,000 fans. None will ever forget what happened yesterday afternoon. From the grand entry until she fought her second bull, she gave me a private bull fight. Unbelievable! When first appearing in the arena, she pranced her proud fighting horse right up to where I was seated—with just a gracious nod to President Camacho himself about a hundred feet to my right—reared her horse back on his hind legs, doffed her flat-brimmed *rejoneador*'s hat, flashed a fabulous smile, then continued her bows to the rest of the *aficianados* of Mexico City as she circled the arena.

Of course, the horses she fights from are enough in themselves to justify going to the *plaza*, for they are all Portuguese fighters of the most noble blood. They are said to love combat and are trained to bait and taunt the bulls even without Conchita in the saddle. Should she somehow be thrown, or gored while afoot (she fights both styles), they will charge in to lead the bull away, offering themselves as a target for its horns. Her aides, the *banderilleros*, will instantly do the same. But often her horse is nearer.

96

Yesterday, she maneuvered and fought her two bulls to within fifty feet of my camera. If the bull moved away she made her *banderilleros* work him back before me. Thirty thousand Mexicans were thunderstruck. It was obvious what was happening. For the top favorite of all Latin America (they call her the Blonde Angel of the Bulls . . . it's better in Spanish, *La Angela Rubia de los Toros*) to do what she did was incredible. From start to finish it was our afternoon. Jim Shirley and his friends who have lived in Mexico for over twenty years had never seen or heard of such a performance. Now their enthusiasm and appreciation rival mine—almost!

If you have never seen a bullfight, you can only partially appreciate the final drama of that afternoon. Conchita fought the second of her two bulls afoot, sending her gallant horse to one side of the ring where he stood alone without a hand touching him, always watching his mistress. She took her handkerchief—silk, I guess—from her sleeve and tucked it into the front of her tight-fitting jacket so that a little white flag stuck out in front at chest level. Then she put her back flat against the boards of the *barrera*, just below me and slightly to one side so that I—only I—had a perfect shot. The syndicate professionals in their basket-seats were out of position as the bull moved closer.

Conchita stood immobile except for the flickering tip of her sword covered by the red *muleta*. There was no sound in the entire *plaza* but the hoarse breathing of the bull—and Conchita calling to him. *"Toro! Bonito toro!* . . . Pretty bull!

"Aquí! . . . Here!

"Toro! . . . *TORO!"*

His tail went out stiff, his head dropped—and he charged.
With her back against the boards there was no escape.
His right horn ripped at her heart.
The handkerchief was torn from her jacket.
She hadn't moved.

The *plaza* exploded.

As she was being carried toward the center of the city on the shoulders of the crowd—the supreme tribute—I tried to shout my thanks over the tumult. She only smiled like a little kid, as though it really was nothing at all—as though every matador did it every day, for a friend.

* * *

Much as I regret the circumstances under which it happened, I am nevertheless in an unprecedented position with our Legation here in Guatemala.

Guatemala City, Guatemala. 13 May, 1942

Last weekend went by special train to Puerto Barrios, on the east coast, then by boat to Livingston across the Bay of Amatique, and up the Rio Dulce to Lake Izabal. That river was the outlet for the coffee country of Cobán, in the highlands, and the greatest German concentration in this hemisphere before the war. Due to our American Minister, Fay Allen Des Portes, every German has been removed from the coast, and all of questionable character have been deported to internment camps in the U.S. This country, which was under very powerful German influence, is now absolutely under control and completely with the Allies.

I went down to the coastal country with Minister DesPortes to do some gratis picture work. With us was a State Department official, Mr. Edwards Murray, in charge of investigating firms and individuals scheduled for the "Black List"—known agents or sympathizers of the Axis powers. Mr. Murray, Georgia born, was a perfectly grand man, distinguished by all of the qualities of the greatest Southerners.

Sunday evening we returned to Livingston, a tiny seaport north of Puerto Barrios, where we were stopping with a gnarled, rustic old Englishman, the representative of local banana and coffee interests. His home was high on the loftiest hill above the sea and surrounding jungle—windswept and peaceful—perfect for the most tranquil or most dramatic scenario.

A storm had gathered in the highlands. It crashed down just as we arrived at the house.

Below us, the wind lashed through the jungle then tore out to sea leaving scattered branches and foam in its wake. We sat down to dinner, only to notice that Mr. Murray was not amongst us.

Our calls brought no answer, so the Englishman started upstairs to call again, thinking he might have dropped off to sleep for a moment. Shouts brought us running. The poor fellow had collapsed at the top of the stairs.

Sure that it was a stroke, I went to work with artificial respiration.

98

Everything was done to make him comfortable. The Englishman headed out into the storm in search of the local doctor, and the Minister tried to contact either Puerto Barrios or Guatemala City hoping to reach another doctor who might come—but to no avail.

The only telephone line had been broken.

Minister DesPortes started out by boat to cross the bay for a doctor from Barrios. The local doctor arrived two hours later, having been released from jail where he had been for two days on a drunkenness charge.

He didn't get to touch Mr. Murray. It was no use, anyway. I had kept him breathing for nearly three hours, then the flickering pulse weakened, that faint spark of life faded, and he went away.

The storm continued, with rain pounding on the attic's sloping tin roof over our heads.

Later, when we carried him down the hill through the rain to the boat upon which the Minister had returned, it seemed like a passage from Joseph Conrad—leaves were dripping and wind ran rampant through the trees, while black shadows scurried away from the storm and the night, and *us*.

After placing him aboard the boat, back under the little roof covering the stern, I watched the others disappear into the darkness, trudging through the storm-born rivulets pouring down the hill. Alone in the stern, awaiting the pilot who had gone for hot coffee in preparation for his third crossing of the bay that night, I listened to the waves on the logs of the wharf and watched the rain sifting down around the single naked bulb lighting the sodden, sagging planks to which we were moored. The night itself seemed to be mourning a loss without words. It was a time between time, a night without perspective—black and oppressive, with only the wind and the water and the loneliness for companions.

Abruptly the rain stopped, the wind lay quiet, and the clouds parted around a crescent moon crowned by Venus. The sea was still. Night faded. We cast off as sunbeams punched through the scattering clouds.

We headed into life anew and another day.

* * *

99

Mr. Nelson A. Rockefeller
Co-ordinator Inter-American Affairs
Department of Commerce
Washington, D.C.

STERLING PRODUCTS INTERNATIONAL
Drogueria Centro Americana
San Salvador, El Salvador
July 17th, 1942

Dear Mr. Rockefeller:

Please be advised that one of your men, Mr. David D. Duncan, saved the life of an employee of this firm on July 16th in a rural section of El Salvador.

May we briefly explain the circumstances. One of our panel delivery trucks, while trying to cross a shallow river, became embedded in the soft river bottom. After many unsuccessful attempts to free the truck it was decided to unload the heavy contents thereby making it possible to pull out under its own power. Our employee, Señor Francisco López, while arranging the material to be unloaded, was overcome by the exhaust fumes and was unconscious in the rear of the truck. Mr. Duncan arrived on the scene and seeing what had happened, carried López out of the truck, forced open his mouth to make sure that the tongue of the victim was not blocking his throat and administered artificial respiration until López regained consciousness. There is no doubt in our minds that López would have died had not Duncan with his presence of mind and knowledge of what to do, arrived when he did. We are, therefore, passing the information on to you, as most likely you would never be informed of the incident.

Yours very truly,

Roberto H. Gruner

Droguería Centro Americana

Now that I am back from the hospital in Panamá, I may as well explain.

Tegucigalpa, Honduras. 29 September, 1942

About eight weeks ago, in El Salvador, I pulled a man out of his truck which was stuck in a river. He was overcome by exhaust fumes. As I wanted to get him ashore fast, I braced the truck door open with one foot, stood in the river on the other, pulled him out and swung him up over my shoulder, all at about the same time. Even as I got him from the truck I knew that something was wrong. It was the abdominal muscles on my left side. Thought they might mend. They didn't. The U.S. Military Attaché for Air, here in Honduras, Captain Paul Miller, offered to fly me to the Canal Zone. Arrived, and went right into Gorgas hospital, the finest anywhere around.

It was done by spinal anesthetic, so I could follow the whole show in the light reflectors overhead. I asked the doctor if it would be too much trouble to reach over and zip out the old appendix while he was at it and had all of his gear handy. Nothing to it! So, with one job now on the left side and one on the right, he fixed me up in truly patriotic style . . . V-for-Victory.

100   * * *

President Somoza is a very congenial man—if one is his friend . . .

Managua, Nicaragua. 29 October, 1942

But I'll bet he's tough as any of the U.S. Marines who were here when he first took over the country. He speaks English perfectly—even with the slang of a guy my own age—and is a real friend of the United States: one of his sons is all set for West Point and the other is at the University of California. I'll have a great time here, for sure.

Two marvelous things happened in the last several days. I was in the country with President Somoza on a "military inspection" trip. Well, we actually drove out to a piece of wonderful woods just so that he might walk around a bit, getting some fresh air after the cigar smoke in his office—mostly from the old ropes of his own which throw off a cloud of fumes so strong they almost fogged the film in my camera. He wanted to test the sights on his new hunting rifle, too. So we fooled around—followed always by his tommy-gun-toting body-guards—shooting at knots on trees, tin cans, and an old crow which kept looking right at us from about 150 yards as we blazed away. Sure, he handed me the rifle, every other shot, just like when Hank Beardsley and I took only one .22 out for an afternoon there at home. Finally, President Somoza handed the rifle to his chief bodyguard, muttering, "You'd better hit him." He did.

Then, while coming home at about six o'clock, in the heat and humidity—two carloads of tommy-gunners in front and two more behind—President Somoza sprawled back on the seat of his limousine mopping his neck and brow, and said how much he wished he had a *milkshake!* I thought I'd gone goofy!

Looking at him, with a huge old Colt .45 on his hip, surrounded by his screen of body-guards—surely one of the roughest, toughest *hombres* in any of the Americas—I thought he was making fun of me, and said so. He just mopped some more, opened the bulletproof window a little so that some of the smoke seeped out, and looked over at me. "Hell no! I love them. I used to live on them years ago when in New York on trips for business [buying guns, from what I gather]. You know where I had the last one?" I told him I could not imagine, unless right here, up at his house. "Here? Are you kidding? Hell no! *In the White House with President Roosevelt.* A couple of years ago, when I was there on a State visit. He made it himself. Had the boys roll his chair into the kitchen and *he* made it. Triple thick chocolate *milkshake!* Then he hooked a bottle with his cane and had a double whiskey. Boy, I sure wish we could be up there right now!"

I asked President Somoza if he would like to have a double chocolate milkshake—"right now." He looked over at me like the heat had really hit me.

"Here! Big joke!"

I told him that I really wasn't fooling, that I had a place where I had been training the guys how to make them. The President just poked a thumb at his driver's neck: "Tell *him*." So I did. We slowed down so that the driver could holler our changed route to the bodyguards, then off we went into the center of Managua which by this time was loaded with people since it was exactly six and all of the offices were closing. I wondered what the bodyguards would do while we drank our 'shakes. General Somoza grinned: "Work."

Our little motorcade swung into that busy back street—two carloads of bodyguards blocking both ends of it—and ole Dave led the President of Nicaragua into an ice cream shop for a milkshake, which he claimed was better than President Franklin Delano Roosevelt's! Of course, I thought the clerks behind the fountain were going to faint, or just plain die from paralyzed breathing. President Somoza perched on his chair, Colt .45 and all, with just the top of his head showing over that 'shake. He really dived into it—like a kid out of school.

It was quite a sight—and one helluva afternoon for Managua.

Then, the next night the house where I live was robbed—well, almost robbed. I stay in a house with Nicaragua's Chief of National Defense and an American "legal officer" from our Legation. The place is right in the center of the most exclusive residential section of Managua. There is rarely a sound along that street unless our friends make it, since between the three of us we know just about everyone in the city and somebody usually drops in almost every evening for a visit if my pals aren't working.

Anyway, I came home about eleven from developing negatives down in my darkroom at the National Police office. I saw a car parked at the end of the street, and if I noted it at the time it was only because I figured it belonged to the last guests of the evening up at our place. But when I got there the whole house was dark. I still thought nothing of it until, as I headed for my room, I saw the figure of a man running low across the patio, into the even deeper shadows, *away* from the front door. Instantly knowing that it was a thief, I yelled for whoever else might be at home and ran to cut him off.

All hell broke then loose. The thief charged around in the gloom of the patio trying to find the front door or a window, my two friends burst out of their rooms with .45 Colts in their hands, no one could hit the light switch for the patio, I damned near grabbed the thief as he tore past me back toward the door with my friends just behind him—then we were all outside . . . and the thief was gone. So was the car. He must have had a buddy who already had gotten out of the house before I arrived. We searched the street and the gardens of nearby homes. No lights flashed on despite the uproar. Guess our neighbors figured it was only another unrecorded Nicaraguan-American fiesta. Poor neighbors! They missed the sight of their lifetime. The Chief of Nicaraguan National Defense and the chief of our FBI bureau for Central America were prowling the street absolutely enraged that *their* house should be a target for thieves—poking everywhere with their pistols—and both stark naked.

102   * * *

No time, dear folks, for much of a letter because as you perhaps realize I have been packing a vast amount of activity into the last several weeks.

Managua, Nicaragua. 29 November, 1942

Upon receiving your suggestion of a letter to Rockefeller requesting army draft deferment, I put in a long-distance radiophone call to Washington. It seemed that Rockefeller was too busy to answer so I talked with others familiar with the entire situation. The result was a waste of money. They would not write a letter unless the Kansas City draft board requested it. Now isn't *that* logical, with the draft board doing everything to grab me! With a couple of exceptions, like photo editor Al Murphy, they in that office haven't any more guts than a garter snake and are getting more and more fearful even of their own shadows.

Still playing with every card in the deck, I then began using my trumps, as the copies of the enclosed telegrams will illustrate. President Somoza radioed both Washington and the K.C. draft board, which floored many even down here who operate only by the rule book.

We had been out in the countryside again, this time checking on a collection point for crude rubber which is then flown to the States. Coming back into Managua, I told General Somoza that I'd soon be shoving off, heading for the States, too. He was surprised, since I had told him earlier that I'd be covering some major Latin American political activities soon to take place in Nicaragua.

He asked me if I still wanted to stay in Managua to shoot the rallies. When I said "Damn right!", he grinned, hunched forward to speak to the driver, then turned back to me.

"Okay! Every time you come around here with that camera you kind of run things. Now, *I'm* taking over—after all, *I'm* the President."

He ordered the driver to take us to the American Legation.

Well, like the afternoon that we had the milkshakes, it was again shop closing time in Managua when we got to town and pulled up at the Legation, tommy-gunners and all. The Americans and Nicaraguans of the staff were just starting for the doors when they saw who was headed toward them. General Somoza is no more than fifty, of medium height, very powerfully built (walks like a heavyweight wrestler), packs his Colt on his hip, sticks a Marine-style World War I campaign hat on the back of his head, would have a thick black beard if he didn't shave for a couple of days, and wears five big stars on his shoulders. By the time we got into the doorway the place was clear. The staff stood transfixed, bug-eyed, life-size dolls pinned upon the walls. At that moment, bless him, playing it for maximum impact, he turned to me and said, "Dunc'. Do you want to send 'em from the message room— or the Old Man's office?"

Minister Stewart was out of the Legation for the moment, so we sent the cables from the office of one of Bill LaVarre's friends, Ed Lawson, the Commercial Attaché who already had helped me with other aspects of my work here. President Somoza sat down at Ed's desk, took his pencil, then looked back at me, doing it again. "Okay, Dunc! What'll we say?"

I thought that Ed and the others who had appeared from nowhere were going to flip, especially when the President suddenly got up and handed *me* the pencil with another grin, saying, "You know what *we* want to say. You write it." So, the signature is straight Somoza—and the words are pure DDD.

TROPICAL RADIO TELEGRAPH COMPANY   MANAGUA, NIC.
RADIOGRAMA   NOV. 24. 1942

NELSON A ROCKEFELLER
COORDINATOR, DEPARTMENT OF COMMERCE
WASHINGTON

STRONGLY REQUEST PHOTOGRAPHER DAVID D DUNCAN BE GIVEN
THIRTY DAY EXTENSION OF DEFERMENT IN ORDER THAT HE BE ABLE
TO FINISH IMPORTANT PICTORIAL COVERAGE OF NICARAGUA WHICH I
FEEL WILL BRING OUR COUNTRIES STILL CLOSER TOGETHER

A SOMOZA
PRESIDENT REPUBLIC OF NICARAGUA

TROPICAL RADIO TELEGRAPH COMPANY   MANAGUA, NIC.
RADIOGRAMA   NOV. 24. 1942

LOCAL DRAFT BOARD NO 8
6247 BROOKSIDE ROAD
KANSASCITYMO

STRONGLY REQUEST PHOTOGRAPHER DAVID D DUNCAN BE GIVEN
THIRTY DAY EXTENSION OF DEFERMENT IN ORDER THAT HE BE ABLE
TO FINISH IMPORTANT PICTORIAL COVERAGE OF NICARAGUA WHICH I
FEEL WILL BRING OUR COUNTRIES STILL CLOSER TOGETHER

A SOMOZA
PRESIDENT REPUBLIC OF NICARAGUA

General Somoza saw the humor in it, too. So reported Minister Stewart, after his and the President's next poker session a few evenings later. Of course, one thing President Somoza could not have known. I have always loathed being called "Dunc." But from him, that evening, it held all of the promise and beauty of Gabriel's trumpet blast itself.

Mr. A. L. Murphy: Photographic Editor
Coordinator of Inter-American Affairs
Washington, D.C.

David D. Duncan
Washington, D.C.
December 19, 1942

Dear Mr. Murphy:

I am here noting those expenses arising from the prolonged duration of my trip through Mexico and Central America for the Coordinator's Office. Also recorded are the costs of making the unnecessary trip to Kansas City and Washington, due to an Office oversight in not advising me that my extension of draft deferment had been granted. No request is being made for the salary of these additional months of work. However, I should like to request payment of $1,500 still outstanding on my contract in order that I might more fully meet obligations that have been created by the already greatly extended life of this assignment.

Sincerely yours,
David D. Duncan

The Bureaucracy forgot to notify their wandering boy! When I walked back in the door —Big Astonishment—and instant discussions about my returning to Central America… despite the hot hairy breath of a not terribly *simpático* Uncle Sam on the nape of my neck.

It was naive planning. No Washington official (except my old friend William LaVarre) would tangle with the supreme voice of the land, the Draft Board of the U.S. Army. So, with all doors to Latin America slamming shut in my face, I made one final pitch even while moving in an entirely different direction—toward a great new life.

WESTERN
UNION

PRESIDENT FRANKLIN D ROOSEVELT   1943 JAN 16 PM 6 57
THE WHITE HOUSE   WASHINGTON DC
WASHINGTON DC

HAVING JUST RETURNED FROM A YEAR PHOTOGRAPHING MEXICO AND
CENTRAL AMERICA FOR THE OFFICE OF COORDINATOR OF INTER-
AMERICAN AFFAIRS, DURING WHICH TIME PRESIDENTS CAMACHO, UBICO,
MARTINEZ, CARIAS, AND SOMOZA GAVE ME EVERY ASSISTANCE IN
FULFILLING MY MISSION, IT HAS BEEN WITH TREMENDOUS
DISAPPOINTMENT THAT I HAVE DISCOVERED THE BARRIERS
CONFRONTING MY MEETING YOU, MY OWN PRESIDENT, WHILE SEEKING
YOUR ADVICE AND ASSISTANCE PERTAINING TO THE PURSUANCE
OF MY WORK IN LATIN AMERICA. ALL OTHER EFFORTS HAVING FAILED
I AM SENDING THIS TELEGRAM WITH THE HOPE THAT IT WILL REACH
YOU AND PRESENT MY CASE. THE COORDINATORS OFFICE WOULD LIKE
ME TO FINISH MY PHOTOGRAPHIC COVERAGE OF COSTA RICA AND
PANAMA, BUT BECAUSE THEY HAVE BEEN DOING THIS WORK ON
CONTRACT THEY FEEL THAT A WHITE HOUSE REQUEST SHOULD NOT
BE MADE FOR MY DRAFT DEFERMENT. AFTER FINISHING THE
PANAMANIAN COVERAGE THE RECONSTRUCTION FINANCE CORPORATION
WANTS ME TO GO INTO THE AMAZON RIVER BASIN PROJECT AS CHIEF
PHOTOGRAPHER, BUT THEY COULD NOT MAKE A WHITE HOUSE
REQUEST BECAUSE I HAVE NOT YET BEGUN WORK FOR THEM.
IRONICALLY THEY ADMIT THAT I HAVE HAD MORE EXPERIENCE FOR
THAT WORK THAN ANYONE ELSE AVAILABLE, AND THEY WANTED
ME ON THE JOB. FEELING THAT I AM BEST QUALIFIED TO HELP THEM
PUT THAT PROJECT OVER SUCCESSFULLY, AND THAT I COULD THUS
BE BEST SERVING MY COUNTRY AS A REPRESENTATIVE IN LATIN
AMERICA, I AM SENDING THIS MESSAGE TO YOU. PRESIDENT SOMOZA
OF NICARAGUA HAS TOLD MEMBERS OF THE AMERICAN LEGATION IN
MANAGUA THAT I HAD DONE AS MUCH AS ANY SINGLE INDIVIDUAL
VISITING HIS COUNTRY IN RECENT YEARS TO SPONSOR
UNDERSTANDING BETWEEN NICARAGUA AND NORTH AMERICA.
PRESIDENT CARIAS OF HONDURAS PROMISED AND GAVE ME AN OPEN

DOOR THROUGHOUT HIS REPUBLIC, AND TOLD ME THAT HE ONLY
WISHED THAT MORE AMERICANS WOULD COME WHO COULD TRULY
REPRESENT THE NEW SPIRIT OF THE UNITED STATES. IN EL SALVADOR
AFTER MY SAVING A SALVADORANS LIFE PRESIDENT MARTINEZ WHO
HAD PERSONALLY TAKEN ME ALL OVER HIS COUNTRY, TOLD ME
THAT EFFORTS SUCH AS MINE WOULD CONTRIBUTE THE MOST TOWARD
REAL PAN-AMERICANISM. TO SUPPORT MY HAVING MADE AS MANY
FRIENDS FOR THE UNITED STATES AS ANY OTHER SINGLE INDIVIDUAL
IN THOSE REPUBLICS I OFFER THE NAMES OF OUR MINISTERS AND
ATTACHES TO THE CENTRAL AMERICAN COUNTRIES, AND THE
PRESIDENTS THEMSELVES. I AM PUTTING THIS EVEN LESS STRONGLY
THAN I FEEL, BECAUSE AFTER HAVING RECEIVED SUCH COMPLETE
COOPERATION IN OTHER MENS COUNTRIES, I DEEPLY REGRET THAT
HERE IN MY OWN LAND I CANNOT BE GIVEN THE SAME ASSISTANCE
AND CONSIDERATION. THE BEST PARTS OF SEVEN YEARS HAVE BEEN
SPENT IN LATIN AMERICA LEARNING THEIR LIFE AND TONGUE AND
FITTING MYSELF TO REPRESENT NORTH AMERICANS AS WE DESERVE,
AND YET NOW THAT I AM BEST QUALIFIED TO USE THESE ABILITIES AND
EXPERIENCE I MUST SEEK SOME OTHER BRANCH OF THE SERVICE, JUST
BECAUSE OF THE HESITATION OF OTHERS TO PLACE THE SITUATION
SQUARELY BEFORE YOU FOR YOUR APPROVAL OR REJECTION.
THEREFORE ON MY OWN RESPONSIBILITY I REQUEST THE PERMISSION
AND PRIVILEGE OF MEETING YOU WHO ARE THE ONE MAN WHO HAS
DONE MORE THAN ANY OTHER TO PROMOTE UNDERSTANDING FOR
OUR SOUTHERN NEIGHBORS, WHO HAS GIVEN THEM MORE THAN
PROMISES OF THE FUTURE, AND WHO THEREFORE WOULD BE BEST
QUALIFIED TO JUDGE THIS WORK AS NECESSARY, AS WORTHY OF
FURTHER EXTENSION, AND A REAL CONTRIBUTION TOWARD FUTURE
RELATIONSHIPS AND UNDERSTANDING OF THE AMERICAS. HOPING
THAT MY FAITH IS NOT IN VAIN, I REMAIN MOST RESPECTFULLY YOURS

DAVID D DUNCAN

Mr. David D. Duncan
% Lt (j.g.) J. G. Watkins, U.S.N.R.
2104 Suitland Terrace, S.E.
Washington, D.C.

Mrs. K. S. Duncan
629 W. 57 St. Terrace
Kansas City, Missouri
January 24, 1943

David dear —

Another year has rolled around. It was wonderful to be able to talk to you last night and *say* "Happy Birthday," instead of wishing it across the miles as we did last year.

I know Jean gave you a good dinner & that you enjoyed having it there with her and Jim. The check we are enclosing brings lots of love to our youngest son. We debated the question of phoning you last night, or this morning. You might be out last night; this morning you might think we forgot till today! I'm so glad we called you last night and you were there.

You have been much in my mind, as you would know. I have realized that like the David of old with his slingshot as a weapon against Goliath, you, too, have gone to battle in the face of heavy odds. I realize that you, a young & unattached man have been making the effort to see the biggest men in our country at their busiest season.

May you have found open doors when you knocked, & men ready to listen.

Jean's letter of yesterday told nothing (she's a well trained little sister!) except that there was again a passing the buck as to who had a right to defer you. That is hard to understand. She also said "he doesn't want to tell you what he is trying to get so you will not be disappointed if it doesn't work out."

We should never be disappointed in any way over you, Dave. You are a source of pride & joy to your Dad and me. You make us feel worthwhile because we have contributed you to the world of your generation. Let's hope that you may be allowed to use your abilities where the most can be accomplished. The Bible says "the fervent prayer of a righteous man availeth much." I'm no man, am not too sure I'm righteous, but I'm praying fervently every day that you may find your right place & be satisfied in it.

You are having a month in Washington—not of your desire. I hope you are making it a business to see the new National Gallery of Art, & to attend a sitting or two of Congress.

Pansies will soon bloom in the beds in the gardens there, never have I seen such masses of them, & Lincoln sits aloft looking with his long vision at the still more confused country that he loved.

Whether you can play your part where you most desire, or where you simply must, Daddy & I are proud & happy to have brought so loyal an American into being.

Mother

108

WESTERN
UNION

WA99 51 GOVT 8 EXTRA=   THE WHITE HOUSE WASHINGTON DC JAN 29
VIA DC WASHINGTON DC 2

                                         1943 FEB 2 AM 10 53

DAVID DUNCAN
629 WEST 57 ST TERRACE KANSASCITY MO=

RE YOUR WIRE SIXTEENTH HAVE CHECKED WITH OFFICE OF INTER
AMERICAN AFFAIRS AND REGRET TO INFORM YOU IT WILL BE
IMPOSSIBLE GRANT SPECIAL DEFERMENT AS YOU REQUEST. ALSO
REGRET ADVISE YOU IMPOSSIBLE ARRANGE APPOINTMENT WITH THE
PRESIDENT JUST NOW=

                    EDWIN M WATSON SECY TO THE PRESIDENT

And it was indeed impossible for *any* American to meet President Roosevelt in the White House, at that time. He was at the super-secret Casablanca Conference with Winston Churchill, where the Prime Minister, and then the world, first heard of his terms for defeating the Nazis and Axis Powers: "Unconditional Surrender!"

ACCEPTANCE

Miami Florida
(Place)
17 February 1943
(Date)

From: **Second Lieutenant David D. Duncan USMCR (AVS).**

To: The Commandant, U.S. Marine Corps,
   Washington, D.C.

Subject: Appointment as **Second Lieutenant** U.S. Marine Corps
   Reserve

1.   I hereby accept appointment as a **Second Lieutenant** in the United States Marine Corps Reserve, dated **6 February, 1943** with rank from **28 January, 1943**, transmitted by letter from the Commandant, U.S. Marine Corps, dated **11 February, 1943**.

David D. Duncan
(Signature)

OATH OF OFFICE

Having been appointed a **Second Lieutenant** in the Marine Corps Reserve of the United States, I, **David Douglas Duncan** do solemnly swear (or affirm) that I will support and defend the Constitution of the United States against all enemies, foreign and domestic; that I will bear true faith and allegiance to the same; that I take this obligation freely, without any mental reservation or purpose of evasion; and that I will well and faithfully discharge the duties of the office on which I am about to enter: So help me God.

David Douglas Duncan
(Signature)

Subscribed and sworn to before me this **17th** day of **February 1943**

G. D. Hartfield
Lieut-Col. U.S.M.C., Ret.

To Be Filled in By Appointee

Place of birth		State or territory of which a citizen	Date of Birth
City, Parish, County	State		
Kansas City	**Mo.**	**Florida U.S.A.**	**23 January 1916.**

110

CHAPTER IV

Coral Gables, Florida.
17 February, 1943

Dear Mother and Dad:

Childhood and my youth are finished. Only He knows how much of my race has been run.

Today, I have been accepted by the United States Marine Corps.

With pride and Love,
Dave

This uniform is a part of me already. Now to learn the life.

Headquarters Squadron, Marine Corps Air Station, Quantico, Virginia. 1 March, 1943

I still marvel at my good fortune.

Being a Marine is enough in itself. But being assigned to Aviation as a Specialist places me in a group of 834 men, no more, for the entire Corps. Even the flying arm has thousands more members. And having been given commissions, we gained positions not only zealously cherished but ranks which under normal advancement take years to earn. It's a real obligation to maintain the reputation that other men have given their lives to establish.

* * *

The most difficult thing to become accustomed to around here is that there is very little individual thinking expected of anyone.

17 March, 1943

I suppose it is because we are still in training, yet it's tough not to be able to pop in on the top man on the post with some idea that seems like a honey. In one way I was spoiled by my other life. I dealt only with the Number One Boss of the whole works, whether overseer or President.

Looking back now, it seems difficult to understand why I didn't join the service much earlier. Of course, I felt that my work down in Latin America was important, work for which I had trained myself to the best of my ability. Anyway, I'm perfectly happy here with the Marines and feel that with them I'll still be able to serve in that capacity for which I am best suited.

* * *

Adiós to that earlier life!

26 April, 1943

Sunday went to Washington for a visit with Captain Paul Miller, with whom I had flown all over Central America when he was Military Attaché for Air in Tegucigalpa. He returned to Honduras on the noon plane, taking the three leather-bound albums of my photographs for Presidents Carías, Martínez, and Somoza, to deliver personally. That will be just about perfect. He'll do it properly, and in style, as I should have enjoyed attempting myself. Since Rockefeller's office told me the books were too costly, and because I didn't consult them before designing and making the books and prints, they figured they just couldn't pay for

112

them. Suits me fine! Now the albums have gone straight from me to my wonderful friends, and are being presented by another great friend.

Paul will also arrange to get my two old suitcases of jungle gear sent up from Nicaragua, partially in his own plane. So, that's that.

And Goodbye, Mr. Tropical Tramp.

* * *

Last week won the Expert's Medal with the Colt .45 automatic pistol. It's higher than Sharpshooter. They aren't very common. I was delighted.

5 May, 1943

It's strange, turning away from a life as vivid as was mine. At night, instead of dreaming of things around here, all scenes and characters have their origin south of the Rio Grande. There are two DDDs under this uniform. The other guys are surely the same.

* * *

Who was the old, old man, a multi-millionaire, who asked to be made a beggar when told that he would be granted any two wishes he desired: "Then I will stand near the cathedral asking for alms . . . of the wasted days in everyone's life."

Air Regulating Squadron 3, Service Group, Marine Fleet Air West Coast, Marine Corps Air Base, Kearney Mesa, San Diego 45, California. 3 July, 1943

After arriving here I learned that Headquarters had under-quoted me one full day on my leave after finishing training at Quantico—one precious extra day.

Kearney Mesa?

It's a pool for aviators and flight personnel. None of us knows how long we'll be here, or where we'll be sent. Some men have been here for months. Others stay but a few days. It's all in the cards. In the meantime we answer muster roll twice a day, eat huge meals, clean our gear, and, as this afternoon, go swimming. We'll be getting out on the rifle range a bit, too, so I hope to target the new-style carbine I drew today. Officers of the Marine Corps now carry them instead of pistols, it being a more versatile weapon. So, we fool around leading wonderfully healthful lives. Just a big resort.

Almost.

* * *

BOOK OF PSALMS

To my dear son
David

May David's songs
bring you comfort
and peace and
an understanding
heart

With all my love –
                    Dad

August 15 – 1943

The start of new adventures!

Headquarters Squadron, Marine Aircraft Group-23, Air Fleet Post Office, San Francisco, California.
25 September, 1943

Since we've already arrived, several incidents can be told without security violation or endangering anyone shielded by our censorship regulations: us.

My entire outfit shipped out aboard an aircraft carrier, the biggest damned ship any of us yokels in the photo-lab (which is now my command) had ever seen. All of our fighter planes were already where they are being used, so we just put cots on the hangar deck and still had plenty of room for movies or touch football, or to wander around looking into the innards of that incredibly complex piece of fighting machinery. The photographic officer aboard was an old friend from Kodak days, a movie specialist needed for the gun cameras of the carrier's own fighter and bomber squadrons. He asked me to shoot some portraits of the carrier's executive officer . . . "the handsomest, toughest s-o-b in the whole fleet." I did—of a grand guy. Captain Fitzhugh Lee, surely of *the* Lees of Virginia. He was just all NAVY.

Ever since arriving here, at Ewa, the Marine Corps Air Station near Honolulu, I have been congratulating myself and receiving commendations from all hands on my foresight. No fooling, that idea of buying a motorcycle and crating it among our other vast cases of photographic "DELICATE INSTRUMENTS" was my one bid to geniushood. At this point, only the Commanding Colonel and ole DDD have permanent, around-the-clock wheels. Having sized up the Brass of my outfit long ago, I figured I'd tackle the Marine Corps just like any other bunch of guys—on my own terms. Well, when I whipped around our new air base as independent as an old jaybird—the same day we arrived—even the Old Timers in the Corps gave me full marks as a scrounger and operator, long recognized as sensible traits, sometimes invaluable, in any *real* Marine. Of course, it's tough carrying all of my gear and keeping balanced on the thing, but I'm learning new ways to make every pocket and tooth count.

Today I also started forth upon the road to becoming a virtuoso of the accordion.

Since I'm now in the business where guys do sometimes get roughed up, I figure I may as well plan for the possible day when I might want something to do while lying around getting back into shape. So this afternoon I bought a beautiful Italian accordion, perfect condition, and, for the instrument, a steal. I'd contacted the best instructor in the area, asking her to look over the little beauty. She knew the dealer, an old Austrian. They took it out, she played —he chuckled—and I bought an accordion. With any ability at all, I should have a magnificent time, next trip to Latin America after the war. Though loving music, I've always had to sit around when friends cranked up tunes. No longer! Wish Conchita were only here to add her personal criticism. A person need be separated from another before he can fully appreciate those special individuals he has known earlier. Only later—when he finds what he seeks—does he learn the price that was paid in fading friendships.

* * *

Talk about luck!

Hdqts Sqdn, MAG-23, AFPO, San Francisco, California.
23 October, 1943

Have been shooting portraits of everybody from privates to generals. Who should our general's executive officer turn out to be but Colonel Al Krieser for whom I did some work—aerial coverage—in Central America. He's one of those terribly reserved, distinguished men who packs authority without raising his voice or a finger. My own gypsy blood is tormenting me. I want to roam. With him here, knowing my background, is like being handed a full deck— of aces!

The accordion is a source of pleasure and confusion! Learning to read music is really something . . . can't get beyond page 13. Trying to make that music come out of the squeezebox is something again. Now, too, I've begun a photographic school for my men and some of the other enlisted men on the base. So far all has gone well and I believe they are getting it. If so, I can qualify them all as field photographers, thus drawing higher rates and pay.

Typical of the kind of men they are, is one—Var Keljik—who before enlisting in the Marines ran a rug shop in St. Paul. He saw how I struggled when carrying gear on my motorcycle. Day before yesterday a pair of beautiful Persian camel saddlebags arrived. His sister had gone through their entire stock to find them, which she felt would be just right. They are works of art, yet Var assures me they will wear indefinitely—even draped over the back fender of my wheels.

Stepping back several years, I have again begun boxing. The men wanted to start ring fighting, so it ended up in my corner. Some of them are very tough guys indeed, but I have yet to find one who knows how to do more than just put down his head and slug. I'm still instructor. Wish you would air express my old shoes and handwraps. Can use them right

116

away. These guys are younger than I, and though I'm in fine health it's far from ring condition. Those shoes will give me a little extra speed. It's curious, though—life with the Marines. Ever since those first days in training at Quantico—which were rough on the men coming from regular civilian jobs—I've been putting on weight. It's like a picnic, after poking around the jungles of Central America.

Being a Marine seems sort of natural.

* * *

Here it is! My request for more active duty has become reality.

Marine Photographic Squadron-254, Marine Aircraft Wings, Pacific, Fleet Post Office, San Francisco, California.
24 November, 1943

It's exhilirating to be on the move again! A Marine Major, Bill Williams, who is making this move with me, already seems like a buddy from all my life. He was a Golden Gloves champion, but as he was fighting mostly around the Middle West and never in the South, we never met. The last night before leaving Hawaii, he appeared with a brand new Harley Davidson motorcycle which he'd scrounged somewhere. I'd just sold my wheels for more than I paid. We took my cameras and Persian saddlebags and shoved them in on top of his lovely new steed—right into the cabin of the plane with us—and away we went. My accordion in its case was our footrest.

Those months with my previous outfit were the finest any guy could ask of the service. Never a discordant note. I was able to leave having finished the qualification school for my men. Their last class was held my final night there. I'd wanted to take them all to dinner as I did in California before we sailed. My orders came too quickly. But just before saying goodbye, they gave me a beautiful gold combination pen and pencil set. I thought it was as fine an expression of friendship and regret on parting as any I have known. You see, even commissioned Marines don't make much money; damned little when a guy's just a private or corporal. Out of what they do earn, most is sent home to families or wives. Practically none goes into their pockets. To have them spend a goodly portion of what they do have, buying the finest set on the market, made every hour working with them seem a pleasure. They must have enjoyed those days, too.

This is the big break toward which I have aimed every hope and effort.

HEADQUARTERS
SOUTH PACIFIC COMBAT AIR TRANSPORT COMMAND,
NAVY NUMBER 140 (ONE FOUR ZERO)
c/o FLEET POST OFFICE, SAN FRANCISCO, CALIFORNIA.

20 January, 1944

MEMORANDUM TO: The Officers in Charge of All SCAT Detachments.

Subject: Cooperation with Lieutenant Duncan, USMCR.

1.   Lieutenant Duncan is being loaned to SCAT to cover the entire SCAT organization, its operations, etc., and he has permission to take pictures of such.

2.   The Commanding Officer, SCAT, would appreciate it if the Officers in Charge of each SCAT station would give Lieutenant Duncan all the cooperation possible.

3.   This memorandum will authorize the officer in charge to place Lieutenant Duncan on any SCAT plane as an extra crew member.

A. C. KOONCE,
Colonel, USMC,
Commanding.

* * *

Considering myself from all angles, I really don't feel a year older at all. Quite a change of scenery since celebrating the day, last year, with Jean and Jim in Washington, yet I feel that I've had great luck this year.

Marine Photographic Squadron-254, First Marine Air Wing,
Fleet Marine Force, % Fleet Post Office,
San Francisco, California.
23 January, 1944

Looking back now, I'm very sure of one thing. I'm glad that I didn't return to South America. Having followed fairly closely the current trend of U.S. policies and efforts down there, it is reasonably safe to assume that I wouldn't have been permitted to stay on the job in Brazil, regardless of the work I might have turned out. To have had someone else do this part of the job while I whipped around those other tropical climes, wouldn't have balanced later, either.

Am now on detached duty from my squadron. Since what I am doing in no way indicates their movements, I can tell you a little more about my work.

I shall now photograph Marine Corps aviation throughout the South Pacific. Perhaps the finest compliment of all is that I've been turned loose on the assignment with no strings attached. Much like those jobs I did for Pan American Airways around the West Indies, Yucatán and South America. No time or other limitations—just from New Zealand and Australia in the south, to wherever the war is in the north. I'm entirely on my own, with the results expected to justify this freedom. It's said to be the first such Marine Corps job.

Getting along toward that good afternoon light—so off I go.

* * *

From: Commanding Officer, 1st. Battalion, Fiji Infantry Regiment, U.S.A. P.O. 709.

To: Major General J. T. Moore, ComGen. 1st. Marine Aircraft Wing, through Lieut-Colonel P. Pennebaker, Commanding Officer V.M.D. 254.

Subject: Services of 2/Lieut. D. Duncan—V.M.D. 254.

1st. March, 1944

        I have the honour to draw your attention to the great services rendered by 2/Lieut Duncan to my Unit during the engagement with the enemy near Sisivie, Eastern Bougainville in February. 2/Lieut. Duncan originally came to our outpost at Ibu to film a SCAT ration drop, and remained with my approval to record the activities of the Unit. When the enemy finally attacked 2/Lieut Duncan proceeded with the advanced elements and was in the thick of the fight. When I arrived as the Unit was breaking contact he was by chance the first Officer I encountered, and he was able to give me a clear picture of the situation. From then on he acted on my invitation as assistant-Adjutant while the Unit was reforming, and was of the utmost help. On the long march back over the Crown Prince range 2/Lieut Duncan rendered many services and I cannot speak too highly of him both as an official photographer and an honorary member of my Battalion staff.

G. T. Upton.
Lieut. Col.
Commanding Officer, 1 Bn. Fiji Inf Regt

CHAPTER V

Nichi Nishino nursed the flame.

He shielded it from drizzly rain while coaxing it through a pyramid of broken twigs toward larger chunks of jungle-rotted vines. After poking the drier center fragments of fallen branches into the spreading blaze, he hung a kettle of rice over the fire and squatted down on his haunches in the middle of the trail. Nichi Nishino, Private, Imperial Japanese Army, was cooking lunch for others of his patrol while they probed deeper along the island path.

Leaning closer to the heat to cut the mountain chill, Nichi huddled under a newly issued raincoat. The rain fell harder. He barely noticed. He was thumbing through a picture book he had found in a pocket of the raincoat. It was a very dirty little book. Nichi smirked happily, lingering over every page.

The rain increased. He was too engrossed to care. Nor did he see the dark, scarcely moving hand when it slid out through the dripping roots to inch his rifle back into the ferns. Nichi's attention had wandered far from his fire and pot of rice simmering on that lonely trail.

He had reached the last two pictures when he tensed, *feeling* someone just behind him. In that instant an iron hand spun him on his heels. Nichi's heart nearly burst. Towering over him stood a bearded, black-skinned giant.

For an eternal second Nichi only stared. Neither man moved. Then the giant grinned. Nichi screamed and dived toward where he had laid his rifle. Yanked, thrashing into the air, he never touched the ground again, alive. A bayonet in the giant's right hand flashed upward through a short, driving arc. Private Nishino was dead when dropped back into the mud.

Eight men of nearly identical size appeared beside the killer. Bearded, black, fern-camouflaged, silent. As one bent to remove all papers from Nichi's body, a second man whispered, "Lieutenant. You promised. I get the next."

Then the trail was empty.

Bougainville, Solomon Islands. Early February, 1944

120

Colonel Geoffry Upton smiled.

"So you're the Marine who hopes to enlist in the Fijian Army! Temporarily, of course. G-2 of the General Staff phoned to say that the request you wish to make has their approval." He offered a cigarette. "Oh! Well, do you mind? Now, just what can we do for you?"

"Colonel, the Marine Corps operates the South Pacific Air Transport Command, as you know. I'm working on a photo coverage of SCAT. Since arriving on Bougainville I've heard mostly about your Fijians and their behind-the-lines-fighting with the Japs. I know, too, that you control an outpost deep in the jungle, in the heart of enemy country. Over at Torokina bomber strip, I was told that your outpost is sustained by parachute drops from SCAT planes. I need pictures of those drops. May I join your garrison?"

At dawn, next morning, I was in the pilots' shack of the Army Air Force's Cub Command, home roost of the artillery's frail, two-man spotter planes. The Operations Officer had the tip of his pencil covering a blue-inked fly-fleck on the map of Bougainville.

"See that?" He looked up at me. "That's Ibu, the Fiji outpost. That's where you're going this morning. Now look a little closer. Here we are at Torokina, on Empress Augusta Bay. There's Ibu, clear across the island. It's about six miles from Jap headquarters at Numa Numa Plantation, on the east coast. To get there in our grasshopper you go up the canyon of the Laruma River, then cut through the pass in the Crown Prince Mountains.

"Thirty seconds after takeoff you'll be over enemy country. In all of those mountains and jungle," he waved a hand to include the entire island, "there's only one place where you can safely land. That's Ibu. You'd better take another good look at this map—and try to remember what you see. If you crash in there you'll need it."

The pilot banked and climbed away from the bomber strip. Peering down, I watched our toehold on Bougainville vanish. We were already beyond the front lines. Just as I was getting well along with a mental picture of being shot down and crawling back through the enemy lines, I began to grin. I was flying to war in a plane so small that kids used to bounce them around cow pastures at home. Not too far below a country was unfolding which I had once hoped to explore as an anthropologist. Now, as a United States Marine I was being flown by the Army to join in a campaign with Fiji Islanders against Japanese. Almost everyone seemed to be in on it, and the war, as I had imagined it, still seemed quite remote.

Wind struck my face when the plane sideslipped into the mountain pass. Weather closed in fast. Sagging black clouds forced us low over the ridges. Veils of rain hid the Crown Prince Range. Bougainville's active volcano, Bagana, was lost in its daily storm.

122

Another squall threatened dead ahead. Pouring on full throttle we flipped over into the next canyon; its walls reared higher than the plane. Diving to the treetops, the pilot followed the zigzagging course of the stream down its floor. Sunlight spilled from the clouds before us. We were blown out of the canyon in front of the deluge that broke all around. Below, Ibu looked like an Ozark woodcutter's clearing in the jungle which choked it from every side.

123

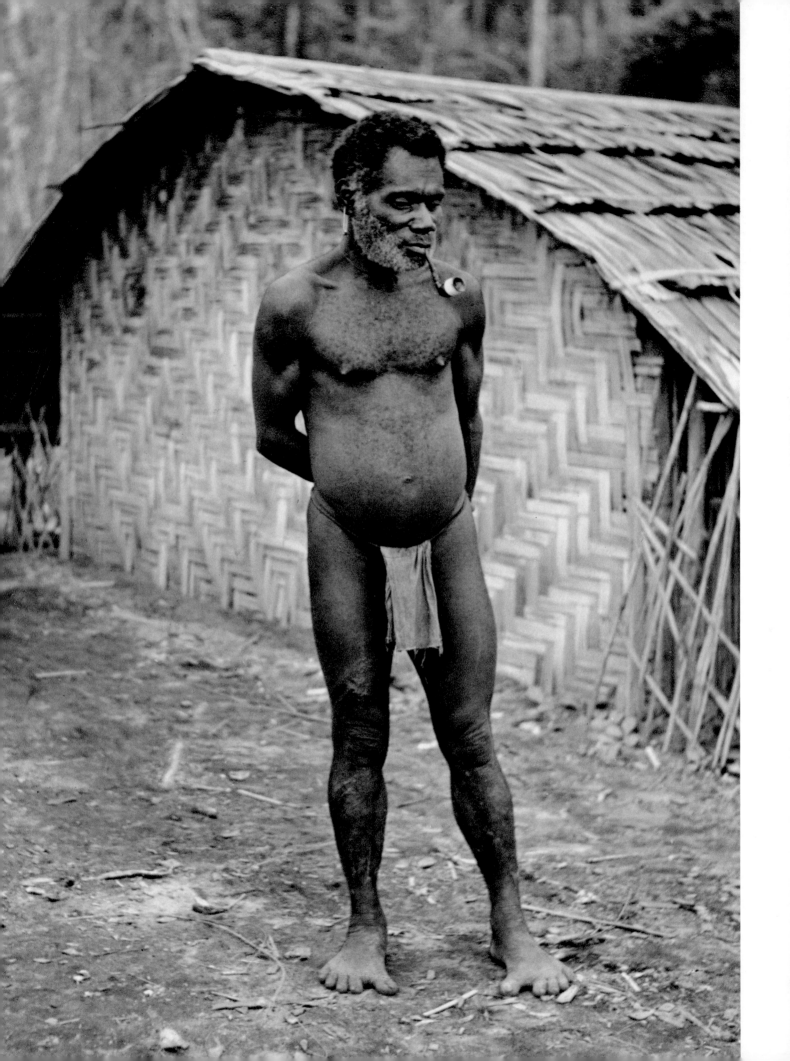

Heavily armed guerrillas roamed the camp in fern camouflage and battle gear. An ancient, lattice-walled, missionary schoolhouse had been converted into the fighters' headquarters. Rough log pilings held the hand-hewn planks of the floor several feet off the ground. The windows were just burlap mats that served as shutters to be closed when it rained—which was often. Front steps had been chopped from tree trunks. Wild ginger and bamboo grew everywhere. An old islander, dressed in his empty pipe, mused before a supply hut nearby.

125

"Do we surprise you, Lieutenant?" A soft voice at my shoulder, where no one had been. Spinning, I stared straight into a vast chest, then up into steady eyes. More than a full head above me loomed a man who casually carried a log as big as a telephone pole under one arm. In the other, a bayoneted rifle.

"Permit me, Lieutenant, to assist you with your equipment. I am going toward our headquarters with this rafter for the medical dugout." I protested only feebly, dumbfounded, first by his English, then that he could carry still more. I had much to learn about the Fijian—and Ibu, my guerrilla home.

127

After supper that evening, as rain beat over the jungle, I sat back from the lantern light and listened to the conversation. Matches flared, highlighting the face of each officer.

The major was speaking, earnestly, so low I could barely hear.

"Tomorrow we do it again. The scouts returned while we were eating. This morning new Japanese troops moved back into the vicinity of the old deserted village of Pipiaia. They still have no islanders guiding them. They must have forgotten our last little party, so we'll give them another they'll never forget."

No one smiled, not even the major. That last "party" was a fire-fight in which twenty-two Japanese had been trapped and killed. One Fijian also lost his life—the first on Bougainville.

"Now, let's check the setup." Pushing back his packing-crate chair he stepped to the chart table. After a quick glance at the large-scale map thumbtacked to the board, he called into the darkness of the verandah. His batman, lounging just out of sight, came running.

"Go down to the camp and tell Bero we must see him immediately."

The soldier disappeared into the rain almost before the major had stopped speaking.

As he turned again to the battle chart other officers moved to his side. Fingers traced lines across the sheet, as though each man was silently choosing his position along the network of trails from which to ambush the enemy.

Naked feet whispering over the floor announced the arrival of Bero.

Squat, barrel-chested, tatooing around his eyes, there was no mistaking the man. He was of the jungle. A pair of khaki shorts with a kris at his waist was all that he wore. In one sweep his eyes covered the lamp-lighted room, the table, and all of the men bending over the map.

His face was expressionless.

Even as his shadow merged with the others on the wall, I realized that I had landed in one of the most drama-filled outposts of the whole war.

Breaking open his revolver, a junior officer moved onto the bunk beside me. Borrowing the can of oil with which I was cleaning my carbine, he quietly answered many of the questions I had been mentally asking about the sinister newcomer.

128

The deep chest, tatooed eyes, and animal tread were superficial. What held me was a feeling. The feeling of something untamed prowling that room amongst us, kept in check only by the frailest thread of a now faraway civilization. The feeling of being *inside* the tiger's cage.

129

"He's tough, that bloke, just as tough as they come. Unlimited endurance. Not much like a Solomon Islander, or had you noticed?" I admitted that I had been wondering where a man with such a build, and such a look in his eyes, came from.

"Bero was a Police Boy before the war, when these islands were governed under Australian Mandate. He and several others in our camp are from Papua, the wildest sector of New Guinea. Watch his eyes and the way he walks." It wasn't necessary. I was fascinated. Never before among any of the forest peoples with whom I had lived and worked had I ever seen that kind of man.

"But what place," I asked, "does a Papuan fill in your battalion? I've been told that no man in the Pacific is better qualified by heredity or environment to make a more dangerous jungle fighter than the Fijian." At that moment, the major sat on the edge of the bunk, having finished his briefing for the next day's action.

"Your idea of the Fijian is entirely correct. You will learn, while with us, that these men possess three remarkable characteristics. First, their senses of perception while in the bush are absolutely uncanny. Out there, they will see, hear, even smell things far beyond the powers of you or me. As you probably have noticed, we officers are divided. Half are Fijians. The other half come from New Zealand. For jungle sense, the Fijians beat us Kiwis every time. Every soldier in the ranks is Fijian, and every one of them is dangerous.

"The second trait is their tremendous good nature. Given the opportunity, raining or sunny, they will convulse each other with stories and jokes, then sing the rest of the day away. It isn't that they can't be serious. Wait until you have lain in ambush, or made an attack, with them at your side.

"It is, perhaps, just that they are happy men.

"Finally, I believe the secret of their warrior ability may be found in their complete lack of fear of the enemy and, apparently, an indifferent attitude toward death. No Fijian would worry about the possibility of being killed any more than he would question the sun not rising in the morning. Naturally, too, we officers believe that the training we have given these men has helped to intergrate their natural abilities with a hard-hitting, lightning-fast unit designed to stalk and deal with the enemy in any jungle of the Pacific." The major put another match to his pipe.

Outside, the rain had stopped.

130

"All of this brings us back to Bero and the other Papuans here at Ibu. Before the Japanese came, the Australian Government conducted a police school at Rabaul, New Britain. Men like Bero were sent from New Guinea to be trained as members of a constabulary force responsible for maintaining law and order throughout the Australian Mandated Islands. These Police Boys were recruited from among the most resourceful, intelligent, and toughest tribesmen of Papua. Their duty was to carry justice into the remote districts of even the most inaccessible islands.

"Some of the tribes with whom they worked were led by men still living in the shadows of head hunting. During their years of moving through these islands, the Papuans developed a knowledge of the trails unrivaled even by local hunters.

"Bero and the others were stationed here on Bougainville. With their understanding of the island and memory of its paths, they are invaluable. Just as you Marines, we New Zealanders and Fijians had never seen the place until a short time ago. To best carry on our campaign behind the lines we needed someone who knew the country as intimately as the floor of his own home. Police Boys like Bero were the answer."

Later, I was to ask Bero whether he or his ancestors had really ever practiced cannibalism. He laughed. When I asked how many Japs he had killed, he gave two answers. First, those he had shot with his carbine. Then, with another laugh, those he had finished in the way of the jungle, using only his kris or his bare hands. Both laughs sounded identical to me.

At Ibu, next day, there was intense excitement. Planes were low over the mountains, coming in fast. I dived for the jungle. Looking back, I was astonished to see the Fijians crowding into the clearing. They ran around hiding their weapons under nearby trees, then tore again into the open. Heads thrown back, they watched the sky.

In a tornado of sound, giant shadows swept across the treetops. SCAT transports were re-supplying the outpost. Propeller blasts stripped leaves from the topmost branches. Directly above the old mission house long cylinders shot into the air. Parachutes exploded in brilliant bursts. The tumbling canisters jerked back and swung down upon Ibu's tiny airstrip and into the clearing. Another plane swooped in, spilling more cylinders overhead. Each was stuffed with military hardware: ammunition, grenades, flares, surgical dressings—everything needed for jungle warfare, even charcoal to deaden reflections on already dark faces. Each parcel averaged three hundred pounds. Released at such low altitudes, many cylinders nearly struck earth before their parachutes fully opened.

One chute failed to open. Its load shot down at over a hundred miles an hour. Upon impact
ration cans sprayed the clearing. Only the old mission's sheet-iron roof prevented total
demolition by those gaudy, silk-tailed meteors, which my Marine buddies aimed right at us.

Several were dropped too late. Their loads dangled uselessly more than a hundred feet above the ground, each parachute glowing brighter than the most exotic tropical flower among the treetops. Padding their arms and legs against murderous thorns jutting from the tree trunks and the ferocious ants that lived in colonies on higher branches, several men were soon aloft cutting down the chutes and their precious cargos. If abandoned, the vividly colored silk would have served as riotous beacons marking the guerrillas' base with absolute precision for all enemy mortar crews and artillery observers within miles.

For the soldiers, every drop became a challenging game.

Each man in the clearing squinted casually up at the plummeting cylinders. Taunting shouts floated from the bordering jungle, The sport seemed hypnotic. Transfixed until the skull-crushing loads nearly clipped their caps, they then corkscrewed away trying not to get squashed—their greatest entertainment in weeks.

When two argued priorities on the next drop, sideline coaching rose to hilarious heights. Neither man gave an inch. One even ignored the pile driving cylinder; instead, he stood nonchalantly lighting a cigarette. As the missile plunged the last few separating feet, two posteriors disappeared over the ferns. Wild applause brought back the victor.

He hadn't snuffed the match.

In the wake of each parachute day, our Ibu Chapter of the Bougainville Porters and Spies Federation usually increased its membership about tenfold. When the outpost was first established, resident Solomon Islanders from that mountainous district rarely came to trade, or offer information about the enemy. But when the Japanese—isolated in their garrisons and nearly starving—started ravaging local villages and gardens, the islanders soon began to appear, timidly, at guerrilla headquarters. To walk suddenly into one of their slowly moving processions on the trails leading to the garrison always produced a gun-gripping shock.

They apparently journeyed without the accompaniment of friendly banter. Unlike most highland peoples of Latin America, over whom the buzz of conversation hangs like a swarm of gnats, the tribesmen of Bougainville move among the ferns and trees of their jungled home without a sound. But for the sighing wind, thunder of storms, crickets and frogs at night, an occasional whistle of a wandering cockatoo, the dull thud of another moldering jungle giant sinking to the floor of the rain forest, Bougainville is a land of deep silence.

133

With the oldest and the wisest in front, tapering to tiny men-children in the rear, the males of the tribe always led the pilgrimage. Out of sight back along the trail, the women followed, maintaining a constant, respectful distance from the heads of their households and the tribe. Backloads of bananas, papayas, taro, or squash bowed each mother from the waist. Perched on the very top of the burden rode her newest addition to the family—a solemn, owl-eyed

134

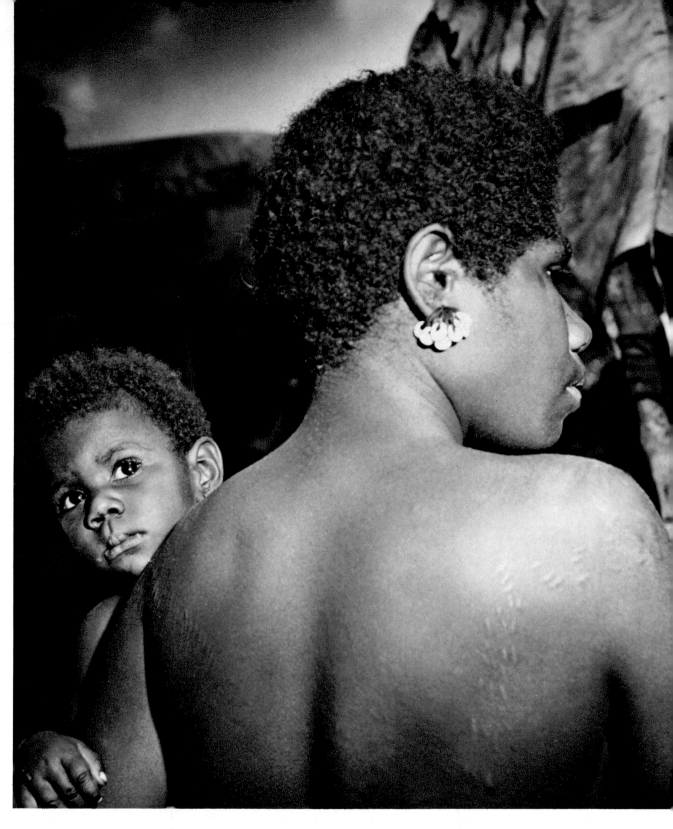

little mahout, prodding his pendulous-breasted steed through the endless wonders of a new world. Except for tribal or ceremonial scars adorning their chests and shoulders, the ladies wore only the prevailing costume of that part of the island—a dusky sheen of complacent serenity. When they arrived with eyes downcast behind the headquarters at Ibu, their men had already begun negotiations for the produce soon to be spread silently around them.

135

Ibu was a changed place the day Colonel Upton flew in from Torokina. Dove-tailing reports from local spies and his own scouts, he had concluded that the Japanese general at Numa Numa Plantation had ordered Ibu exterminated.

"There will be no more para-drops for several days," he told me. "If you wish, you may accompany another of our patrols into the bush." The "bush," I learned soon after landing at Ibu, was the Fijian term for any country away from headquarters. It originated in Australia, among frontiersmen speaking of the desert heart of the continent. At Ibu, whether meaning the open plantations on the east coast around Numa Numa, the lianas, ferns, mold and decay around the jungled Allied beachhead at Torokina, or even the deep canyons and razorback ridges of the volcanoes, it was all "the bush." Bush or jungle, we cut into it on the trail leading to the outer edges of the Fijian domain—and the Japs of Numa Numa.

Colonel Upton personally led that last patrol. His adjutant, Captain Merven Corner, was a stocky, tireless administrator who left nothing to chance. Before the war he had been one of New Zealand's greatest rugby stars. Like the others of the small group of officers temporarily based at Ibu, the colonel and his adjutant were an unemotional, rigorously trained, easy-going pair of jungle fighters. Within forty-eight hours they—and every other man in the outpost—were to be thrown upon their own resources for simple survival.

Winding down along the Numa Numa trail, we stopped in the gorge of the Wakunai River. There was only one ford for miles along the stream, and it was flanked on either side by high bluffs. The colonel quickly chose ambushes, to be manned by Ibu's daily Numa Numa patrol should the enemy launch an attack over that approach. Machine-gun fire lanes swept the trail and river for three hundred yards in both directions.

We then pushed closer to Numa Numa and Sisivie—just an obscure jungle knoll—the Fijians' most outlying command post.

In Sisivie, as at the earlier ambushes, Colonel Upton and Captain Corner relocated the positions of all weapons interdicting the trail. The trap below the nearby ghost-village of Tokuo was a terror—a masterpiece of guerrilla cunning. After seeing it, I understood more clearly why the Fijians were credited with nearly four hundred Japanese, against the death of a single comrade at Pipiaia.

Rising from the canyon of the Wakunai, the trail stretched over a spine of ridges approaching Tokuo. The gradient was so steep that even Bero and the other mountain-born Papuan

136

scouts grunted for breath as the colonel combed the slopes for ideal sites in which to plant his three-man Bren-gun teams. The trail's flanks were fern covered and dropped away into deep crevasses. Tremendous trees from below towered far overhead, throwing a confusing maze of shadows onto the trail.

For nearly fifty yards in front of the first Bren gun the track lay straight and narrow as a bayonet blade. Corporal Malakai Mo and two gunners burrowed down into the ferns until all that remained visible from the path was the gun's black snout. Barely an inch jutted from the gnarled root in which it was cradled. Nothing in front of the trap betrayed its presence. No spider web torn. No bit of moss dislodged or crushed. Not a fern leaf broken. Nothing had been touched.

After passing that first position the trail veered slightly for another forty yards. Only a woodpecker could have found the second Bren. It protruded from the trunk of a lightning-struck tree. Any force driving up from the Wakunai would be dropped on the ridge or blown aside to perish in the ravines below.

At that ambush the path dog-legged, then straightened to run for over a hundred yards along the crest of the ridge before dipping slightly to pass through the vacant huts of Tokuo village. The third Bren was dug in so that it could blanket the ridge with lead. Reversed, it commanded fire lanes that swept the village.

Leaving nine charcoal-blackened, fern-camouflaged bushmasters lying quietly behind those three Bren guns, Colonel Upton headed for Ibu.

No sooner had he arrived than the Japanese attacked. Within twenty-four hours the Fijians were engulfed in fighting that threatened to transform their record of incredible success to one of disaster.

Allied Headquarters at Torokina reported powerful enemy forces moving around Empress Augusta Bay. They soon overran the Torokina end of the Numa Numa trail, cutting that escape route. Colonel Upton's Fijians had to evacuate Ibu or face annihilation. Everything but the old mission house was left in flames.

At the first trail-block below Tokuo, Corporal Malakai Mo and his Bren gunners were hit by a full Japanese company. For six hours the enemy tried to shoot and claw their way past that knife-edge ridge. Machine guns and grenades rocked the jungle. Each time the Japs charged, single file—the jungle terrified them—they were cut down. Finally, behind mortar bombs, they hit the ambush again, but it had been abandoned. They sprayed the ridge with heavy machine-gun fire, not sure where the next ambush was hidden—then drove in with bayonets, screaming. The Fijians waited until they were within three yards. Bren-gun fire sent them cartwheeling over the edge. Other enemy soldiers appeared immediately upon the lower trail and attacked, again behind heavy machine guns which chewed the old lightning-struck tree trunk to splinters. The second position was deserted. The third ambush repulsed another massed attack. Then the Japs, having gained the sloping top of the ridge but fearing the Fijian fire more than the jungle, infiltrated around the trail. Their three-sided Banzai charge carried them over the position. Empty.

Corporal Malakai Mo and four buddies waited behind Tokuo village itself. Malakai had ordered the other four men of his team into the jungle, to report back to Sisivie. The last attack came at dusk. Bren and sub-machine gun slugs and grenades poured from the trees around the huts, lifting the leading Japanese soldiers into the air, driving the unwounded back into the darkness. Tokuo belonged to the night, and the Fijians. The enemy had lost more than one hundred men that afternoon. Not a Fijian was hit.

Reinforcements reached the Japanese assault company during the night. They regrouped noisily below Tokuo village, where Corporal Malakai Mo and his four friends had been taking turns sleeping while awaiting the next attack.

With dawn, heavy clouds seeped down from the volcanoes to blanket the ridge under dreary mist. On the forested knoll of Sisivie, a mile from where Malakai Mo and his gunners were again under enemy fire, Lieutenant Bruce Dent and a trail-block handful of men quietly waited. A thin ridge connected Sisivie with another hillock three hundred yards to its rear where a supporting Bren-gun was in position. Should the ridge be overrun, any men still in Sisivie were trapped.

Colonel Upton called on the walkie-talkie. His two full-strength guerrilla companies had evacuated Ibu and were racing to reinforce Sisivie when scouts reported a vastly superior enemy battle group holding the Numa Numa trail between his position and ours. Bero was now leading him into Sisivie from the rear over a long-unused and nearly forgotten trail. He hoped they would arrive within the hour. So did we. Sisivie had been under attack since noon. The mist had become a deluge. Even on the brightest day Sisivie was a dismal place of perpetual murk in the rain-forest gloom. With the downpour, visibility was failing as though it were night.

Bringing enemy fire, and all of his men, Malakai Mo filtered back into Sisivie. Everyone looked much the same in the rain. The Japanese, like the Fijians, wore olive-drab battle uniforms. They also pulled cloth caps low over their eyes to shield them from the storm. They even used black face paint. But they never stuck ferns around their heads, and all wore knee-length leggings—if one could see them.

At first, the Fijians stood motionless under the giant trees. As the enemy appeared from out of the rain they were shot through the head or chest. When the Japanese fired from below the hill their bullets only ricocheted among the branches overhead. Then they scaled the slope and broke into the lower camp area. Their shooting improved.

Everyone in Sisivie was busy. Riflemen dropped many Japs as they darted between the trees. Two Bren gunners poured bursts into the mouth of the trail. Sprinting around the hilltop with a sack of grenades slung over his shoulder, one soldier pulled the pins with his teeth, hurling the grenades and wild bellows into the faces below.

Beaten back, the enemy regrouped under the hillock. Each of the twenty Fijians on the knoll seemed to be living in a little world of his own. All except six-foot-four Malakai Mo. After returning from Tokuo he had stayed at my side with his sub-machine gun, handing me grenades when mine were gone. The other men waited among the ferns. One team of Bren gunners burst into loud laughter over some joke known only to themselves; no sense in remaining quiet any longer—the Japs knew exactly where we were. Guerrillas guarding our flanks hummed wordless tunes of their own creation, *in harmony*. An unmistakable sound came from a clump of bamboo. Someone was opening a ration tin with his bayonet.

Malakai Mo tapped on his tommy gun, grinning. He pointed to the grenade thrower who stood a little to our rear sheepishly tying together his dungarees. Machine gun slugs had ripped away the seat.

The Japs pushed forward again through the lower trees. Everyone threw grenades. Malakai Mo pointed into the rain. The six-foot-seven mortar man stood braced with feet far apart, completely exposed to the enemy, slamming one bomb after another into his weapon, *firing it from the waist*. Each shock twisted his massive body, but his feet never moved.

Lieutenant Bruce Dent roamed the hilltop checking ammunition, shifting weapons to strengthen weak points in the tiny perimeter, giving quiet orders to the men of his command. The enemy was cleared from Sisivie, their assault again stopped. Checking for casualties—there were none—Dent called two men and slipped out of Sisivie onto the ridge to the rear, leaving the comparative security of his massed fire to check personally if the way of escape was still open, should the order come. He also hoped to contact Colonel Upton's troops.

The Fijians in Sisivie lounged against trees.

Rain fell even harder.

The enemy returned.

They stormed the little hilltop without a sound. Their rifles were high-pitched, almost barking. Two heavy machine guns opened up from the trail below. Sniper shots sprinkled in from trees on the flanks and rear. Sisivie was being surrounded.

In the near-night and the rain, the Japanese were only elusive blurs advancing among shadows. Until the dripping painted face came rushing from the ferns one could never be sure. A pistol bullet twisted the limp cap and the face vanished, but then another arose to take its place. Now the cap flew off as though snatched aside by an invisible hand.

Malakai Mo touched my shoulder, shouting in my ear. Sisivie was to be abandoned, orders had come to withdraw. Colonel Upton's men were now behind us. With Bruce Dent, they were holding the ridge.

Half of Sisivie's Fijians vanished. The remaining ten men backed slowly, shooting. A flare glowed overhead. The first guerrillas had escaped. Those still in Sisivie shouted jeers out into the dark, firing parting bursts from every weapon on the hilltop. Then we ran like hell.

Sisivie was left forever. There were no regrets.

Colonel Upton's two infantry companies were spread out along an ancient path over which Bero said he could lead the way back across the mountains and down to the sea within a few miles of the Allied Perimeter. Captain Corner counted casualties. One Fijian was nicked precisely across the center of his scalp. Another had lost the camouflaging ferns from his cap —clipped short—and the tip of an ear. Machine-gun bullets had singed our grenade thrower when the burst had blown away the seat of his pants. He was now being heckled by other guerrillas who wondered what he had been doing when it happened.

Security guards moved out through the dripping mountains, into the night.

140

The rain stopped in mid-morning of the third day of marching after we left Sisivie. Just before noon, word reached the rear guard that scouts had crossed the divide and were starting down the other side. They could see the ocean. Jubilation temporarily numbed all hunger.

Then, it rained. When the tail of the column reached the divide there was nothing to be seen but more bamboo, ferns, low-hanging clouds, and a thin line of faltering men.

The descent was worse than climbing.

During the first two days when a man slipped, he struck only the vines and rocks of the mountain with his chest and face. Now when a soldier fell, he collapsed, twisting and rolling, to smash into the bamboo thickets below. My universe narrowed to the pair of plodding legs ahead. Ferns, arched over the path, hid the feet. As the column advanced hundreds of boots churned down through the mud, freeing nets of intertwined roots. Men disappeared over the edge of the trail when they tripped. Nobody stopped.

The world was the back of the man ahead.

As the Fijians slithered down the ridges and canyons, one hundred and fifty Solomon Islanders shuffled along in the center of the infantry column. They had aided in the evacuation of Ibu knowing that if captured by the Japanese they would be shot. They carried everything from radio transmitters to babies. Barefoot, trudging unhappily along, bending low under their burdens, tripping and falling with the Fijians, no Islander—not even a baby—ever voiced one word of complaint.

At dusk it was still raining.

Night closed over the bivouac. Colonel Upton passed back permission to light the first fires in four days. It still was bitterly cold on the lofty flanks of the volcanoes. There was nothing to eat. It made no difference any more. No one even mentioned it, or the cold. No one spoke at all. Perhaps the Fijians were thinking of one of their officers, Lieutenant Isireli Korovulavula, who had crashed in the jungle with an American Cub pilot when the weather suddenly hid Ibu and they ran out of gas while flying back toward Torokina. With the American on his back, Lieutenant Korovulavula slid down from the treetop into which they had smashed, then carried his wounded companion for a week across the mountains until the pilot, sure that he was dying, refused to continue. The Fijian survived, walking out of the wilderness twenty-one days later. He had lost seventy pounds but checked in immediately at his infantry battalion headquarters for duty.

The fifth morning of the march was beautiful.

We stood on the beach of western Bougainville watching Navy landing barges plow across the sea to pick us up. Marine fighter planes roared low overhead. Platoon after platoon of haggard, bearded, proud men assembled on the sands. The First Fiji Battalion was intact. Not a man had been lost, and two only slightly wounded, since the Japanese of Numa Numa had attacked Ibu.

Their campaign had not been the toughest, or the longest, and would never become famous. Indeed, it seemed most unlikely that anyone other than Fijians or New Zealanders would ever remember or hear of Ibu at all. Yet in fulfilling their mission, Colonel Upton and his jungle fighters planted the seed of a legend of black ghosts in the Solomon Islands that was told, changed, then retold by those soldiers who left Bougainville to follow the war north through the other islands of the Pacific. But however much it was changed, no one could ever tell the story better than simply the way it was up at Ibu with the Fijian guerrillas.

Oh lovely special day!

Bougainville, Solomon Islands.
19 February, 1944

Safely inside the Allied perimeter,
after walking across
this unfriendly island—
and today, the 18th
on the other side of
the International Dateline,
Dad's birthday.

Today was terrific! I got my mail. Ninety-four pieces all told.
At last I know, dear family, what's been happening outside my little world.

Marine Photographic Squadron-254,
Marine Air South Pacific,
% Fleet Post Office,
San Francisco, California.
7 April, 1944

So brother Ken is now in the Navy, the service he desired, and their house in Memphis sold. That Mona and the kids will now come home to you is wonderful! All concerned should welcome these coming opportunities for getting reacquainted. How grateful you must be, too, that you didn't sell the old house. Seems funny, doesn't it, that the eldest and the youngest should be in uniform.

Ken should soon enjoy the life, if he is capable of overlooking the youthful crudeness and vulgarity of the kids. Surely his draft classes are running toward men of his own age, so he should find much in common with his new comrades. Again, physically, he'll gain after the first fatigue wears off and be in the best health he'll have enjoyed since his ice-wagon days.

Thinking of those younger guys who seem to assume that by being incredibly coarse they are acquiring toughness—slipping into the "hero's" role of a cheap, intellectually cheap, novel through obscenity—they are never *really* tough at all.

In my life I have had the pleasure of knowing some truly tough men: Captain Allie Ebanks, Michael Lerner, General Somoza, and a couple of enormous Fijians about whom you have not yet heard—and except for an occasional "hell" or "damn" they never swore. Heck, I'm not so very tough but I have yet to meet one of these self-announcing "toughs" whom I won't challenge with pistols, knives, sub-machine guns, swordfish harpoons, or my bare fists.

Speaking of one non-military aspect of your overseas gypsy, I have, as of yesterday, severed all connections with my immediate career as a wandering accordionist. Traveling always by air, never in the same place more than a couple of days or weeks, I simply had no time to teach myself to play it. Only arrived at page 13 of Book One and then had to fill in by ear. Besides, it was beginning to pick up mildew. Sold it for $55 more than I paid. The Marine who bought it will soon be going home, where he plans to give it to his wife. Really was a beauty. I hope someday to find another and start again. The desire is still wide awake.

* * *

143

At last! The job is finished. Six months to the day. One thousand matched enlargements covering the combat-transport division of Marine Corps aviation in the South Pacific. A thousand prints, single-handed!

Marine Photographic Squadron-254,
1st Marine Air Wing, Fleet Post Office,
San Francisco, California.
28 July, 1944

During the few hours that I took off from the darkroom in Sydney, Australia—where I did all of my lab work in the photo setup of the *Sydney Sun*—I either went for walks, shopped for black opals, or slept.

My walks from the darkroom brought me into contact with most of the jewelers and gem polishers of Sydney, who first gave me the benefit of their knowledge, then helped me find what I sought. To describe the black opal is quite impossible. But when I think about what they *seem* to be, well: multiple rainbows shimmering within midnight tears . . . happy tears. When I get home you'll see the finest black opal to leave Australia during the war, and one of the finest just plain ever. You know I have always wanted a beautiful gem stone in a ring. I have it now.

So help me, I sold my Honolulu accordion before I left the Solomon Islands and decided to get a very inexpensive small one that I could toss in my seabag. You know me! I now own a really magnificent 120-bass job; an Italian Soprani with four tonal shifts on the piano side and one on the bass. Absolutely brand new. Very beautiful, too. Sort of Moroccan red and silver. Even though I can't play a darned thing, you'd be surprised, even amazed, by the quality, depth, and variety of sounds I can get out of it—all pleasing. Who knows, perhaps I'll get off page 13 in that instruction book!

In Sydney, I met a *girl*; one you would adore, unlike any ever to come into your home. She would have fitted. Georgie is half French and half Japanese. Her hair tumbles below her shoulders, polished ebony. When she smiles, a flash of white dims any other illumination around. Dusky apricot complexioned with highly arched jet black eyebrows over languid, or fiery eyes, she might easily have been Queen of the Nile, or of Polynesia. Capable and

144

smart as any girl has a right to be; truly radiant; fingers so tiny I can span her entire hand with my first three fingers. Georgie embodies those qualities I have always hoped to find.

Like the black opal, Georgie is unique.

Yes, I fell in love.

Had I not been going back to where I am now, in the business in which I am now, weighing my feelings for her against the responsibilities that this uniform imposes upon me *now*, I should have reached for that slender hand—yesterday, and every day of the future.

Thanks to my search for black opals I became the close friend of an astonishing man. Czech refugee, now a diamond tool maker; slender; sallow; hair falling continually as a colorless screen hiding pale, almost flat gray eyes; master of nine languages; my age, Kovi Bomba smiles only when handling black opals or recalling the ways young men of his homeland, in the thirties, faced the dangers of life under Gestapo agents.

When I once said that Prague must be a beautiful city, Kovi agreed. "Beautiful! I remember it as the place my father—an ornamental iron worker, a real artist—used to stand in the streets before the main hotels, early in the morning or at dusk, looking up at the windows hoping to catch the eye of a tourist who would let him carry the luggage to the station. There was no other work."

Kovi left Czechoslovakia, wandered across Europe, was jailed in Spain during the Civil War (where he added fluent Spanish to his list), somehow got to China where he acted as bodyguard to a warlord (his days of facing the Nazis had not left him unfamiliar with weapons), then, finally, caught a grain ship to Australia where, without papers or passport, he was given sanctuary. In Melbourne he took up his father's old craft, ornamental iron working. There, too, he saw and became enraptured with black opals. He also began handling industrial diamonds, which are indigenous to Australia.

Shortly thereafter he made a discovery of considerable significance for all craftsmen who cut iron or other very hard materials. He learned how to infuse powdered diamonds into the bronze edge of rotary-saw discs. Always before, it seems, diamond chips were embedded in the edges of such saws, making them rather thick. The fusion of diamond dust and bronze permitted saws to be made as thin as the metal blade itself, allowing much finer work than before. Sales from his blades—which he had patented—brought in more money than he had ever had before. He saved nearly a thousand Australian pounds. Then, one fine morning, he walked out of his shop with his savings, caught a train to the place—the only place—where first-water black opals are mined in the world: Lightning Ridge, New South Wales, a cluster of prairie dog mounds northwest of Sydney, hundreds of miles from nowhere.

The village taxi at Lightning Ridge drove him out into the arid countryside to where he could see the mounds of the mine shafts ahead, just low gravel heaps. Stopping and paying the cabbie—who took off for town—Kovi stripped, put on his most tattered work clothes, then, after putting his thousand pounds in his pocket and his city clothes under a flat rock, he headed for the miners' clapboard shacks.

He knocked on one door after another. There were several dozen opal miners living in the place, mostly cantankerous old men, semi-hermits, known throughout Australia for their ill humor, and as "gougers." Many never even opened their doors. Others listened to his plea for work, but still slammed their doors. It was suppertime. He was not invited in. Then he found a door blocked by a tall, sturdily built, white-haired and bearded man, probably in his seventies, who casually beckoned Kovi inside with the flick of a finger. The door was left open behind them. Two plates were already on the supper table. Kovi met Bobbie Reynolds, an English poet of rather noble lineage turned opal gouger.

Kovi stayed with Bobbie Reynolds at Lightning Ridge for seven weeks, learning about black opals, mining for them himself. He dug his own mine shaft: simply a narrow, vertical hole down through alluvial earth and gravel, riding in a bucket suspended by block and tackle from a rafter spanning the mouth of the shaft. At depths ranging from eighty to one hundred and twenty feet he struck a horizontal stratum of gun-metal black stone—probably a type of limestone—which was terribly hard, called "steelband" by the gougers. Cutting through that —usually about a yard thick—he found himself in opal gravels, in theory. In fact, he never found a black opal during his entire back-breaking apprenticeship. But he didn't care, for that wasn't his reason for being there.

However, he learned that opals are the residual mineral salts that were deposited infrequently

146

in sacs beneath the steelband, aeons ago, when dikes of volcanic water tried to escape to the earth's surface. Blocked by the steelband, the rivulets turned back, formed pockets, cooled ever so slowly, and, under perfect geological conditions in a few sacs, formed black opals, the mineral precipitate of the volcanic water.

In some places the mineral-laden water precipitated opalescent deposits upon the bottom of the steelband stratum, beautiful but extremely thin, too thin to be polished into solitaire gem stones. The gougers cut these opal-encrusted sections free from the surrounding stratum, then, during periods of bad weather or at night, tediously polished away the base of drab steelband, leaving just a thin veneer of gem stone affixed to a mirror-like backing. These thin veneers were later glued to heavier pieces of low-quality opal and sold as "doublets," sometimes sold to the unwary or to the novice collector as the real, full-bodied gem. Of course, the difference in price between a solid black opal and a doublet was enormous. Yet the doublets helped the gougers to earn their daily livings, since the finding of a great black opal was a rare event.

At dinnertime, as the weeks passed, other gougers in Lightning Ridge began calling at Bobbie Reynold's shack. Kovi had become an accepted sight around the mounds. The others apparently were curious to discover what, if anything, he had found. When they saw that he had still to make his first strike, they were more tolerant, even showing him the opals they had found. Each carried his year's finds (they sold to the Sydney market just once a year) in a chamois pouch around his neck or in a cotton-padded snuff box in his pocket. Testing Kovi's new knowledge of opals—and Bobbie's role as a teacher—each would hold out one stone at a time, asking Kovi's opinion as to its weight, quality, and value. It seems that with each test Kovi under- or over-estimated the stone's weight and value—he could *never* hit it on the nose. The gougers were fairly crude in their scorn and laughter. It also seems that almost every time, during such a cross-examination, Kovi had to excuse himself to slip out to the privy behind the shacks—where, in a tiny notebook, he itemized every black opal in Lightning Ridge, appraised by the gougers themselves, in front of gougers, as to weight, quality, and value.

One night, again just at suppertime when each gouger was in his shack, Kovi ran from door to door, explaining that a relative had just died, left him a few pounds, so here, here are X number of pounds for your nine-carat green opal, and another Y pounds for the blue, and Z for the tiny red one with purple flashes. He cleaned out Lightning Ridge . . . and was gone into the night. He pulled off the greatest coup ever known in the opal fields, unlike anything heard of among those rough men since the gems were first mined in any quantities, starting before the turn of the century.

All of this has a direct bearing on my magnificent jewel.

As months passed, Kovi, back in his diamond tool shop, kept thinking of those crusty old gougers spending their nights and rainy days slowly polishing doublets by hand. So he rigged a foot-driven potter's wheel with a set of his diamond disc saws and shipped it to the opal miners of Lightning Ridge. With it they could slice through the hard, worthless layers of steelband supporting the thin veneer of opal, cutting away in seconds what had taken days before. The gougers, in their appreciation—and respect for a man even more canny than themselves—decided to send him, once a year, the single finest stone each of them had found. The price? The price to a fellow gouger.

Kovi had told me that he expected the year's parcel momentarily, and that, if I wished, I might choose one stone. The day he called me at the darkroom I shot out of the place, down the street, and into his place—leaving spinning Sydneyites in my wake. He had an unopened snuff box on his workbench; a dozen long boxes of rough industrial diamonds had been shoved aside. He opened the flat tin container under a single naked light bulb—and held molten fire in his hand. Twelve black opals.

We said absolutely nothing. He just moved the tin slowly under the light. Then, gently touching a glowing combination of scarlet and indigo flashes polished into a regal, slightly cabochon almond, he whispered, almost in prayer, "It's a miracle!"

My agreement was complete. "Super! Really incredible!" I reached into the far end of the snuff box to brush cotton away from the great curved cornea of an emerald-green eye sprinkled with flecks of pure gold staring at both of us.

Kovi straightened slightly from the table, turned his own colorless eyes on me, then looked again into the snuff box: "You learn fast."

148 * * *

Lieut. D. D. Duncan
VMD-254
1st Marine Air Wing
% Fleet Post Office
San Francisco, California

Lt. Colonel Geoffry Upton
Commanding. First Battalion
Fiji Infantry Regiment
Suva, Fiji
12 November, 1944

My dear Dunc—

Your letter with the pictures & stories gave me a great thrill.

I am enclosing shoulder patches & Fiji titles of our Regiment & would be very proud to have you wear them. Don't forget the patch is worn as a square. I enclose a spare set for good measure.

I have passed on your regards to all the boys & they were excited to hear from our old friend. I am getting the big battalion set of photos you gave us framed & after they have been exhibited in Suva they will adorn the walls of the officers' mess. They are marvelous.

We are now in a good permanent camp with nice quarters & no tents. We are all training hard for new campaigns & hoping for the best. Hope you will be along with us again.

Am afraid there are no air-mail facilities from here but this should go quite fast. Hope you will get your spell at home old son & have a really good time. You deserve it.

Drop us a line again & keep us up with your wanderings. Until then Da Moce, as we say in Fiji. Happy Landings, Dunc. Come see us soon.

Your friend,
Geoff Upton

* * *

Captain M. E. Corner
2nd N.Z.E.F.
Attchd 1st Battalion
Fiji Infantry Regiment
N.Z.A.P.O. 250
12 November, 1944

Dear Dave,

The C.O. showed me your letter and the coloured prints, also the articles you wrote. I think you have made a great job of them all and am pleased that your facts have been kept so true to things as they really happened. Although some of the incidents will be hard for some people to believe we know that as you relate them they are true to facts.

At the moment we are in a wooded camp, training and reorganizing for another job should we be called on. The life of a permanent camp is not the free and easy life of active service. Where in combat the big thing is to get a job done and that is all, in training there is so much red tape that one gets very fed up with army life. I suppose once having been through the mill of training we find our second threshing a bit wearisome.

Well Dave if I can do anything for you at anytime let me know, and if you hit New Zealand again after this mess is cleaned up, contact me at the Auckland Savings Bank and we will continue our friendship where we left off.

Kind regards,
Merv Corner

First Endorsement   (Date) **Dec 23 1944**

From: Transport Commander.
To: **1st Lt. David D. Duncan, (018021), USMCR (8500),**

Subject: Orders.

1.   You reported for transportation on **5 December 1944.**

2.   Subsistence was furnished without cost to you.

3.   Transportation completed this date.

Irwin E. Farington
Major, T.C.
Transport Commander.

HAPPY NEW YEAR!

BOQ, Hdqts, Marine Corps Air Depot,
Miramar, San Diego 45, California.
31 December, 1944

It is already—just being here, exactly a year and a half since I went through from Quantico on my way to the Pacific. At that time everything seemed so new and strange—not frightening, really—just so different from anything I'd known before. Now that vast Pacific Ocean seems like an old, old friend, and several of its islands are almost like home. Not *your* kind of home, certainly. Yet home in another way, a way that one who has never been there—under these peculiar circumstances—will ever understand or know. I wonder how many of the other guys miss it already, too.

What a Christmas! Just hearing your voices! It truly sounded as though we were all around the tree together. What could any material gift add to our joy. Surely, that is exactly the spirit intended originally—the gifts borne to Bethlehem by the shepherd kings were simply pagan offerings acknowledging that they were bowing before and servants of a Sovereign come to rule over the *hearts* of all men who accepted the prophecy of His birth.

Let me tell you, now, of another gift made to each man aboard our transport—and to their families—this Christmas week. Shortly before midnight our last night out—eighteen days after sailing from Guadalcanal—we were approaching San Francisco Bay on a calm ocean, under a cloudless, moonless, star-filled sky. At the most, we were no more than fifty miles off the Golden Gate. The ground echelon of our squadron was aboard. All of the remaining space was filled with wounded men. Our escorting warships had dropped us somewhere around Hawaii. Most of the guys were asleep below. Since I usually slept on the planks over the aft hold, I was quietly visiting with the gunners of nearby weapons, which were manned constantly during the voyage. We were probably talking about where we hoped to spend Christmas if we could just get cleared through San Francisco quickly the next morning, after we docked.

Suddenly, as I sat on my heels listening to one of the gunners at the rail, a monstrous blacker-than-the-night *shape* appeared over the gunners' silhouettes. I spun and threw myself flat upon the boards of the hold, trying to dig my fingers into those planks—waiting. Nothing happened. Slowly, unbelievingly, I got back up, ran to the stern, then to the prow. At that moment GENERAL QUARTERS sounded throughout the ship (that's the TOTAL alarm). It was unnecessary. Disappearing into the night across the tranquil sea, two of our destroyers held their course—while we serenely continued on toward the Golden Gate. With no running lights showing, our jammed-to-the-gunwales transport had sailed directly between them.

The helmsman of the destroyer that I had seen loom over us, had apparently ordered full-speed astern when he saw us appear dead ahead—which threw his bow up and back just enough for us to slide under. Our tail gunners on the fantail claimed later that they could have touched the steel nose of the other ship in that frozen moment before we moved apart.

The second destroyer passed in front of us with only a slightly greater margin of clearance.

Our bridge rang ALL CLEAR almost immediately, passing it off as a false alarm so that the wounded were headed back to their bunks and starting to sleep again practically before the orderlies and medics had begun evacuating them to the deck.

If the three captains involved had not been maintaining radio silence, I would have loved being in the communications shacks when the red lights went on and their receivers warmed up.

So, my dear Mother and Dad, this is indeed a

Merry Christmas!

Dave

Start baking those pop-overs!

I should be out of here within a week, headed for a month's leave—and home.

UNITED STATES MARINES CORPS
HEADQUARTERS, AIRCRAFT, FLEET MARINE FORCE, PACIFIC,
℅ FLEET POST OFFICE, SAN FRANCISCO, CALIFORNIA.

5 April, 1945

From: Commanding General.
To: First Lieutenant David D. DUNCAN, (018021), USMCR (VS-PR),
           (5401), (HqSq, AirFMFPac).

Subject: Orders, special temporary aviation duty.

References: (a) CMC letter, serial MC-410923, dated 24Feb45.
            (b) PacFlt letter 12L-45, dated 8Feb45.

1. On or about 8 April, 1945, you will proceed via first available Government aircraft to such places as the Headquarters First, Second, Third and Fourth Marine Aircraft Wings may then be, where upon arrival you will report to the respective Commanding Generals thereat, for special temporary aviation duty in connection with photographic matters concerning combat aviation.

2. The officers to whom you are directed to report are requested to assist you in your mission as communicated to you orally, and to provide you with government aircraft transportation to various echelons under their commands and to other Wings.

3. You have been directed to photograph all phases of Marine Aviation, both land and carrier based.

4. You are authorized to report to the above designated officers in any sequence deemed expedient.

5. You are authorized to carry and use cameras as an official photographer of the Marine Corps.

6. Class II priority air transportation for travel by air and excess baggage allowance of two hundred (200) pounds, consisting of Government equipment, are hereby certified as necessary in the execution of these orders.

7. You will keep this office informed of your whereabouts at frequent intervals. Upon completion of this special temporary aviation duty, and when directed by proper authority, you will return to your regular station and resume your regular duties.

8. Your detail to duty involving flying is continued in force for this duty.

9. A per diem of seven dollars ($7.00) in lieu of subsistence will be allowed while absent from your regular station, except when government quarters are available, when three dollars ($3.00) will be allowed.

10. The travel herein enjoined is necessary in the public service.

James T. MOORE

Those dream orders are mine!

You see—as I tried to explain when I was at home—the entire secret of my job out here, if it works, will be to go into the forward areas armed with orders from the top brass of the Marine Corps which say, in effect, even though this guy DDD is only a lieutenant he is to be given the green light for his work; he *must* be given air or surface transport when he requests it; he can take photos anywhere he desires; he must have top priority when changing stations—in short, he must be given the consideration a combat general or admiral receives.

Some dream!

Incidently, censorship has now been removed from disclosing where we are, so you *know* that the war is moving in our favor—at last.

Guam.
21 April, 1945

Here, as everywhere I'm sure, the death of President Roosevelt came as a chilling jolt. Who knows what he was carrying in his head! His personal contact with Churchill. His extraordinary *image* of leadership in times of crisis. That voice which put shape to dreams, and dreams to lofty purpose. These have nothing whatsoever to do with Roosevelt the peculiar political creature that was formed by our times, the Depression most of all.

Now, with Harry Truman, another purely political creature sits in the White House. Fellow Missourian. Fellow Kansas Citian. The ultimate product of the Pendergast powerhouse and machine. With Tom Pendergast a near-neighbor for so long, up on Ward Parkway; with our knowledge of his machine's blackjack methods of handling labor and opposition voters' businesses around Kansas City throughout my lifetime, and much of yours, we should all simply pray that *President* Truman—like Man himself—will evolve into something finer than the muck that spawned him.

My plane soon takes off. So this note and I part—going opposite ways—filled with excitement for the future. Who knows what lies ahead?

153

Visibility was almost zero.

Okinawa Shima, Ryukyu Islands.
21 May, 1945

Thick curtains of rain swished past the windows as we roared in from Guam. The pilot held the big transport low, nearly clipping the waves. Strings of aircraft carriers burst through an open patch in the storm—and instantly disappeared. Okinawa lay straight ahead. We couldn't see it. Then the wheels rumbled and locked, our plane banked, engines surged, and we went in—splattering mud, skidding to a stop. Yontan airstrip, that April morning, was all of the grimness we had ever heard about the place.

Until we invaded—Easter morning—few stories had ever been printed about the island, and they were unkind. Now, with its cloak of enemy secrecy torn aside, Okinawa appears to be one of the better places revealed by the war.

While most of us were unprepared for the beauty of Okinawa, its people have proven even more of a surprise. After the battles in the Marianas, where thousands of civilians chose mass suicide to surrender, we had every reason to believe that the Okinawans would follow the Japanese soldiers' example with equal fanaticism since this was an integral part of the Japanese Empire. Nothing could have been farther from the truth. Okinawans scarcely consider themselves Japanese. And, ethnically, they scarcely are.

It's not a very big island. Only sixty-seven miles long and about five wide. On maps of the United States it would cover little more than the sand dunes between Palm Beach and Miami. Like those two resort cities, it is exactly the same distance north of the Equator. The East China Sea, separating Okinawa from Shanghai, even vibrates with the same intense blue of the Gulf Stream. There is, however, one tremendous difference. Were we to fly four hundred and fifty miles north, instead of Savannah, Georgia, we would be over Nagasaki, Japan.

154

For more than fourteen centuries Okinawa has fed the families of immigrants from a dozen foreign shores. Most recently, the Japanese sent boatloads of settlers to the island, which they annexed from China at the end of the nineteenth century. But there were many other peoples here long before the Japanese.

Through a thousand years of obscurity Okinawa was a step-child of China. Merchants, traders, fishermen, farmers, coolies came here in an unending stream, although few on the mainland knew much about the place. During earlier centuries it was never called Okinawa; in those days it—and the other islands of its group—was heralded as the Kingdom of Loochoo, which bowed to a local dynasty of Chinese emperors.

155

Through those centuries too, sampans, junks, freight canoes, schooners, and the surf itself brought hundreds of Malayans, Indo-Chinese, Filipinos, a few Russians, and a sprinkling of nearly every other race of the Far East. Still earlier, the island was peopled by fair-complexioned, heavy-set, thickly haired aborigine Ainus, the first-known residents of the islands of the Western Pacific. It would take considerable imagination to call Okinawans Japanese.

A final confusing element to throw into the racial *bouillabaisse* which is Okinawa is the fact that many of its people speak Spanish. Nothing has surprised me more during the Pacific war. My first inkling that some Okinawans spoke the tongue came one morning while I was out in the civilian internment sector on the Katchin Hanto peninsula. An old man, seeing me on a dike in the rice paddies, hailed me with a frantic wave then plunged into the knee-deep water to overtake me. Waiting for him to catch his breath after he hopped onto the dike beside me, I naturally wondered just what underlay his excitement.

His hands spoke first. Then his voice. Neither told me a thing I could understand. Finally, he got them synchronized. Clenching then popping open his fists with a devastating flourish, he indicated that something had blown sky-high. Obviously not my newly acquired friend. Then two words registered hits from the wheezing and spluttering of his verbal barrage. Both were apparently Spanish: *peligro*, which means "danger," and *cuidado*, which is "beware" or "stop." Astonished, I asked, in Spanish, whether he spoke the language. His face showed no glimmer of understanding. I had been mistaken. Still, his agitation made me curious.

My tottering guide took off through the paddies. Instead of following the dikes we sloshed up into a sweet-potato patch. I saw nothing under his pointing, gnarled finger . . . then my pulse went up three hundred percent.

Booby trap!

Nearly touching my toe, practically hidden by leaves, lay a hand grenade. Looking up at the old man, thinking a multitude of jumbled things, I found his expression one of sublime serenity. I was expected to do something. I did—with a gut-full of misgivings. The leaves made it impossible to see the booby trap's wires.

No rattlesnake back in the Florida Everglades was ever approached more gingerly.

Slipping my knife into the leaves, I tried to find the wire. Old Patriarch Pedro, looking over my shoulder, acted as though I was giving a lesson in panning gold. The blade had moved through a nearly complete arc around the grenade when my confederate leaned too far forward, fell upon me—and the knife slashed the remaining distance. Nothing happened. There were no wires, nor was it a booby trap: only an American grenade dropped by a passing Marine on patrol of the peninsula. Had he so desired, the peasant could easily have pocketed it, waited, then blown the daylights out of a jeep-load of Seabees or Army engineers. Instead, he pleaded with the first "enemy" he saw to take it away . . . typical of so many of the world's peasants, caught by wars they never understand but cannot escape.

The next day I met an entire family headed for the Katchin Hanto internment camp. Though at first shy and speechless, they melted when they saw the matches and chocolate I offered in exchange for their photograph. Then the smallest boy shot away in pursuit of his goat. The mother called to her son. There it was again! She was telling him to come back—in Spanish. They were in no hurry to arrive at the internment area, and were surprised we could understand each other. They had lived in Peru for twenty-six years, where they and many other Okinawans had gone as laborers. Tales of high wages had lured them from the constant hard work in their own fields. Thousands of other Okinawans sailed to Argentina, Chile, Brazil, and Hawaii, where stories of wealth beckoned them, too. By the time they discovered that wages abroad were indeed somewhat higher than at home, but also that life there was vastly more expensive, it was too late. With no other honorable escape possible, they stayed and worked and reared their children, and prayed and saved for the day when they might pay for a ticket home. Many never got away. They remain scattered throughout the tropics of Latin America today. Others finally made it, taking home broods of Spanish-speaking children, dozens of unmistakably Latin traits, and even substantial numbers of Latin American husbands and wives. Their return added a pinch of *mañana* and laughter to the heterogeneous Okinawan character.

Another day I was again out on the Katchin Hanto, waiting in a cluster of deserted huts, hoping to catch an old nanny goat and her two kids browsing among the hibiscus lining the path. To me the scene reflected the loneliness and heartbreak of the homes that had been abandoned in the path of our invasion. The only trouble was that the goats refused to come out of the bushes. And everything about that day was beginning to seem absurd—with the southern half of the island still engulfed in a flaming war.

158

My patience was about gone when a whisper of voices floated from the flowers behind me. Slowly, with the faintest of rustles, they crept around me. I didn't know who they were, but I knew exactly what they were doing. The she goat sauntered out into the sunlight, stood on her spindly hind legs to browse on some brilliant blossoms—and I had my picture.

When I stood up, stretching foxhole kinks from my knees, two jet-eyed brothers slipped from the bushes behind the goats. With hilarious chuckles they slapped the animals' rumps, sending them bouncing out of sight. Now solemn faced, they walked straight to me to give my camera their most professional attention. When I placed it on the ground, they peered intently into the hooded top, as they had seen me do. The image on the ground glass thrilled them speechless, a priceless reward for their efforts. Then, while the smallest of the two was taking his second look, I felt someone behind me. Big brother, so small his head barely reached my belt, was carefully brushing the dust of the path from the seat of my campaign-faded pants. Slipping into my pack I walked slowly to the main road. I stopped and looked back. They hadn't moved. They waved, and I waved. Then we turned and went our ways.

159

CHAPTER VI

Thick red mud spewed off the tires as the truck hauled us to the airstrip. The stuff splashed into every face, to be only half-heartedly wiped away. It was a lousy morning to go hunting.

On the field, even in the semi-light, you couldn't miss our plane. Long-bellied, ponderous, machine guns hackled out from each bulging muscle, it squatted against the ground a giant of deadly strength. Through the murk its tail fin soared alone, a vast gray sail dwarfing the other bombers and fighters clustered around the runway. This was the heavyweight of the Navy—Consolidated's Privateer—the newest weapon in the ocean war against Japan.

The morning before, I had taken off from Yontan aboard an identical bomber. We flew up past Kyushu, Japan, and the east coast of Korea. Business was only fair: one harbor holding three freighters bombed, and a lone oil tanker sunk. Returning south, the pilot was on instruments for nearly five hours. Twisting, climbing, swooping back down to the sea, we prowled the pinnacle-studded Korean shore, hunting, but found nothing more. That was yesterday.

There was something curious about *this* morning. During the past two years I had made numerous flights over enemy territory having no premonitions of any sort. This day was different. It could have been just the rotten weather. Yet I made sure my little wooden lucky bear was snuggled in her corner of my pocket—then shoved off.

160

Yontan Airfield, Okinawa.
30 May, 1945 – dawn.

Today, for the first hour, we stayed low over the East China Sea. The water, normally liquid cobalt, lay sullen and drab, hammered flat by the rain. Lieutenant Joe Jobe, flying the second Privateer of our team, moved up until the two bombers' wings seem entwined. We had no escorting fighters. Looking straight ahead from my temporary station in the nose turret, the world choked down to a narrow chute of clouds and rain through which we hurtled but never escaped . . . a wide-eyed version of childhood dreams where I ran forever, but stood still.

Back in my assigned place across from the radar operator, life on the Privateer was the same as on most four-engined bombers. Two turret gunners were on the inter-phone haranguing each other with memories of last meals Stateside. Listening in, I found it difficult to remember that I was with one of the Navy's crack search crews in the Pacific—looking for trouble.

This massive plane had just sunk a Japanese destroyer, and before that had given birth to a whole litter of battle reports listing enemy transports, tankers, and merchantmen destroyed or damaged. Except for the destroyer, their targets were not for headlines; they were aiming at the veins through which flowed most of the enemy's supplies, reinforcements, and even evacuees from now nearly isolated garrisons; lesser targets, each armed to the gunwales and waiting for a pair of the wave-skipping bombers to appear in their sights.

Now, except for those laconic orders that made our huge plane a compact, finely tuned destructive instrument, there was no evidence that we were roaring straight toward the heart of all Japanese troop concentrations on the mainland of China. Friendly banter bounced around the inter-phone as we climbed through the overcast. We broke out. The sunlight was blinding. It changed the whole world. My constricting chute of gloom was gone. Cloud dunes stretched to the horizons. War and bombing, and recurring sadness, seemed of another life.

The inter-phone popped, then a voice called for me. Lieutenant Leo Kennedy, our pilot, knowing that pictures were my sole reason for accompanying his mission, had asked the second bomber to come up close again for its portrait. Then he invited me into the cockpit. It would be rather snug, but he offered to slide open his window so that I might get what I wanted by shooting over his left shoulder. The combination worked. We decided to use it during any possible attacks against enemy shipping.

We didn't have long to wait. Radar came in to pilot. He had the Chu-shan Islands on his screen. We were within thirty miles of China. The cloud cover had begun to break, but we still couldn't see the water. Kennedy waved off our sister ship, gave his co-pilot the nod, wheeled over, and started down.

162

The warm contentment of a moment before was gone. Low, just over the water, visibility was about five miles. Islands were everywhere, little knobs of earth covered with tiny farms. I saw many peasant families bending over their crops of grain. Most never looked up even though we flew just overhead. It was harvest time—earlier here than on the Kansas plains.

Out among the fishing craft reaction to us was different and immediate. Tales by survivors of attacks by these shark-tailed, winged battleships must have bred deep terror in the hearts of all who sailed the China Sea. Nearly clipping the rigging of larger sampans, we could see their crews lying huddled in the bilge or crouching behind masts. Some jumped overboard. Except for strafing the few showing radio antennae, our gunners never touched most of these boats. Though their catch was probably confiscated by the Japanese, the majority of the fishermen were undoubtedly Chinese who had no choice but to serve the invader.

Kennedy and Jobe were now half a mile apart heading straight toward the mainland, so low that the fishing boats boiled around us as blurs. Then we saw land. What a disappointment! Instead of being wild and mountainous, as was Korea, China was checkerboard flat. Most fields were planted in cane. Sugar refinery chimneys bristled in the distance through the haze. Shanghai lay beyond.

We veered north before crossing the shore. The sea below was now a vile brown, as though all of the GI khaki on earth had just been washed there. We were in the Yangtze estuary. It seemed impossible. We had gotten in undetected.

I saw the first target only after Leo Kennedy banked hard to port and his machine gunners began hammering. There really were two targets: a lightship, and its escort. Jobe led the attack. Kennedy followed close on his tail. We were up about two hundred feet, circling, the two boats held in the center. From over Leo's shoulder I could plainly see the tracers from both planes stabbing through their hulls. Other bursts chopped cups from the sea all around, and ricocheted off their decks. There was no need to waste bombs. The lightship lay dead, sinking. Her escort was lost in smoke, its stern aflame.

Wagging his wings to his partner, Kennedy slipped down once more to wave level, headed for another sector of the estuary. He made contact immediately. With a shy smile he turned and shouted in my ear. He now had a couple of good ones for me. Following his glance I saw two more forms swimming from the haze. They didn't look like much—until we closed in. Then all of my earlier apprehension welled up again. These were 4000-ton, armor-plated, attack-transports, deep in the water—escorting each other.

For a couple of minutes our Privateers circled, well out of gunners' range. Kennedy and Jobe apparently decided to attack each transport individually but under the combined total fire-power of both bombers. Down at two hundred feet, they straightened out, with our plane again trailing. We went in strafing.

164

Out only a couple of hundred yards, the entire bomber began to throb. In my camera finder the tracers were an endless stream of glowing hypo needles punching at the hide of the thing below us. Its decks were swept clear. Not one burst of ack-ack came back. That ship was anesthetized. Ready for bombing. We banked into the second transport. A jeep-size flack hole appeared in Jobe's tail fin.

Kennedy rammed up his throttles, banked into his strafing run, a little farther out this time. Tracers spun fire cocoons around the ship, which looked gaunt and venomous. We were abreast. Kennedy turned to watch his tracers, his shoulder gouging against my chest. Muzzle-blasts of flack fire sparkled from the target, from bow to stern. Centering the ship in my finder I started to—all Creation exploded!

Lying there on the life jackets was pleasant, but I got up—and was knocked flat. As I crawled out from under the steel footplate of the dome gun turret, something snagged my pants. A slender metal fragment had caught in the cloth. Its other end was buried in my left wrist. It wouldn't move. One side was nicked. I pried with my knife. It had struck the artery.

Tourniquet . . . everything fuzzy . . . camera gone . . . everybody gone . . .

Hey . . . Marine! . . . navigator Jim Marshall backing, tugging someone . . .

Leo Kennedy had been hit. The cockpit was half destroyed.

An anti-aircraft shell had torn under my chest, hit Leo in the left hip, and exploded. The blast blew me backward, out of the way. Leo Kennedy pulled his crippled bomber level. His controls broke. He was unconscious. Co-pilot Bill Wassmer held the Privateer above the Yangtze, close. Spray raised by the propellors drenched the plane.

Flight jackets kept Leo warm. Harlyn Bakko, plane chief, and Harry Horton, turret gunner, made a bed of their parachutes as the Privateer faltered back over the China Sea toward Okinawa. They had flown only with Kennedy since entering the Navy. They couldn't speak. We worked that we might save him. It was hopeless. The squadron report for that night cost a terrible price.

Half of its controls shot away. Nose tire gone. No brakes or hydraulic system. Bomb-bay doors jammed open by a second shell that had ripped through the waist, missing an overloaded bellyful of 100-pounders intended for small-fry targets along the way . . .

The Privateer was a flying time-bomb.

Rain still flooded Okinawa when we finally circled Yontan. That was luck. We would skid.

The great plane hit. Deafening.

Runway grids chewed through our metal skin. Then the nose wheel went down, nearly broke, held, tail lifted—we stopped. The tail gunner had blood running from his chin. There wasn't a sound. Now sirens wailed across the field. Someone reached over, twisted open the escape hatch, and dropped into the mud.

We were home.

166

One is rarely aware of the luck that governs life. Yet, sometimes, there are incidents which make these whims of fate glaringly clear. When I was released from the hospital after an overnight's routine checkup, an orderly returned my uniform and gear. Seeing me fully dressed and headed for the door, the doctor-in-charge called me back. He asked whether I had examined my Colt .45, which I always wore in a shoulder holster under my left arm. A quick glance. "No, but it's okay." He repeated the query, in a strange, rather prodding way. So I unwrapped the waterproof sleeve in which I folded the weapon during overocean flights. Just as I'd said, everything okay. I began rewrapping the pistol. The medic stopped me again.

"Look more closely."

I did—and saw it.

An inch-long, cashew-nut-shaped fragment of metal—anti-aircraft shell—lay encircling the steel trigger guard. During that instant when the Japanese gunners had shattered our Privateer, killing Lieutenant Leo Kennedy, my old shoulder-holstered Colt had been hanging slightly forward, shielding my heart.

Upon developing the film taken on Squadron VPB-109's last search-bombing mission, I was surprised to find, as the final picture on the partially exposed roll, a photograph that I'd intended to take but never took: a portrait of the Japanese attack-transport. I'd been saving the last half of the film for closeup shots while we made our bombing run, hoping for a sequence-series leading right up to the bridge of that enemy ship as we bored in just overhead, Since I'd never seen such a sequence, this seemed a perfect chance—maybe my last—for it was the squadron's final mission.

Leo Kennedy was killed and his plane nearly destroyed before the bombing run was made— yet I had a picture of the enemy target. The Japanese gunners took their own portrait. Concussion from the shell burst that killed Leo Kennedy also blasted the camera, tripping the shutter, to record the counter-firing Japanese, the smoke puffs of their anti-aircraft guns, and their ship.

168

Everything else is like walking!

Yontan Airfield,
Okinawa.
16 June, 1945

At last, all of my work and hopes and past experience in the Marine Corps are paying off. I've been receiving complete cooperation from the very top on every proposal yet introduced. Within the next weeks I feel sure I'll have put the finishing touches to the most exciting pictures yet made of combat aviation as applied to support of the infantry. On two special missions involving a fabulous Army Air Force pilot—Major Ed Taylor—and his single-seat P-38 fighter, I've already shot the most technically difficult aerial photographs I've ever attempted. We slung a special, plastic-nosed tank under his left wing, I slid inside, and we went for a little sightseeing around some historic spots on this island. It was incredible, the closest I'll ever be to total aloneness—high in the sky, then streaking down to just over the treetops—better than a bird, for they *must* be aware of their own wings and the effort of flying. Ed and his plane and everything of my earthly bonds were invisible behind me when I lay looking straight ahead. Perhaps the landing was the most tingling part of all, for Ed set her down on the runway with plenty of throttle since my tank created a drag at slower, normal landing speeds. So he took her in at well over a hundred miles an hour, with my nose seemingly an inch off the ground and about to plow that steel-grid runway from end to end.

The only thing we forgot before taking off the first time was to adapt airscoop ventilators for the tank. It got rather warm inside. As I sweated, all of the moisture condensed on the inside of the tank and plexi-glass nose, and I had trouble wiping away the water so that I could make pictures—the reason for Ed Taylor going to so much trouble in the first place. You see, he's the commanding officer of a P-38 photo-reconnaisance squadron with plenty to do other than go joy-riding with a gypsy Marine. Bet I drank a bucket of water when we landed. The old radiator was really dry. In fact, I lost eleven pounds during that hour and forty-five minute flight. Now it's the only way I want to fly. And pictures! Ed nuzzled right up to each attacking Corsair as the boys blasted enemy artillery positions with broadsides of rockets and fire-bombs, so close I could look right over the fighter pilots' gunsights. Then Ed poured on full throttle and flew us straight through the exploding targets—at 400 mph.

171

Big Brass needed some close-ups of flamethrowing tanks clobbering enemy pillboxes which infested the Shuri Castle-Naha Line, and of napalm silencing mountain guns hidden in caves on the forested slopes of Kushi Take.

The generals got exactly what they wanted, thanks to some kid Marine torpedo pilots and Ed Taylor—who dived down among the targets, then flew around right over the fire.

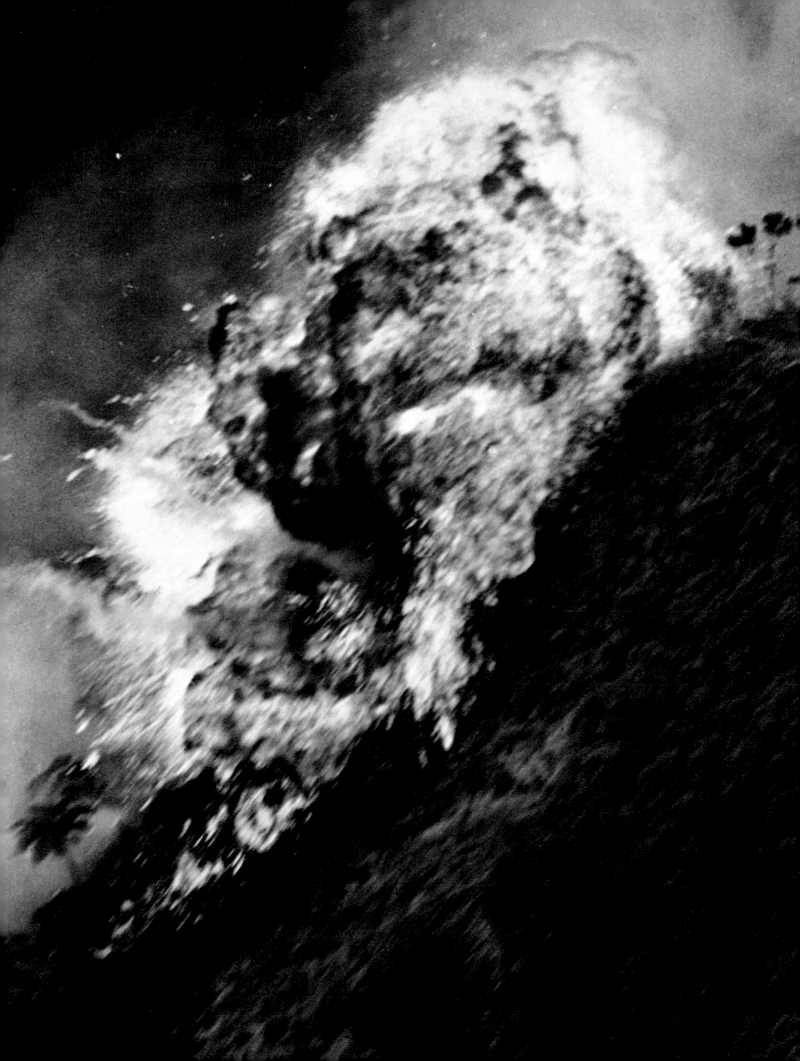

2nd Marine Aircraft Wing, Fleet Marine Force, Pacific,
% Fleet Post Office, San Francisco, California.   22 June 1945

1st Lt. David D. DUNCAN, USMCR (018021) (VS-PR), fulfilled the following photographic missions over enemy-held Okinawa Shima in pursuance of his basic orders:

6 May 1945: OY-1. Naha. 500 feet. Small arms fire over target. 0940 to 1000.

10 May 1945: OY-1. Naha harbor and airfield. Bombing assessment. Small arms fire. Pilot of control plane wounded. 500 feet. 1357 to 1505.

11 May 1945: OY-1. Artillery barrages hitting enemy positions south of Yonabura. Scattered light ground fire behind Japanese lines. 1008 to 1058.

12 May 1945: OY-1. Okinawa below Shuri and Yonabura, no sign of enemy. 0838 to 0938.

24 May 1945: TBM. 1000-pound bomb strike against Shuri Castle, primary enemy strongpoint on Shuri-Naha Line. Five passes over Castle. 100 feet. 1520 to 1555.

29 May 1945: PB4Y-2. Bombing and strafing shipping in Straits of Korea, the Japanese Sea, and on east coast of Korea to 38 : 30 N Latitude. One oil tanker sunk off central Korea. 75 feet. 0618 to 1633. Navy Squadron VPB-109.

30 May 1945: PB4Y-2. East China Sea to estuary of Yangtze River off Shanghai. One small cargo ship strafed, left sinking; one lighthouse ship strafed, left dead in water; one medium (3000 ton) transport strafed; one 4000 ton gunboat strafed. 400 to 200 feet. Aircraft struck by 20mm or 40mm antiaircraft shells. Pilot Lt. Leo Kennedy, USNR, killed. Lt. Duncan struck by shell fragment in left wrist. Copilot Lt. Wassmer, USNR, crash-landed aircraft upon return to base. 0915 to 1645. Navy Squadron VPB-109.

1 June 1945: TBM. Parachute supply drops to forward patrols of First Marine Division. 200 feet. 1410 to 1500.

1 June 1945: TBM. Parachute supply drops to forward patrols of First Marine Division. 200 feet. 1620 to 1645.

6 June 1945: OY-1. Para-pack drops to forward patrols of First Marine Division. 100 feet. 1240 to 1605. Pilot 1st Lt. L. Stein, Squadron VMO-3.

7 June 1945: TBM-3. F4Us making napalm and rocket attacks south of Shuri Castle-Naha Line. 100 feet. Also 500-pound bomb attack against enemy positions on Senega Shima. 50 feet. 1238 to 1545. Pilot 2nd Lt. L. T. Iglehart, Squadron VMTB-232.

12 June 1945: TBM-3. 500-pound bomb, napalm, and rocket attacks against Segana Shima. Photo aircraft hit by 20 mm antiaircraft fire. Radio-gunner, sitting between Lt. Duncan's feet, struck in back. Making emergency landing because of wounded crewman photo-aircraft made downwind landing and ground looped. 1225 to 1445. Pilot 1st Lt. R. J. Ferris, Squadron VMTB-232.

13 June 1945: P-38. 60 aircraft F4U napalm and rocket strike against Headquarters Japanese Army Okinawa. 10 runs. 100 to 25 feet. Lt. Duncan in belly tank under wing of P-38 shooting pictures through tank's plexi-glass nose. 1415 to 1600. Pilot Major E. H. Taylor, USAAF, 28th Photo Reconn. Squadron, Commanding.

15 June 1945: P-38. Napalm and rocket attacks against Kushi Take, central Okinawa. 75 feet. Lt. Duncan in belly tank with plexi-glass nose under port wing of P-38. 1330 to 1515. Pilot Major E. H. Taylor, USAAF, 28th Photo-Reconn. Squadron, Commanding.

18 June 1945: TBM-3. 500-pound bomb and rocket attacks against Mabuni area strong-points, southern Okinawa. 50 feet. Photo-coverage of strike curtailed before last bomb run completed because Marine ground strike observation officer killed by enemy fire. 1358 to 1517. Pilot 2nd Lt. O. R. Baird, Squadron VMTB-232.

20 June 1945: OY-1. Marine tanks attacking, following aircraft assaults against strong-points southern Okinawa. To make target pictures aircraft flew over enemy positions in cliffs while tankfire and artillery shelling hit target. 100 feet. 1038 to 1145. Pilot 1st Lt. D. W. Manley, Squadron VMO-3.

21 June 1945: OY-1. Flamethrowing Marine tanks moving against enemy strongpoints southern Okinawa. Marine infantrymen moving up to cliffs. Enemy troops killed in attack, or who committed hara-kiri, under cliffs on beach. 100 feet to nearly altitude zero. 0830 to 0917. Pilot 1st Lt. D. W. Manley, Squadron VMO-3.

21 June 1945: TBM-3. Tanks shelling enemy strongpoints southeastern tip Okinawa. Mortar strikes on targets. 100 feet to nearly altitude zero, below level of cliffs. 1057 to 1138. Pilot 2nd Lt. O. R. Baird, Squadron VMTB-232.

21 June 1945: TBM-3. Artillery shelling, tank attacks, infantry assaults against strong-points in cliffs where enemy made final stand Okinawa. 100 feet down to nearly altitude zero. 1223 to 1330. Pilot 2nd Lt. O. R. Baird, Squadron VMTB-232.

OY-1, designates Marine Piper Cub, artillery observation plane.
TBM-3, „ Marine torpedo bomber.
F4U, „ Marine Corsair fighter.
P-38, „ Army Air Force, single-seat, twin-engine Lightning fighter.
PB4Y-2, „ Navy Privateer, 4-engine search bomber.

To have won, today, was to pull off boots for the first time in weeks—and to sleep until dawn under silken tents made of discarded ammunition parachutes. To have lost, today, was to sprawl lifeless in the sand beneath those coral cliffs where the battle stopped—and to be carried away on the next tide.

21 June, 1945. Okinawa Shima – late afternoon.

Enemy resistance on Okinawa was officially declared ended at nightfall when Marines, in tanks and afoot, smashed through the cliffs and out upon the southern beaches of the island. This —the first day of summer—was to become the final day of infantry fighting between organized armies in World War II.

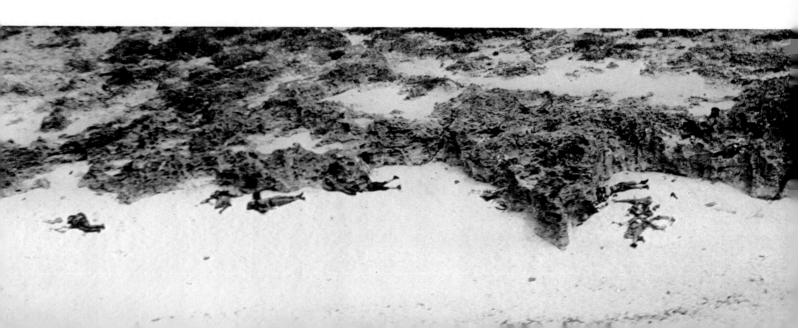

Even though "organized" enemy resistance has ended in the Philippines, there are still plenty of Japanese soldiers around who seem not to understand General MacArthur's press communiques. So there's yet work to be done by the U.S. Army, and by Marine airmen, in this remote tropical area. I arrived from Iwo Jima and Guam only a couple of days ago; started shooting pictures today.

Zamboanga, Mindanao,
Philippine Islands.
4 August, 1945

For the second time on this tour I've had occasion to be grateful for my Spanish. Naturally, I knew they spoke it here, but I was surprised to learn how little it varies from the Latin American brand. The Moros themselves are the most sinister-appearing characters I've met since Bero and the other Papuan scouts who ran interference for the Fijian guerrillas on Bougainville. With a few breaks, I may be able to scratch around and uncover another somewhat offbeat story. It'll all depend upon how long I can spend here. What I really want is a sort of vacation. Should it develop that I can shove off, then I'm going back into the interior with the Moro guerrillas. They are still most active. I might get a powerful finishing-up report from this theater. Of course, I'll have to get some Marine pilot friends to drop some ammo or chow to my boys in the center of the island, to make my presence there conform with the wording of my orders. You know, of course, that it was the Moros who fought our Army with such fanaticism during the Spanish-American War. Since they were almost inhumanly tough, the Colt .45 pistol was designed specifically to stop them. Hope they remember that we're all big buddies, this time, this war.

This last tour has emphasized one fact: it proves the worthiness of a set of orders such as mine. Not only am I accorded total cooperation from the highest ranking officers of the Corps and Navy (and the Army, too, really), but when I want to move fast to cover something that I feel is important, I'm usually on my way almost as soon as I decide my destination. It's really incredible—and fun—to watch the reaction when I walk into an outfit's headquarters and ask for the commanding officer, usually a colonel but several times a general. The duty officer on the desk will almost always start to give me the routine of the "Old Man" being busy, so, "What's your problem?"—the duty officer often being a captain or major. When I tell the guy it's a mission to be discussed only with the commanding officer, orally—well, I see those eyes go to my lieutenant's bars, and a flush appear around the collar line. That's when I sort of ease a copy of my orders across the top of his desk. The eyes, invariably, bounce back to my lieutenant's bars, then glaze over when they take in my old roll-brimmed, Fijian campaign hat with its gold-and-silver full-dress Marine Corps emblem on its prow which I've worn ever since Bougainville. After a fast phone call, I'm on my way in to see the Old Man. Each time it happens, I bless those orders—in black and white. Now, no matter what happens, I can sharpshoot my way through the whole damned war.

CHAPTER VII

What a week!

Guam.
14 August, 1945

Was at Zamboanga, in the southern Philippines, when the surrender scuttlebutt came over the radio. Maybe you heard us—and the other guys all over the whole wide Pacific. It *must* have been the same every place!

Thanks to my "Open Sesame" orders was put on a special plane to come here, expecting to board another going north for Japan to cover the signing of the surrender. As of this date, I'm still standing by, as is everyone else out this way. Should know within twenty-four hours what the future of the war will be. But if the atomic bombs that destroyed Hiroshima and Nagasaki are as frightful as claimed by those first announcements, then this war is now history . . . and so are they.

One bomb—one city.

Hiroshima was about the same size as Kansas City. I wonder if it had a Country Club Plaza or Mission Hills residential district. With parents like you at home awaiting a son who has been waiting for me down in these islands, to settle the war between *us*—after which one of us would go home. But homes there would be, forever. Yet from this week on—never.

When I came back up from Mindanao, I brought out pictures of an event so unbelievable that had they been taken at any time prior to *this* particular week they would have shocked the world. I photographed the naked act of treason. Pictures are on their way to Head-quarters showing a Japanese officer (who walked into the American lines on Mindanao) voluntarily leading a Marine bombing mission of 36 planes against his own friends and headquarters deep in the jungle. We—and he—hit the place for three straight days with everything (no *not* everything) in the book. Through an interpreter, he even briefed the Marine pilots for the strikes. Only my camera, never words, could record the expression of glacial contempt in Colonel Ridderhof's face as that enemy soldier carefully revealed the emplacements of his former base on the operations map for the fighter and bomber crews.

178

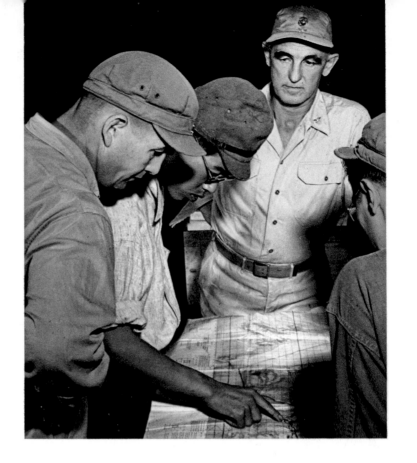

Finally, to tangle the web of war and history and our lives even more irrevocably, that enemy officer and I were seated side by side in the waist of our bomber, the second day's attack finished, when the interpreter cut in on the navigator's headphone. Flight control back at the Marine airbase had just picked up the news: Russia had declared war against Japan.

182

My pathetic little companion, skeleton thin and arms still raw with the jungle sores of mal-
nutrition, sat squatting on his heels amid the Mae Wests and machine gun belts and a tropical
ration chocolate bar cluttering the floor of the plane. He huddled there, holding his head in
his hands, staring down toward the faded drab paint of the bomb-bay doors . . . at nothing.

CHAPTER VIII

It's *OVER*!

Guam.
15 August, 1945

We're on our way!

Word just hit here that the Emperor has accepted our terms of surrender.

It's all over—at least in the Imperial Palace. Let's just hope that all of Mr. Hirohito's emissaries down through these islands get the word, and agree. Also those manning the coastal defense guns around Tokyo Bay, because that's where I'm headed, right now, aboard a Navy transport bulging with Marines.

They will be the first fighting men to step ashore in Japan since this thing began—other than prisoners-of-war.

That's one thing we're not!

184

When you read this I shall have gone ashore well, happy, and very proud.

Yokosuka Naval Base,
Yokosuka, Japan.
30 August, 1945

Knowing that every Marine couldn't make this final landing I like to feel that we represent
all of those who will come later, and those who earned it, but will never make it . . . ever.

U.S.S. "Missouri",
Tokyo Bay.
2 September, 1945

Dear Mother and Dad:

This is the Day.

Love,
Dave

CHAPTER IX

One complete lifetime of emotions and drama and memories has been crammed into eleven days, and a new world begun, since the Marines landed at the Yokosuka Naval Base below Yokohama making that first beachhead on the home island of the Emperor.

U.S.S. "Ancon",
Tokyo Bay.
10 September, 1945

The surrender terms demanded that every shore artillery position be marked by a white flag. Well, as the invasion fleet sailed—I should say crept—into Tokyo Bay, whose hilly slopes are heavily forested, it looked as though thousands of housewives had just hung out their laundry on the trees to dry. Everything from handkerchiefs to bedsheets seemed to be flapping all over the place in the morning breeze. But, as you already know, not one shot was fired. And as we steamed ever closer we didn't see a soul—just those spooky white flags.

Since I, personally, had waited a couple of years for that morning, I decided to document the historic moment of the final landing by shooting it in color. Well, after clambering down the nets of the transport into my landing barge and bouncing merrily over the waters of Tokyo Bay—banging pictures left and right—suddenly, while still about a quarter-mile offshore, I started listening to my camera. It's something every professional does subconsciously. Historic morning it surely was! I was photographing the invasion with a pair of empty cameras.

It's true! After yanking the black and white rolls out of each of the two cameras being used, cleaning their lenses and gears, I had slapped them shut again to await the Big Moment—minus color film—stark empty.

Luckily, I still had time before we hit the embankment of the Naval Base, so was functioning somewhat more sensibly when we went ashore.

Should anyone ever in the future ask whether I remember the morning the Marines landed in Japan, the answer is a curt, "Damned right!"

Once ashore—with no one shooting at anyone—and the commanding officer of the Japanese Naval Base wandering off with the commanding officer of the American invasion force, for talks about the surrender, or the Yankees and the Dodgers, or to have tea—anyway, they disappeared very casually and I *knew* that the war was really over—at that moment I turned tourist. And toward Tokyo.

General MacArthur's orders to the invasion force had been explicit: no member of the first echelon naval assault troops was to enter Tokyo until permission came from his Supreme Headquarters. Well, I was there as a representative of Headquarters, U.S. Marine Corps, Washington, and had only the Commandant to answer to; besides, I was attached to the landing force only until I got to Japan. So I scrounged an ancient alcohol-burning motorcycle from a battered garage at the Naval Base and soon had it running. Not fast—maybe 10 miles an hour—but faster than walking. Then I ran into two marvelous characters who didn't give a damn about MacArthur and his quarantine on Tokyo, or anything else. Sam Dietz is a huge Navy lieutenant who once played All-American football for Alabama, and Bernard Perlin is a slender, quiet, but good-natured *Life* magazine war artist. Sam had a Thompson sub-machine gun slung over one shoulder. Bernie had a rucksack filled with paints, and a sketchbook under his arm. I, of course, had my old Colt .45 in my shoulder holster, my Fijian campaign hat on my noggin, and a side-car on my new motorcycle. So off we went—not having any idea where Tokyo was except to the north of us, about 30 miles up the road.

Outside the main gate of the Yokosuka Naval Base we were met by an extraordinary sight. A totally lifeless city. A lovely day, not much bomb damage among the low wooden buildings, and not a single civilian. But we weren't alone. Stretching along the road, in both directions as far as we could see, the way was studded with a line of black-uniformed policemen standing about fifty paces apart, with their backs to the street and us. We turned right, to the

190

north, and chugged slowly toward Tokyo, surely the first of the invaders to pass that way. Not one man moved as much as a finger—or turned to watch us go.

At that moment our motorcycle exploded and died.

Bernie, who is extremely well-mannered and proper, saved the day. Turning to Sam and me as we pushed the smoking, lifeless motorcycle to the roadside, he said, "Gentlemen, as we New Yorkers would say, 'When lost or in doubt ask of the first gendarme the way' . . . so let's ask that first black-booted b-------." We did. That is, Sam did, looking down from all of his six feet four at that first policeman, who was about five feet four. Something like, "Say, fella. Wheresa da way to a-Tokyo?" Bernie almost flipped. I came out with something like "For-Christ's-sake Sam make it so's he can understand—or at least so *we* can—we're not looking for Rome!" The little cop just stood looking up at Sam, as if he was trying to memorize what was before him so he could tell his wife all about what *he* had seen on the beat that sunny morning.

Funnily, really funnily, another cop then marched up, saluted, and wondered whether he might be of assistance—in perfect English. We explained, very seriously (as though we were accustomed to such situations just as much as he), that we were strangers in Yokosuka, that we had lost the way, that we were looking for the best way to get to Tokyo. "But that is velly easy." He looked at his wristwatch. "Go back two stleets. Go light one stleet. You will find on the reft the station. Next expless to Tokyo—seventeen minutes—on time." And it was.

Roaring along to Yokohama, then Tokyo, we rode in a train not unlike a New York subway. Except all of the windows had been either blown out or removed to prevent glass flying during our bombing raids. Each car was stuffed solid with Japanese—soldiers, more cops, children, parents, old, old, old folks, mothers nursing their babies, and three Americans. At the station stops more local people shoved their way inside, then, abruptly aware that they were confronting no ordinary barrier of kimonos and cotton suitcoats, some of them found their eyes climbing slowly up and over a vast barricade of Navy or Marine Corps khaki. To their everlasting credit and honor, each, upon finding himself, or herself, looking squarely into the eyes of an enemy soldier, simply bowed, ever so slightly, as though to excuse himself, and his countrymen, for having so inconvenienced us by providing such crowded transport at a time like this.

From Yokosuka to Tokyo, none of us heard a single word spoken on that train. Tokyo . . . home of the Emperor . . . target of our devastating fire-raids . . . the end of the line in this war. Tokyo, that afternoon, was a place where three Americans got off the express train from the south—along with thousands of Japanese passengers—and walked down from the station ramp into the streets of a city that was no more. Or so it seemed at first.

We found what had been the main drag, the Ginza. Except for a couple of sagging, rein-forced-steel-and-concrete buildings, gaunt and gutted, our view of the city center was one of unadorned chaos. The place was burned flat. Only the abandoned, rusting safes of long-gone or dead shopkeepers, and the blackened scarecrows of jutting brick chimneys marked what had been the heart of Asia's greatest city.

Then, we wandered farther abroad in the desolation. We found that life still survived, rustling amid the ashes. Old couples were farming vegetables in bushel-basket-size plots of earth behind fallen walls. Others lived in holes beneath the walls. Flotsam houseboats choked the canals that crisscross what had been Tokyo.

Just before sunset we found the Imperial Palace, apparently quite undamaged behind stone ramparts and deep moats. It seemed forlorn and totally unrelated to the world war just ending, with its violence already faded into a long-gone yesterday.

Down the street, we walked into the lobby and across the polished floor of another also nearly intact, low, rambling palace—Frank Lloyd Wright's Imperial Hotel. We were met by the manager, in striped morning pants and cutaway—and with a bow. We explained that we were interested in the biggest, most comfortable, room or rooms—with beds to match our heights, and hot-water baths. The manager listened politely and imperceptibly raised a finger in response to which three bellboys shot out from nowhere. We had neither baggage nor gear, but they still led us to our rooms. However, just before the procession began into the plush innards of Mr. Wright's masterpiece, we were presented with, and signed, the register of guests.

192

We each signed in the same way: name, rank or title, organization. Then we each added the brief postscript: "Present bill to Japanese Embassy, Washington, D.C."

And dinner? Three trays of soup and rice arrived while we were soaking.

For nearly two weeks of glorious sunny autumn weather I photographed the cinders of Hell —the charred hulk of Tokyo—in color. Other photographers hurried down to Hiroshima, naturally, but I saw that as the final grisly equation on a remote physics blackboard. Tokyo, to me, symbolized the enemy—the fallen dragon—beaten in combat by mortal men.

During that period, General MacArthur flew in to one of the airfields, coming from the Philippines, and set up staff headquarters in Yokohama. Tokyo was still out of bounds to the occupation personnel, at least to the levels below Super-Brass. Sam Dietz headed back to wherever he came from, so Bernie Perlin and I had the place pretty much to ourselves, sharing it with only a handful of other guys in uniform who flitted through the Imperial, and, of course, some of the old professional news correspondents. The day General MacArthur made his first grand entry behind his 1st Cavalry Division MPs as escorts, Bernie and I wandered down to a good conspicuous street corner where we rested comfortably on the curbstone, on the tips of our spines, watching the conquerors sweep past. I just sort of felt that a lot of other guys, starting back at Pearl Harbor and Corregidor and Guadalcanal, were sprawled out on that curbstone alongside me.

Of course, when the Brass poured into the Imperial I got booted out. Not by the really *simpático* Japanese manager—he kept switching me from room to room for several days so nobody could at first catch me—hell no, I was tossed by a *full* colonel, the army's new billeting officer. Anyway, by that time I didn't care because Bernie, as an accredited *Life* war artist, had been assigned a cabin, with two bunks, in the communication ship "Ancon." He somehow fixed it so that I was given the other sack—and that's where I'm writing this letter right now. Then, through Bernie, I met two of the greatest guys in my profession, men whose work I have followed and admired and sort of aimed at for years: *Life* photographers Jay Eyerman and Carl Mydans. They're in the cabin across the corridor. Finally, half way around the world from where I started, I have met two of the men who look at this old earth with my kind of vision—and as a common challenge.

When Surrender Day was set for September 2nd, Carl and Jay tried desperately to get a camera position assigned to me aboard the battleship "Missouri," but it was hopeless. I had no press accreditation, and with Brass flying in from all over the Allied world, a crummy lieutenant photographer didn't have a prayer. Even as it was, there would be so many official representatives aboard that battle-wagon that only a miracle would keep it afloat or from capsizing into Tokyo Bay.

"Besides," growled someone else who had no position, "the whole show is locked up tight. Nobody is going to sneak aboard *that* ship. Everything is in the hands of one guy—the handsomest, toughest s.o.b. in the whole U.S. Navy."

Something started spinning forward through my memory . . . and I grabbed it. Turning to Jay, I asked just one question: "By any chance is the officer in charge of this show a Navy captain named Fitzhugh Lee?"

Jay looked up from cleaning his cameras and nodded. "Yeah, Dave. Only it's Commodore Fitzhugh Lee. And he *is* really a tough guy. He's gotta be for this thing."

I was already headed for the ladder and topside, toward the holy of holies, the commanding officer's quarters of the communication ship, so I only half heard Carl agreeing with Jay on the character of the commodore.

Commodore Fitzhugh Lee received me almost immediately, although for sure he did not place my name until we were again face to face. That's right! He was executive officer of the aircraft carrier "Essex," aboard which I first shipped overseas, and whose portraits I shot and printed while we ran from San Francisco to Honolulu.

How could *anybody* have my luck!

He explained graciously and carefully that he was being besieged by the biggest guns from Washington to London to Paris and even Moscow, to get *their* representatives aboard. That was at the governmental level. At the press level he was being depth-charged around the clock. While telling me this he kept right on working at his desk, writing. Then he stood up

194

again and handed me a card, with a lean smile. "Don't worry! You're aboard. Surely no man here deserves it more than a United States Marine."

Of course, everyone has seen the newsreels taken aboard, and probably heard the radio broadcasts during the actual signing ceremony. I was upon a five-inch gun turret, back slightly from the deck where it took place. Just below me a catwalk connected the captain's quarters with the lower deck, where the surrender documents waited. There was a slight commotion atop one of the gigantic sixteen-inch gun turrets that had been converted into a press stand. One of the baggy-pantsed, leather-booted Russian cameramen tried to shove his way to the front, ignoring the place number marked on his card. Much to my joy, two lanky Marine MPs grabbed him by the scruff of the collar, and by the seat of those pants, and tossed him back to where he started from—and belonged.

A moment later, to my astonishment, General MacArthur and Admiral Halsey walked out on the catwalk right beneath me. Commodore Fitzhugh Lee really fixed me up royally! I certainly wasn't the person closest to the surrender signing table. But I did have one of the greatest overall views of the momentous pageant taking place aboard that battleship.

That she should be the U.S.S. "Missouri," of all the ships in the fleet, made that day an extra-ordinarily personal page in this old world's life story.

Yet for all of the glory and profound elation felt by all of us aboard, there was one sad and unnecessarily cruel aspect to the ceremony, which the movie cameras perhaps did not show. It was the moment when Mamoru Shigemitsu, the top-ranking Japanese civilian of their surrender signing group, came alongside the "Missouri" in his launch. The sea was calm but he had a terrible, humiliating, and probably painful time trying to climb the ship's stair-ladder to the main deck, and then get from there over to the table where he was to sign the surrender document. He is a very old man. Like the other Japanese civilians aboard, he was dressed in formal morning clothes. But somewhere, either fighting as a youth against the Russians, or the Chinese, or the Koreans, someplace, he had been critically wounded. He could scarcely walk—for he had only one leg.

No one went forward to help him.

The National Geographic Magazine
Washington, D.C.
Melville Bell Grosvenor
Assistant Editor
September 13, 1945

1st Lt. David D. Duncan, USMC,
Hdqts, Aircraft, FMF, Pacific,
FPO,
San Francisco, California.

Dear Dave:

I was really thrilled to receive your letter with the U.S.S. MISSOURI, Tokyo Bay, September 2, 1945, cachet on the envelope. That is a collector's item. You couldn't have sent me anything that gave me a bigger kick. I have waited a long time, some 25 years, for just such a cachet. Even when I was a midshipman at the Naval Academy we were fighting the war with Japan. We all knew it was coming someday. So this letter and envelope put an end to that bugaboo.

By the way, are you making any Kodachromes? We do hope that you are able to make some color pictures of the Japanese people and Tokyo. Also did you make any of the Fleet anchored in Tokyo Bay beneath Fujiyama? There have been several pictures published in the papers but not many. We would like very much to see a series of color pictures, even black-and-white, of the Fleet in Tokyo Bay and of the Japanese people.

Your Okinawa Kodachromes were a splendid contribution to the October number. An advance copy has been sent to you and I hope it will reach you soon.

In your last letter you mentioned Philippine and Borneo surveys. Were these postponed by VJ-Day and the exciting events which followed? I imagine your plans were changed abruptly. Can't you let us know what you have produced so that we can be on the lookout for it.

All of the family ask to be remembered. We hope to see you soon. Your bunk here is always waiting. But bring home a collection from Tokyo and Japan, please!

Sincerely,
Melville Grosvenor

196

CHAPTER X

This is as nearly the glamorous, legendary tropical isle as I can imagine.

The girls really wear grass skirts, flowers in their hair, ankle bracelets, and nothing else.

They and their men—who are clean-limbed fishermen—radiate the simple charm of a humor-loving life, close to the sea and nature. Apparently, they were not too ill-treated by the Japanese soldiers who have been garrisoned here since before the war actually began.

Yap,
Caroline Islands.
20 September, 1945

My getting back down here in the tropics was a typical streak of DDD luck.

Left Tokyo on the 11th for Guam to transmit all of my pictures to Headquarters, since so much stuff was moving from Japan on the surrender I felt there existed a definite danger that mine might get lost.

You just can't imagine the organized confusion out here now with the war suddenly all finished, millions of guys figuring out ways to get home, Japanese commanders and troops trying to find someone to surrender to, Stateside characters trying to get a quick look at the combat areas before they get rid of their uniforms, other Stateside characters streaming toward Tokyo with their slide-rules and economics books to administer the Occupation—and your ever-loving, ever-nomadic offspring trying to see the rest of this part of the world while the transport, anonymity, and my orders make it possible.

Luck? I landed on Ulithi—was there only 25 minutes. I hopped right in one of the LCTs leaving for Yap (and I not even knowing they were due to leave at all: I meant only to ask about the latest scuttlebutt on Truk). Arrived here, went ashore, just in time to step in the launch carrying the Marine colonel to the Jap colonel for the ceremonial surrender luncheon deep in the forested interior, at the former enemy headquarters, which was also his home.

The lunch was a model of conduct for professional soldiers who had just been trying to kill each other, but now sat opposite each other according to the conquered officer's code of honor—with every man in the room at armed ease. Even though no Japanese weapons were visible, one could not help but sense that they were not too far from easy reach.

The thing that most interested me was the low, rambling headquarters house itself, with its tropical open-verandah. Above the portals of each sliding-screen doorway, in the space separating the cross timber and the ceiling, someone had tediously, and lovingly, polished great sections of driftwood into fragile, nearly transparent lacework. The panels were just the natural colors of the wood. Light from each adjoining room shone through them, so that even while sitting on the floor during meals, one could clearly follow the whorls and veins in each old sea-bleached log. They were the work of a dreamer and a great artist.

Through the interpreter I asked the Japanese colonel whether it was work of Yapese craftsmen of earlier times. He looked up at them for a moment, then replied, "No. It was I who made them. We have been here a long time."

The Japanese colonel also knew Yap intimately, not just as a military commander in charge of its defenses but as an anthropologist interested in the islanders themselves. He sent me across the island with two of his aides (one ahead, on the trail, and one behind me—so you can be *sure* the war has ended!) to villages where there still remained several dozen of the objects that aroused outside interest in Yap during the age of Pacific Ocean exploration. These are the enormously heavy, four- to five-feet-high rings of "stone money." They look somewhat like great millstones leaning against the trunks of cocopalm trees, or abandoned alongside the trails. Their origin is lost in the mysterious past—which is what I like best.

Now, the Marines are demilitarizing this place.

So back to another kind of past far from lost to us, yet.

* * *

Lord, it's been so long since I last wrote, the old fingers scarcely function. To tell it all right now will be impossible, so lots will have to wait probably until I come home (and when that'll be I still have no idea—there's so much to do).

Shanghai, China.
16 October, 1945

As I remember, I last wrote from Yap. Well, after that I went back to Ulithi on a sub-chaser, caught a plane for Guam, another for Okinawa, and boarded the ship carrying the first occupation force to Tientsin, China. Landed in the late afternoon of September 30th at Taku, which is the port for Tientsin. Went ashore with Marines of the 1st Division. An old train carried the men into Tientsin station, where we arrived long after dark. A sagging line of derelict, alcohol-burning trucks coughed and wheezed and waited outside the terminal doors to carry the Marines to barracks recently vacated by the city's Japanese garrison. Tientsin's electric power plant had either broken down or was inoperative because of lack of fuel, so the streets beyond the feeble lantern light of the station were pitch black. The guys threw their gear into the trucks, then climbed in, too, and that creaking cavalcade started out into the night with only God and the battalion commander knowing where we were bound in the silent city ahead.

Eerily, when the nose of the truck-train disappeared into the tunnel of the night, a ghostly sighing rushed back toward us who were riding in old wrecks at the tail of the caravan. It rose higher and higher and higher and ever louder, then we also were deep in the streets of Tientsin—and a cloudburst of human voices crashed over the trucks, sweeping us along our way. Over a million and a half Chinese stood banked in tier upon tier of themselves that night in Tientsin, shouting, singing, weeping, offering flowers, fruit, their hands. What a reception! *We* had won the war. China was "Free!"—"Free!"—"Free!"—"Free!" And that very word *free*— in English—rose as a chant until it soared and dipped and flew above the heads of those million and a half ecstatic Chinese like a night bird broken out of its cage.

And that night, "free" sounded Chinese. Everyone went *crazy.*

Since the Marine battalion had been ordered to stay in Tientsin, I spent a day there looking over the city (a rather drab industrial town with pleasant parks outside the manufacturing sections) and another day helping Allied and American prisoners-of-war to move from the

Japanese stockades onto a hospital ship anchored off Taku Bar. Curiously, one of those new-ly liberated prisoners was a Russian-American fur merchant who had been behind barbed wire during the entire war, and yet he still wanted to stay in North China a bit longer, through autumn. Apparently it was the peak of the season for stone marten pelts in that part of China and Manchuria, and since he was the only professional buyer within thousands of miles he didn't want to lose his chance of a lifetime for a coup. I went with him for a couple of hours when he bought strings of pelts. Most looked identical to me until he laid several of them side by side, then explained specific characteristics which made them vary so greatly in price. Features obvious to the professional—as in every trade or craft—but unseen or ignored by the novice. I asked him whether there was any secret formula whereby an amateur could be assured of buying beautiful furs, and he replied, yes, there is: "Buy them in New York."

Late that second afternoon I was in Peking.

No Allied commanders or troops had yet moved into the Forbidden City, where the Japanese commanding general for North China was said to have his headquarters. But I figured that he and his soldiers had already surrendered in principle, if not in fact, like those enemy com-manders still stuck on their islands in the Pacific and throughout Southeast Asia—just waiting for someone to appear who would accept their swords. Anyway, although some of the Marines in Tientsin observed that it might prove a bit too festive going sightseeing so far inland so soon—it's only about seventy-five miles west of Tientsin—I wanted to see that fabled city, the sooner the better. If there would be no Allied troops tearing around in their jeeps, better still. How'd I get there? Simply rode the train. If nothing else survives from these first months after the surrender, I shall still have those several days' memories when as a nearly lone Westerner I walked through Peking in the autumn. Winter's threat was in each evening's breeze from the Gobi Desert and Mongolia, just beyond the Great Wall to the north.

Marco Polo could have been no more elated after journeying across Asia from Venice, to arrive at the Court of Kublai Khan.

For two weeks I roamed Peking. As in Marco Polo's time, the entire city seemed to be one vast treasury whose arcades and bazaars glowed with the riches of the Eastern world. Brocades embroidered with silver and gold; shimmering bolt upon bolt upon bolt of pure silk—every color known to nature, from the softest pastels to blood red; trays of bracelets and rings and ear pendants and exotic fingernail guards of sky-blue enamel; pearls, rubies, sapphires (star and clear), diamonds, rose-coral figurines, one mammoth Ceylonese cat's-eye of total purity, alexandrites, moonstones, and overflowing hampers of lesser gems of all cuts, all sizes, all colors. Other treasure glittered, unseen even by Marco: case after cabinet after window loaded with Leicas, Contaxes, Rollieflexes, Ikontas, all in their original boxes, for the Japanese received these professional jewels from the Germans as a part of their Axis arrangements—cameras lost to the West since before the war. Street markets were literally carpeted with multi-hued oriental rugs—Persian, Bokkhara, Beluch, Afghan, Turkish, and magnificent local Chinese. Teas and spices were offered in wondrously decorated sections of bamboo-and-paper cylinders, handiwork as delicate as ever adorned a Pope's parchment in medieval times. I walked through it all in a near daze, for *this* was what the horizon had promised when I was a kid.

Oh, I shot pictures as I wandered—in color. But, mostly, I was filling special chambers in my memory, forever.

I had no money. I bought nothing. No one cared. My obvious love for what I saw and that which was placed—also lovingly—in my hands seemed ample reward for every shopkeeper. You see, almost every object offered in those ancient bazaars had, in some mysterious way, been buried from sight during the entire Japanese occupation of China. Their owners were surely even more thrilled than I on seeing them once again in pure sunlight, instead of by a flickering candle in some remote basement cave.

The language barrier was easily hurdled. I was introduced everywhere by the diminutive daughter of the ex-director of the Bank of North China. Nearly all of the shopkeepers were elderly gentlemen who had known Fu Yeng since she was an infant holding tightly to her father's finger when *he* had roamed the bazaars. They revealed even their personal treasures for her, and my, pleasure, having seen her only infrequently since her father had died in front of a Japanese firing squad.

Am leaving for Okinawa in the morning and returning to Shanghai the following day. I have been staying here with the *Time-Life* people after running into Bernie Perlin, the *Life* war artist with whom I covered Tokyo before the occupation and surrender ceremony. The food in Peking and here is a dream, with chopsticks! I have my own. Silver, too. A gift from Fu Yeng. I carry them always, in an inner pocket of my flight jacket together with a menu from

Sun Ya, one of the great restaurants of Shanghai. Now I can walk into any restaurant in China, point to what I have test-flown, pull out my chopsticks, and be in business.

Immediately upon returning here I'll fly back to Peking. I hope to get into Manchuria while the opportunity offers. The Russians have moved in and are said to be stripping the land bare, especially of all former Japanese industrial plants. You see, even though the press there at home may not yet be reporting it, there have already been fire-fights between the Nationalist Chinese soldiers and other Chinese guerrilla bands which are said to be Communist. No wonder the Russians moved so quickly to declare war after we dropped that first atomic bomb on Hiroshima, then crossed the Manchurian border in massive strength. Just before I left Peking the city was suddenly teeming with Nationalist troops who were being airlifted in by our Air Force transports. Could it be, with a World War just finished, that a Civil War is brewing?

* * *

Since I've again missed my mail, I can't do much sensible observing on the home news. Going well into three months that I've been out of touch with Stateside, but such is the job. It'll take equally as long to answer everything once I finally get my hands on that package.

Peking, China
2 November, 1945

When I returned to Shanghai after going over to Okinawa (I actually flew down from Peking only to search for my mail; more than two thousand miles round trip), I had intended going right back to North China. However, when at the sentry gate of Shanghai's airport—miles from the city—scrounging a jeep ride into town for the night, I was picked up by the flight surgeon of an Army Air Force transport squadron based at Hsian, way to hell'n'gone out in central China. I explained that I am a photographer for the Marines and that I'd just gotten in from Okinawa where I'd gone to get some cash out of our paymaster so that I might clean up some of the camera bargains just sitting in the bazaars of Peking. He immediately asked about the rate of exchange for a dollar against the Chinese dollar issued by the Japanese in their occupation zones, and still used there by the merchants. He snorted when I told him what I last heard the dollar (U.S.) was worth. Then he suggested that I rejoin him at dawn the next morning at the airfield, to fly in one of their planes to Hsian, where the rate

202

was much higher. It would add only an extra day each way on my proposed flight to Peking. So I met him at daybreak, and off we went—still stuffed to the gills from a Sun Ya dinner with Bill Gray, Carl Mydans, Bernie Perlin, and the rest of the Shanghai *Life* magazine crew of photographers and war correspondents.

We arrived at Hsian just in time for a late lunch, and for the doctor to receive the sad news that one of the squadron's pilots had been killed the day before in a crash. Preparations were being completed to fly the poor guy's body to the major American air base at Kunming—down on the border of Burma. Other pilots of the outfit, after asking what the heck a Marine was doing out in their part of China, suggested that I ride along to Kunming, too, in the plane carrying the coffin. The exchange rate was far better in Kunming than Hsian. I'm aware of how callous all this must sound back in Kansas City, but out here it's a harshly realistic world where the untoward loss of friends is bitterly noted, while those who survive continue along the road of their military and private lives. Thus, next morning I was en route Kunming, which is the Chinese end of the famous Hump air-supply corridor over the Himalayas. As there were no seats in the transport, I sat on what was available. He surely would have done the same, had our roles been reversed.

At noon we put down at Chungking for gas and chow. Was standing in line at the Air Force mess hall when a terrific blow nearly put me on my knees. Paul Miller, with whom I flew all over Central America while on the Rockefeller assignment, stood right behind me with a grin seven miles wide and his right arm raised to belt me again. He's now Major Miller, assigned to Brigadier General Larry Randall, our Air Attaché for the Embassy in Chungking. Paul had a stripped-down B-25 light bomber and was on a survey flight for General Randall, checking the landing conditions of fields all over China. He was headed east, toward Shanghai. When he learned that I was aiming for Kunming, southwest and hours in the opposite direction of his flight plan, he simply sent his crew chief over to the tower to file a new flight plan—to Kunming.

That night we changed all of my money, all of his, and all of General Randall's which Paul was holding, sort of like his banker. We carried away our Chinese dollars in a two-foot-deep Coca Cola carton. Once we had the money we continued according to his instructions, namely landing and taking off at fields near Hankow, the great bomb-ruined, inland port; Nanking, the puppet capital; Shanghai once again; and then, after two more days of Sun Ya dinners with the *Life* magazine guys, Paul delivered me—staggering under even more money, since everyone seemed to want something from Peking—bright and shining, and much more widely traveled than a week before, to my original destination—the Forbidden City. By this time it seems quite folksy, like home.

Within one 24-hour period, acting as purchasing agent for General Randall and many of his colleagues at the Embassy, and for Paul Miller and his friends in the Army Air Force, I had the extraordinary experience of crisscrossing the bazaars of Peking buying almost everything I had seen beckoning to me during the weeks when I was there nearly alone, except for Fu Yeng. She joined me, coming from her mother's home in Tientsin. Together we bought seventeenth-century brocades and eighteenth-century mandarin gowns of flaming Imperial yellow embroidered with gold; end-to-end rainbows of silk; the figurine of an old and wise fisherman in rose coral *nearly a foot high*. We bought that 21-carat Ceylonese cat's-eye in a ring set with diamonds around its shoulders; pairs of rings, each with tremendous star sapphires mounted as twins facing each other across a bridge of diamonds; jade necklaces, rings, bracelets, figurines, ear pendants, and more necklaces. Fu Yeng knew every dealer, who knew every object being considered, and I knew something of what we were being offered and exactly what might be spent.

During the one day of shopping, Fu Yeng and I paid the old gentlemen of Peking more than $10,000 for their treasures—$10,000 prior to Paul's and my work in Kunming . . . possibly $100,000 in equivalent U.S. dollar values that day in the bazaars of the ancient Manchus. I only prayed that each object bought might be going into a happy home, where it will be loved even fractionally as much as it was in the eyes of the man who permitted me to buy it.

No attempt was made to touch solitaire diamonds—I know too little. But I did spend my own couple of hundred bucks in a manner that would have stunned Barney and others in his camera shop there on the Country Club Plaza. Am now figuring ways to haul Stateside four Leicas, four Rollieflexes, four Super Ikonta Bs, a Contaflex, and some other little items. All brand new. Shall keep a few, then offer the rest to friends in labs and darkrooms at various bases all along the way, guys who have helped me tirelessly because they are of that breed.

And Fu Yeng—what did she desire? Not a thing. She made only one request. A company of Nationalist Chinese soldiers had just marched past us, toward the foothills outside Peking. Watching them disappear, she took my hand. Then, after a long moment, she said, so low that I barely heard her, "Remember us as we are now."

204

Peking,
that autumn of '45,
drowsed under a faded, dusty sky.
Her bazaars exploded with laughter,
caravan bells,
silks and jewels, and persimmons
yellow as a setting Gobi moon.
The entire Forbidden City seemed mine.
I was welcomed much like Marco
—the Venetian himself—
by a girl
and her murdered father's friends—
greeted as in the court of a Manchu princess . . .
Fu Yeng.
Yes, I remember.
Perfectly.

CHAPTER XI

Lieut. David D. Duncan, USMCR
Division of Public Information
U.S. Marine Corps
Washington, D.C.

The National Geographic Society
Washington, D.C.
February 14, 1946
Gilbert Grosvenor
President and Editor

Dear Lieutenant Duncan:

Herewith we have pleasure in handing you The Society's check for $1,750, in payment for the material on the Island of Yap and that on the city of Peiping, which I trust will be acceptable. The amount of $750 has been allocated to the Yap material because of its lesser quantity—eight or nine pages instead of sixteen or eighteen. The amount of $1,000 for the Peiping material is in line with the rate established with you for similar features.

We appreciate your cooperation and are well pleased with the material you have contributed. I hope that you will continue to keep the Geographic in mind on your travels.

With personal regards,

Yours truly,
Gilbert Grosvenor

The last day in uniform—and what a finish!

Washington, D.C.
28 February, 1946

Doctor Grosvenor and his son, Melville, have accepted my final stories from the Pacific, stuffed my pockets with money, and whacked me on the shoulder wishing me a happy civilian career. It's almost like leaving home. Curiously, like home, nobody mentioned that I might stay and work for them here. Guess they saw the gypsy gleam in my eyes. I want to go someplace—anyplace—*prontissimo!*

Cairo in the morning, then Tehran for my first assignment.

DDD, Life Magazine Photographer
Luqa, Malta.
27 March, 1946

That old lucky star preordains everything! In New York, I ran into *Life's* chief photographer, Jay Eyerman, who had helped me in Tokyo at the time of the surrender. He asked what I was planning to do as a civilian, a casual question which has irrevocably changed my life, just as when Jean gave me that toy camera for my birthday, years ago in Arizona. Jay explained that *Life's* Executive Editor, Wilson Hicks, was desperately trying to find someone to cover Iran where the Russians are threatening Tehran with tanks. The big war now ended, most of *Life's* staff photographers are rather reluctant to accept new foreign assignments, being finally at home with their families. Jay felt there was a chance that I might land the job, if interested. Imagine asking a guy whether he was interested in having his dream of dreams come true!

I spoke with Wilson Hicks, who seemed glacially elegant—on first contact. He's a silent, peerer-over-glasses type of editor, painstakingly dressed, and maybe just a fraction slow in greeting an aspiring stranger (although, the Lord only knows how many arrive at his door). He is also the most imaginative picture editor in the magazine world today. He seemingly wasn't too impressed by my photo albums of those pre-war Lerner expeditions which I'd borrowed. However, since it is a newly hatching war that he wants covered, I was on familiar ground and told him so. He appeared far from convinced. I returned to the *Life* darkroom where Jay had gotten permission for me to work on some portraits of a friend.

The next morning, Jay charged in and dragged me up to the editorial floor of the magazine. Mr. Hicks met us in his shirt sleeves, *outside his door*, and with a half-smile. "David. Can you be in Persia this weekend? You are our newest *Life* photographer."

* * *

Tehran, Iran.
27 April, 1946

. . . camel caravans, bells tinkling, plod along the main drag. The wealth of rugs is staggering, and the jewelry striking—yet, for the most part, those gems that I've seen here were not of first water, although they made up for it in Oriental splendour. Pearls are smuggled by the turbanful from Arab fishermen on the Persian Gulf. So, this is quite a place; peaceful, too, since the Russians loaded their tanks on flatcars and hauled them back into Soviet Azerbaidjan, after the UN Security Council members stood up to them. Now, I seek other stories. One of them in the mountains could be terrific.

Tribesmen *everywhere* . . . 200,000 Qashqai
nomads migrate—plus one Yankee nomad
from faraway Missouri. What a life!

The Valley of Beaza, southern Iran.
13 May, 1946

Donkeys, camels, huntsmen, mothers with
infants or lambkins in their arms—and
sometimes both—surge past amid pageantry
and din on a colossal scale. Silhouetted
atop the highest ridge, Malik Mansour,
Khan of the Qashqai, sits astride Sharak,
his great Arabian stallion, and scans the flow.
He awaits the cavalry squadrons, just as
his ancestors once watched over *their* tribes
on the wind-torn steppes of Turkistan,
before the Vikings sailed down from the north,
or the Roman legions landed in England.
Even now, each spring as they wind into
the mountains from the Persian Gulf, then
return in autumn to escape the snow, the
Qashqai *must* follow the sun and new-born
grass, and the eternal cycle of their own
rootless lives—or die.

211

Tribal strength,
among the nomad khans,
is measured in terms of
armed cavalrymen.
In their tents, around
the fires at night,
after the great silver
platters have been cleaned
of roast gazelle, grilled
partridge under crushed
pomegranates, pistachio
pilaf, snow-chilled melons
and Shiraz cherries,
and after tea
when their talk shifts
from events of that day's
trek, to hunting and
horses—as it always does—
the hunters and horsemen,
who are of course the same,
often refer to their rifles
as "the brothers of Allah",
and to their horses
as their own brothers.
Thus, the Qashqai, who
own thirty thousand square
miles of southern Iran,
and roam another fifty,
are a vast family of
hawk-beaked men, barrel-
chested, tireless horses,
and countless kin of Allah . . .
rifles fired by men
who wait until dusk before
competing with each other—
when they shoot bats
and swallows
out of the night sky.

Nasser Khan Qashqai—Buddhalike, six-feet two, the Khan of Khans—rules as a benign monarch over his summer domain where children learn of life with army rifles and pure-blooded horses as companions. Here, too, Khardijeh, Nasser Khan's mother, Khosro, Malik and Hosein, his bear-coddling, backgammon-playing Khan brothers—and the other tribesmen—spread their black tents and visit each other in meadows that will be home until frost drives them south. Also here, as throughout his realm, every man bows to Nasser Khan, men loath to acknowledge any sovereign but the sky, yet willingly give him three percent of their flocks and herds. In return, he shields the nomads from government senators in Tehran who view the tribal lands with avarice—leaving each Qashqai free to pursue his lonely, unsheltered, wandering life.

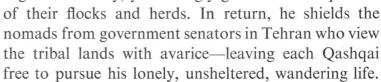

CHAPTER XII

Jerusalem, Palestine.
14 June, 1946

Arabs versus *Jews:* Oh, troubled Promised Land!
Every time I start out the door something blows up.

It's everywhere! The danger. Barbed wire and guys with burp guns are everywhere, too. Orthodox, fur-hatted Jews from within the Old City, Arab donkey drivers, kids playing tag, and girls from the "foreign" quarter . . . all get hung up on the wire. But I'll bet they can't smell *it*. Or maybe they can but just ignore it, like out in the islands during the war. Jerusalem looks better over the cupolas of the church in the Garden of Gethsemane, from the rocky slopes on the Mount of Olives, and perhaps a bit as it did when Jesus met with His disciples for the last time—where the cypress now grow—the night before He was crucified.

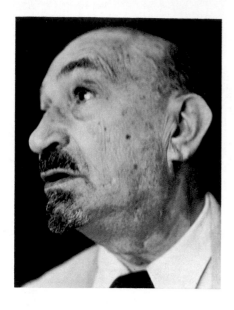 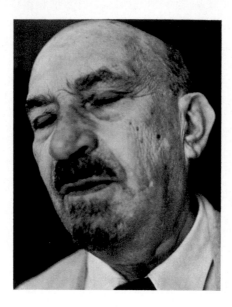 

Rehovoth, Palestine.
17 July, 1946

Poor Dr. Chaim Weizmann labored since his youth for free Israel, Now, failing in sight and health, he surely understands that violence is the way to his State. Like the light at dusk, the idea seems more than he can bear.

Moshe Beigen also shuns light. He is master tactician of the Irgun, Jewish terrorists who are battling the British Army (here trying to keep peace), local Arabs (here by birth), other Jews who abhor fighting, or *anyone* who gets in the way. After being blindfolded, I met him in a blacked-out Tel Aviv hideaway, then photographed a rough map of *their* Israel— Mediterranean to Euphrates. Less extreme—as dedicated— Haganah, the Jews' clandestine army, has made arsenals of the kibbutzim (raided by British soldiers who intern the men), while everyone in the country awaits *the* day—coming soon.

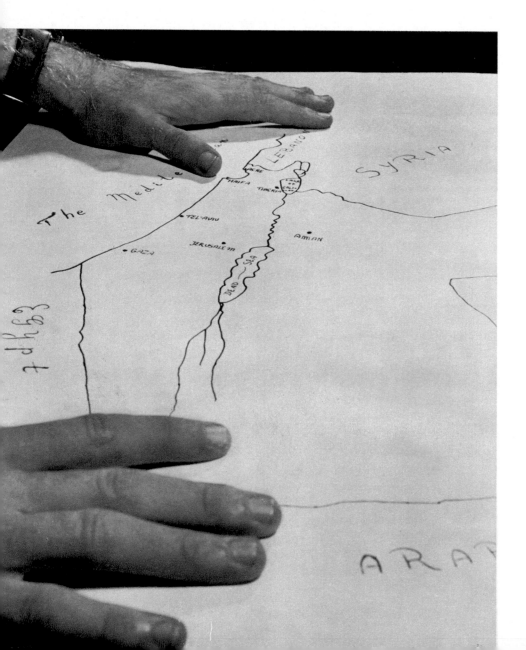

Those b------ !

Jerusalem. 22 July, 1946

Irgun dynamiters blew
British Headquarters in
the King David at noon;
English, Arabs, Jews.
No warning. Cordite
and blasted bodies . . .

LIFE MAGAZINE Cable & Wireless JERUSALEM
NEWYORK 13 SEPT 1946

HICKS: SHIPPING UNDEVELOPED FILM. EXCLUSIVE.
TERRORIST ATTACK OTTOMAN BANK IN JAFFA, CAR
COVERING OPERATION, GUNMAN BACKSEAT WHO
WAVED ME TAKE COVER FRACTION BEFORE SHOT
THREE ARABS BESIDE ME, CAPTURE OF THREE
TERRORISTS, WHOLE SHOW. ACCURATE REPORT
STILL MISSING. YOULL GET IT BEFORE PICTURES.
WHAT A BEAUTIFUL DAY STILL TO BE ALIVE.

Roll I; Pix 1–12 & Roll II; Pix 1–6: Irgun raided Jaffa Ottoman Bank at 1120 today Friday.
Firing echoed down street but hard locate. Saw three Arabs hiding behind corner. Bank out
of line their vision. Joined them. Saw Chevrolet sedan ('36), green, parked next intersection
one block right (north) of target (bank). Two men front seat one in rear. Just as saw them gunman waved me take cover (apparently thinking me a Jew, in khaki) moment before opening
fire automatic weapon killing Arab my right, critically wounding Arab my left, probably
fatally wounding (riddled groin) third Arab slightly behind me. Ran halfway up street
toward car dived into doorway made picture of car pulling through intersection, gunner
firing, to pick up other terrorists escaping from rear bank. Police moved in firing, passing
Arab sprawled in street (others fell or crawled into doorways). Three plainclothesmen round-
ed corner covering two men hands in air (cops also thought was Jew and camera my gun;
yelled) Firing again started near bank. Accompanied police now arriving through movie
house (show today is two-gun "Captain Midnight"). In bank found general manager James
Annett shot through left leg above knee. Very calm. Helped carry to ambulance picking up
wounded and dead. Ten minutes for whole show. Trying get this aboard 1520 Cairo plane.

*. . . despite all terror, others kept pouring out of shattered Europe aboard vessels which seemed
to date from the Middle Ages. For, even at its worst there would be the fulfillment of a promise
that was repeated each year for nearly two thousand Passovers—"Next year, Jerusalem!"*

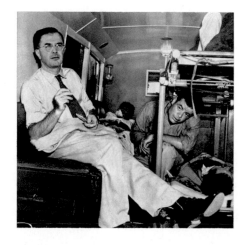

The Hills of Galilee.
20 September, 1946

It has been a summer
without clouds.
Nothing broke the pattern of
empty blue and naked stone.
Four months of curfews, searches,
immigrants running the blockade,
gun battles, explosions and
murders; visiting sheikhs and
settlements; driving over nearly
every road in the land and flying
over most of the rest; guest of
everyone from the Irgun
to the High Commissioner
—and Arabs so secure in the
isolation of their Biblical era
they know not what is happening—
trying to see each side as they
see it, yet not permit the camera
to be partial. Now, there is
nothing to add, not one word.
The story should be woven of the
same fabric as the lives of the
Palestinians who made it possible.
The land, which they both claim
as home, will be self-evident
and should make many there in
America pause, for a moment at
least, in wonderment—trying to
grasp something of the fortunes
of others who must turn
to such a calloused bit of earth
for support, or refuge,
and here sow their dreams.

Istanbul, Turkey.
27 November, 1946

That offer from the Sheikh of Huzayel, down in Beersheba, sounds tempting: two hundred sandy acres and a wife, "brand new"! My last story is almost finished, and I'm now quitting *Life*. That Palestine essay seemed both unfair and misused. I know of no other way in the future to ask for help in portraying confused issues between two or more factions, unless this is fought out right now, in the beginning.

LIFE MAGAZINE   **TURKISH TELEGRAPH**   ISTANBUL
NEWYORK   27 NOV. 1946

HICKS: JUST RECEIVED COPY OF PALESTINE ESSAY. STUNNED. HOW IT CAN BE OFFERED AS COVERAGE OF PALESTINE PROBLEM IS BEYOND COMPREHENSION. YOU PRINTED 18 PIX: 11 JEWISH, 4 ARAB, 3 GENERAL. 11 PARAGRAPHS OF TEXT: 10 JEWISH, 1 ARAB. YOU LEAD WITH TEXT FROM A PARTISAN AUTHOR, LABLE WHOLE THING "PALESTINE" THEN HAVE THE GUTS TO SIGN MY NAME TO IT. WHERE ARE THE MILLION AND HALF OTHER PEOPLE WHOSE REPRESENTATIVES I IMPOSED UPON, IN THEIR SHOPS, SCHOOLS, CLINICS, AT THEIR DINNER TABLES, AND AT WHOSE SIDE I WAS STANDING WHEN MEMBERS OF OTHER SIDE TURNED THEIR MACHINE GUNS LOOSE? SURELY THEY DESERVE SOME VOICE. UNTIL TODAY I HAVE NEVER SHOT A STORY WHICH, WHEN PRINTED, MADE MY RETURN TO THAT COUNTRY IMPOSSIBLE EITHER BECAUSE OF OMISSION OR PARTIALITY. TO ME THAT LITTLE BIT OF PERSONAL PRIDE CARRIED A VALUE FAR BEYOND THAT WHICH OTHERS MIGHT DREAM, AND YOU HAVE TAKEN IT FROM ME. CONGRATULATIONS. THAT'S ANOTHER EXCLUSIVE. YOU STILL HAVE AN UNTOUCHED STORY ON ARAB PALESTINE, JUST AS NEWSWORTHY AS WHEN TAKEN, SO HOW ABOUT NOW SHOWING THEIR SIDE OF THE ISSUE AND THEIR COUNTRY? UNLESS SOMETHING IS PRINTED TO BALANCE THE GROSS OMISSION, HOW IN GOD'S NAME CAN YOU ASK ME EVER TO SHOOT ANOTHER STORY INVOLVING MORE THAN A SINGLE SIMPLE ISSUE? BELIEVE ME WHEN I SAY THAT I'VE BEEN MY HAPPIEST WHILE DOING THESE ASSIGNMENTS FOR YOU AND AM COMPLETELY AT HOME AT LIFE, BUT BELIEVE ME I'M ALSO COOLEST I'VE EVER BEEN WHILE FIGHTING FOR SOMETHING I BELIEVE IN WHEN I SAY THIS TURKISH STORY IS MY LAST FOR THE MAGAZINE UNLESS YOU BALANCE YOUR SIDE OF SCALES. SURELY YOUR EVERY SENSE OF INTELLIGENCE AND INTEGRITY WOULD HAVE BEEN OFFENDED HAD I SUBMITTED SUCH A LOPSIDED SET OF NEGATIVES AND TOLD YOU, HERE IS PALESTINE. I'M ENTITLED TO SAME RESPECT AND PROTECTION WHILE YOU HAVE PRIVILEGE OF SIGNING MY NAME WHILE I'M GONE.

232

WESTERN
UNION

DAVID DOUGLAS DUNCAN   NEWYORK
PARK HOTEL ISTANBUL   5 DEC. 1946

DISTRESSED AT YOUR ACUTELY UNHAPPY REACTION TO PALESTINE ESSAY
AS PUBLISHED. AM SURE YOU AND YOUR ASSOCIATES HERE COULD FIND
COMMON UNDERSTANDING IF WE COULD SIT DOWN QUIETLY TOGETHER.
WE DID NEXT BEST THING. TUESDAY MANAGING EDITOR THORNDIKE
CALLED TOGETHER ED THOMPSON WHO MADE ORIGINAL LAYOUT, BILL
WALTON WHO WROTE TEXT AND CAPTIONS AND MYSELF TO DISCUSS
YOUR MESSAGE WHICH MADE TREMENDOUS IMPRESSION ALL AROUND.
HERE ARE POINTS ASSEMBLED EDITORS MADE: ONE, ARAB PICTURES WERE
FINE BUT JEWISH PICTURES WERE STILL FINER SO WITHIN LIMITATIONS
NINE PAGE ESSAY OUR PROBLEM WAS WHICH SHOULD GET BIGGER PLAY.
JEWISH PICTURES WON DECISION. TWO, ARTHUR KOESTLER IS NEWS
HERE. HIS NEW BOOK "THIEVES IN THE NIGHT" PROVIDED MOST
EFFECTIVE NEWS ANGLE POSSIBLE. IT HAD NOT BEEN PUBLISHED WHEN
ESSAY APPEARED BUT NOW MONTH LATER RANKS SECOND ON BEST
SELLER LISTS THIS COUNTRY. ALSO BECAUSE OF FIGHTS SHIP DIVERSIONS
ETCETERA JEWISH NEWS HAS RECEIVED MUCH BIGGER PLAY HERE THAN
ARAB. SO I BELIEVE IT WILL BE UNDERSTANDABLE TO YOU WHY WE
PLACED EMPHASIS AS WE DID. THREE, THERE WAS GENERAL AGREEMENT
FULLEST ADVANTAGE WAS NOT TAKEN OF SOME SURPRISING FACTS SET
FORTH IN ARAB PICTURES AND BEHIND OUR REGRET FOR THIS WAS
SPACE PROBLEM WHICH HELD ARABS TO COVER PICTURE AND TWO
PAGES. IT IS NOT LIKELY WE CAN GET BALANCING ARAB STORY FROM
MATERIAL NOW AT HAND BUT I CAN ASSURE YOU LIFE WILL PRINT
OTHER ARAB STORIES WHICH MIGHT WELL INCLUDE MORE OF YOUR
PICTURES. WE REALIZE YOU DID LONG AND ARDUOUS JOB TAKING MANY
PICTURES VISITING MANY PEOPLE INCLUDING MOST IMPORTANT ONES
BOTH SIDES. LET ME SUGGEST THAT YOU MAY BE READING THINGS INTO
THE ESSAY OUT OF YOUR GREATER KNOWLEDGE THAT NOT EVEN MOST
RIGOROUS PARTISAN MIGHT GATHER FROM IT. IN VIEW DIFFICULTY
DISCUSSING THIS SUBJECT AT SUCH DISTANCE HOW ABOUT FILING THIS
ONE FOR DETAILED DISCUSSION WHEN YOU NEXT VISIT NEW YORK?
I HOPE YOU ARE NOT SERIOUS IN SAYING THAT THIS MIGHT BE YOUR
LAST STORY FOR LIFE. WE LOOK FORWARD TALKING ABOUT TIBET AFTER
TURKEY. I SENT YOUR DAD SOME PRINTS YOUR PICTURE WITH SHEIKH
OF HUZAYEL. BEST REGARDS

                                                         WILSON HICKS

When choosing photographs for Nomad *taken in Palestine during those final months before Israel was born, emphasis would again fall upon a phenomenon unseen for two thousand years —militant Jewry.* Life's *editors had been on solid ground, the week their story was published.*

CHAPTER XIII

Nothing moves as night sifts down
upon the winter world where Europe
and Asia nearly join—nothing but
glacial water and Russian mines,
which flow from the Black Sea
and Stalin's darkness beyond.

The Bosphorus, Turkish Straits.
20 February, 1947

After daylight, double lookouts stand
on every prow. They watch for those
monsters, lost during wartime,
which too often still lurk below.
Icy-handed Turks in kayiks
fish amongst Red-flag merchantmen
ploughing past them to fight
the current at the Bosphorus net.
Even Soviet seamen edge warily
around this barrier which seines
the water pouring toward
the Dardanelles, and a world
few of the crewmen have ever known.

Far to the east, beyond Kizilçakçak,
sunlight glistens upon frozen grass.
To the right looms Ararat, where Noah
beached his Ark; to the left, Georgia,
where Stalin was born. Straight ahead,
just behind the barbed wire,
Russian soldiers wait each day
—patrolling with dogs at night—
to shoot anyone who steps upon their
well-raked strip of earth.
Turks call it the "Carpet of Death".

Paradise—My God! Happy Bulgarian Youth Brigade members form endless lines in Ninth of September Square, awaiting a holiday week of "volunteer" farming in the countryside. Above them is Premier Gheorghi Dimitrov, their lord and mentor, in heroic profile on every wall. Naturally, he is overshadowed by *his* lord and master—Stalin. This makes issues rather clear. Local Communists, backed by the Red Army, are now overrunning the land.

238

Bringing in cameras was easy. I simply tied gift parcels (pressed caviar and Turkish delight) and letters from the Bulgarian military attaché in Istanbul to his superiors in Sofia, onto the lid of my camera case, then rode the Orient Express—being saluted all along the way.

Sofia, Bulgaria.   *1 April, 1947 – hand courier.*

239

It's chilling! The difference *really* shows. They wear their way of life on their faces. It's written all over broken-down Premier Dimitrov, who stooges for the Soviets; and toothless Vasil Kolarov, Bulgaria's President, Dimitrov's stooge; and Tzola Dragoïcheva, Secretary-General of a coalition Fatherland Front which runs the country—no stooge. She directs the purges. "Coalition"? A farce! Those joining with the Communists are in hiding, jail, exile, or graves. Now, other Bulgarians sit quietly aside: Russia has won.

Many traces of an earlier life still exist in this Balkan land, but the image is fading. Lovers roam spring nights—until the curfew drives them home. Perhaps no other group can excel the Gusla National Choir, European champions before the war—even though some members have now disappeared for being politically off-key. Nearly every farm is worked by aged peasants who own the soil they till, but are apprehensive of Party bureaucrats trying to collectivize each hectare. Most Bulgarians pray under ikons of their own Orthodox faith—whose Metropolitan now accepts Moscow's historic religious treasure as gifts. How long will *anything* survive? The Kremlin knows.

When the Gusla singers perform,
each embroidered shirt reflects the country's
passion for color and traditional design.
An aura of nostalgia—and pathos—
also surrounds the work of a craftsman so naive
he continues providing elegance in fashion
for an era already dead.

Reality is the loss of personal identity
suffered by every Bulgarian at the door
of the National Assembly, where he is frisked
of weapons such as corkscrews, pocketknives,
and measuring tapes—before he can watch
members of his "coalition" government at work.

What a difference from the Communists' conquest of Bulgaria!
Two weeks from today, Lord Mountbatten—the last viceroy—
will bless the independence of India and Pakistan.
Though an Empire dies, a new world is born.

New Delhi, India.
1 August, 1947

Partition has paralyzed this hate-filled land. Four men race to divide India peaceably before it is too late. Mahatma Gandhi has now emerged from among his untouchables, consulting with the Viceroy. Jawaharlal Nehru guides tactics for the Hindus, while Mohammed Ali Jinnah, alone, speaks for Pakistan. Mountbatten sets the pace. Still, Moslem tailor and Brahmin schoolgirl make their flags at home. Shops are bare, farms lie fetid, mail piles up undelivered and entire trains have disappeared, side-tracked by crews sure to be on *their* side of the Demarcation Line that final day. Fear contaminates everything. Meanwhile, pages are ripped from calendars which show that both the end, and the beginning are near.

245

Yesterday was Pakistan's day in Karachi. With a curt nod, and a simple speech, flame-eyed Jinnah became Governor General for the Moslems. It took about an hour. Returning for the ceremony here, staged with imperial splendour, Lord Mountbatten again stood for the Crown, and justice, in a way that has made *him* hero both of Moslem and Hindu, this summer.

This day belongs to Nehru; and to a wizened little man seated at his spinning wheel in another part of the city.

New Dehli, India.
15 August, 1947

Today, the last viceroy, with his Lady at his side, walked into Durbar Hall—and freely returned India to the Hindus. It was an act of statesmanship unparalleled in world history. Where yesterday's ceremony was held in the makeshift, Karachi Parliament building, this morning's pageant took place in the marbled throne room of immense Durbar Hall, probably built during Queen Victoria's affluent reign. Over a million and a half brand-new citizens jammed the city, hoping to glimpse the men who are viewed as being barely mortal by their countrymen. Now, it is over.

Now, with the British gone, Moslem faces Hindu: it begins.

This morning a few clouds covered the sky, marking the now-dying efforts of the monsoon to break the heat that has been stifling Central India for months. Flocks of squawking parrots swirled among the treetops outside my window. Standing naked in the bathroom, shaving, I wondered whether the plane that was to take me to Egypt would arrive, despite all of the recent communal massacres around Delhi.

Old Delhi, India.
10 September, 1947

Machine-gun fire slammed across the garden behind the hotel. I ducked down flat, half under the tub. Other machine guns opened up. Off the floor, running, throwing on clothes as I went through the lobby, I tore into the room of Price Day, veteran combat correspondent of the *Baltimore Sun*. He was naked too, just dressing, but had not heard the firing. It looked like the old days, the way we went out of that hotel, only we dived into a taxi instead of foxholes and headed toward the bazaar district. I left my camera behind. Hindus, Sikhs and Moslems all know and fear the danger of pictorial evidence; a man with a camera would stand little chance of survival in one of their race riots.

Housetops were black with people, all looking in one direction and yelling. The distance was still too great to tell whether this mob was Moslem or Hindu, since it was on the boundary between neighborhoods of both faiths. The trouble center was directly ahead. Across the center of the road a *tonga* (passenger horse cart) was burning oilily. I wondered whether the driver had saved his horse before they fired the cart. I had almost passed by when my guts contracted with that nearly forgotten nausea. "God, he's still in it!" The driver had been killed at the reins and was now burning with his little cart. He was crouched as though trying to hide under the floor boards, so small that he must have been just a boy.

The crowd was mixed Hindu and Sikh, the latter a particularly warlike sect. Each was armed, with the strangest assortment of weapons I had ever seen. This was a mob with no predetermined intentions. When we first walked down that street it was not even a mob but simply the menfolk of one neighborhood brought to their doorways by fear. They, too, had heard the firing and now rumors had just warned them of an imminent attack from the adjacent Moslem quarter. Their first response was that of brave men. Each grabbed whatever household article might best serve for a weapon and rushed out to join his neighbors in the street. There was neither organization nor leadership. They only knew that they were in peril.

248

Looters started breaking into shuttered shops whose Moslem owners had just fled. At first, only boys pilfered. But then, seeing mere children stagger away under such prizes as office chairs, wall mirrors, stems of bananas, fans and even small safes, temptation shattered all restraint of the squeamish, young and old alike. Except for the shouting, as doors came down, there was no mob feeling other than to loot and burn.

Then the Sikh arrived.

Dressed in faded khaki shorts, an old sport shirt half-open down his chest, a turban and Roman sandals, he dashed from one gang of looters to the next. Nearly a thousand men were either in the streets or their doorways. Shouting exhortations, he ran through them all. Strangely, for a Sikh, he was unarmed. But here was leadership.

Over the swooshing sound of the flames and the snapping crackle of sparks as power cables burned through, the tone of the mob noise changed. Individual voices disappeared. Under the herding of the Sikh separate bands of looters merged into one. Once it started moving as a whole, he would leave a gang, then—churning the air with his arms that they were to follow him—hurl himself into another group farther along the street. Soon the Sikh had hundreds of men moving down three streets into the bazaar intersection. The fourth street lay empty and deathly quiet. It led into the adjacent Moslem quarter.

The intersection was now jammed with men. Most of them were Hindus, with only an occasional Sikh waving his sword overhead. The majority had no idea of what was actually happening. These were clerks, small merchants, government workers, schoolboys. One man, wearing only a loincloth and with his head totally shaved except for a wild-looking top-knot, ran by screaming, punctuating his scream by sliding the back of his wrist over his open mouth, as in western movies. He disappeared into the front of the mob, threshing the air with an ancient sword. Someone nearby grinned and explained that he was a milkman.

The Sikh stood shouting for a moment from the pedestal of the intersection's clock tower, then leaped down and charged into the deserted street, where he began tearing at a doorway with his bare hands. Behind those doors were Moslems who had not escaped.

The doors came off their hinges. A tiny six-year-old, hugging her baby brother in her arms, darted into the street. Hockey sticks, bamboo poles, hatchets, spears and swords flashed and fell, to rise and fall again and again and again. Only an animal voice and smell filled the morning, for the mob sound turned deep, crushing all other feeling beneath it. The child sank in the middle of the street, her arms thrown protectively over the body of her brother. Swords and war axes flailed their bodies and, in a frenzy of madness, the ground around. Then they found her twelve-year-old brother and her sister, her mother and grandfather. They found the little neighbor boy next door, and both of his parents. Each made the same heart-bursting sprint. The young reached the middle of the street. The old fell into the filth of the hard-packed earthen sidewalk. Their murderers had no idea of anatomy. Instead of piercing their brains or hearts, giving them a merciful death, the mob simply butchered and beat them to pieces. The two boys, despite having their heads and arms and legs nearly severed from their bodies, were still alive when their executioners left them. A new sound arose. Someone had finally seen the police patrol, now slowly advancing upon the intersection from the side street leading to New Delhi. The Sikh was already upon the clock-tower pedestal judging the distance and time that separated those quietly moving men from his riot. They drew nearer. I counted seventeen men, each with his rifle slung backward over his shoulder. They were *talking* their way down the street, into the heart of the riot. Murdering men filled the intersection. The patrol kept advancing The Sikh jumped down and raced again into the body-strewn street. Just as breakers eventually crash upon a beach, swirl around rocks, then retreat back into the sea, so did that mob of men when they knew it was finished. As they swept back out of the narrow street, they too broke and parted around what now lay crumbled in their path.

While talking with the constable in command of the patrol, I learned that he had moved through the heart of the trouble zone where I first had heard the machine guns. He had fired five rounds to restore order.

A choked cry spun me to face again that narrow street. Holding a dinner basket in one hand, the father of the tiny girl stood among the mutilated bodies of his family. He had returned from some all-night job, knowing nothing of the trouble. Price Day and I started back to where we had left the taxi. The sobs of the father followed us. Men still jammed each doorway and others of the recent rioters lined the street as we drew away from the intersection where the police and military were now taking charge. Then the Sikh himself fell in alongside to escort us out of the neighborhood. He had seen us at the intersection and now apologized for his lack of hospitality. He had been too busy to get us chairs so that we might be more comfortable. He also regretted that he was so far from his own house that he could not give us something cool to drink. It was such a warm morning!

We had only two more blocks to go. As we moved back along the road the crowd pressed forward, but upon shouts from our chaperon the faces remained impassive and we passed. Perhaps it was their knowledge of what we had seen, now with the frenzy burned out, which brought that look into their eyes as we walked through them. The Sikh was explaining that he was an astrologer, that he had spent two years in England, that he was deeply indebted to some Americans who had been based in Delhi during the war, that—the same sound twisted Price Day and me on our heels. There, the three steps away needed for its stroke, stood a near-naked Hindu fanatic with a great war axe gripped in both hands. We had heard a bamboo pole strike the axe when another Hindu stepped from his doorway to block the blow. The face of the fanatic was devoid of all expression. But his eyes never left us as we continued, half sideways, toward the car. The Sikh muttered, with a shrug, "He's a very ignorant man." We passed the *tonga*. There, just ashes, knelt the driver... as if praying.

CHAPTER XIV

Trust Dave to find secrets in distant houses: Conchita; Georgie; Fu Yeng—now, Leila, who looks straight at you like a trusting child, while searching for answers still unknown to her.

She laughs with her head bent slightly to one side. It sounds like a glass that Pauline has dropped at the top of the stairs, with all of its pieces bursting as they hit the steps in their fall. Her hair looks black but is deep, burnished auburn. Maybe it was her walk that I first noticed, for it is as though she is stepping amongst smaller creatures under her feet, trying not to crush their wings. Her bearing is that which one sometimes sees in the woods when a fawn bounds into the sunlight of early morning, then stands quietly, scarcely breathing, totally aware of her immediate world and almost quivering to its promise; straight-legged, completely alone. After God flecked the brown thrush, which used to sing those mornings in the sycamore tree, He must have tossed the same colors high into the sky in a burst of joy, for they fell as a delicate mask of freckles across her face. She meets *my* idea of beauty.

Her mother is of Lebanese origin, from a now no longer landed family in the Nile Valley. Her father is a gentle little Turk, one of the most respected lawyers in the Middle East and a Napoleonic scholar, who fished faltering but precise English from his background of family languages—French, Arabic and German—learned before my Freckle-face was born, twenty-three years ago. They are Catholics, yet one evening, when talking of religion and her father, she mused for a moment, then answered, "Father's religion? His mind! His work is his prayer on earth to that God of both this life, and the next." He, and her mother, and older brother and sister, will be with her today. I shall be alone.

Shepheards Hotel,
Cairo, Egypt.
20 September, 1947

Tonight, at six o'clock, Leila and I will be married.

When Ibn Saud visited here last year, we clicked from the start. He threw a cookie party for the kids where—nudging bodyguards aside—I shot pictures even *behind* him. Aramco boss, James MacPherson, okayed my saying good-bye. We were received after evening prayers. Explaining what it meant to me, I unfastened the St. Christopher that I had worn through the war—and dropped it into the King's hand. It was like hitting every man in that tent in his solar plexus. I had touched the guardian of Mecca with an infidel's talisman. Ibn Saud lifted the worn bit of silver to his one good eye . . . then slipped it inside his gold-and-camel hair robes with a smile, "Ashkurak"—Thank you. MacPherson's blue eyes were still tightly closed, but color slowly returned to his cheeks and he started breathing once again!

Arabian-American
Oil Company.
Dhahran, Saudi Arabia.
27 June, 1948

It's great to have as a friend one of the last monarchs on this earth! I have been invited to be Ibn Saud's guest at his fortress-capital of Riyadh, when he greets Abdullah of Jordan. With the Arab world now fighting Israel, practical Abdullah is apparently coming to patch his fences with Ibn Saud, after feuds of a quarter-century.

Abdullah seemed lost in Riyadh. Ibn Saud towered over him when leading the way to celebrations in the mud-brick royal town. They walked slowly, Ibn Saud because of wounds accumulated while conquering this desert peninsula which now bears his name. The visit lasted three days, traditional among Arab chiefs. Roast baby camel and skyscraper pastry overflowed rooftop tables. Poems were recited in palace gardens. The kings surely dealt with more serious problems, but on one question Abdullah failed. I had just made a flash-shot. He glared toward me, "Who is that?" Ibn Saud raised his massive head: "My friend."

Princely sons, wall-to-wall:
what a legacy! Faisal, Saud,
Mishal, Talal, Fahd, Turki,
Sultan, Abd Allah, with
more nearby. Princesses,
too, however in this court
they really do not count.
There are other legacies,
like a land where almost no
rain falls; and poor folk
who line the road between
the Red Sea port of Jiddah
and Mecca each Friday, in
expectation of their king
whose attendants dole out
silver *riyals* by the sackful
when he passes by to pray.
Of course, under the hot
sand lies nature's legacy—
seemingly eternal. With
it, Arabia is being made
into a place unknown by
the Old King, whose world
will vanish when he is gone.

257

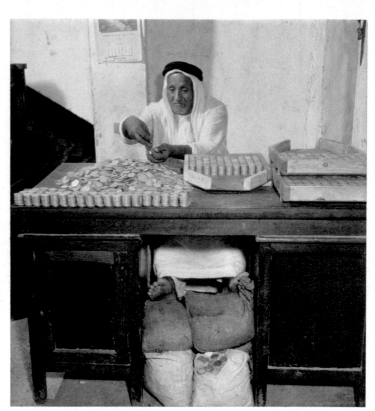

The dream is cornucopian! *Three hundred thousand* barrels of oil pumping daily into the Trans-Arabian pipeline, Persian Gulf to Mediterranean—1,100 miles—a black river across the desert. Pearl fishermen have now beached their *dhows* to work in the refinery; shepherds herd trucks; cameleers weld pipe; local merchants keep *bags* of money under naked feet— banks are new—and Aramco pilots meet check crews where only caravans passed before.

259

  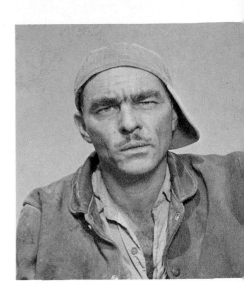

Everything about Aramco's desert operation is special, the men most of all. Drillers, welders, geologists, long-range truckers, Arabic experts, the boss himself . . . Davis, Tindall, Washburn, Inman, Mahoney, Barger, Ohliger, MacPherson . . . not as royal as the Old King's sons, but just as regal in another sort of way—which they earned. Giant convoys haul sections of pipe—nearly one hundred feet long—through blistering wastelands where, if a tire explodes, everyone aboard moves with the smooth precision of a bomber crew under enemy attack: Arabia's midday summer sun can broil a man alive before nightfall. Yet, despite all caution, when guys get lost, feeder lines break, oil escapes, there's hell to pay at Aramco.

At Aramco's trade school
Sudanese, Somalis, Arabs,
Eritreans and men from
as far as Afghanistan,
learn of a new life with
other men who will
never speak their
tongues, but whose
knowledge of their crafts
is so profound that
almost no barrier
prevents total
communication.
Master ironmonger
Harry Johnson
is no exception,
his Arabic being limited
mostly to his hands—yet
his students work as
professionals in nearby
oil fields, usually in
record-breaking time.

262

Only seconds more, and jackals
tonight would have snacked on
well-barbecued tidbits—me—
because of my ignorance of the
oil fields and their many dangers.

When MacPherson learned I had
missed *the* shot for my story,
being with Ibn Saud at Riyadh,
he told drillers: "Do it again!"
It cost Aramco about $100,000.
He burned *Abqaiq 44*, a new well.

Geologists were to run to it
with panels of cobalt glass as
they do each time gushers come
in then are fired to burn sand
and water which, with mud, jam
the pipe. Through his glass an
expert judges by the inferno's
color when pure oil is flowing.
Valves choke off the fire, and
a new oil well has been born.

Abqaiq 44 was Aramco's baby.
Then Mac's veterans charged in.
They paused an instant, and ran.
I was shoving film into my old
view camera, with eyes down,
my face covered by wet towels.
I glanced up! A burning geyser
of oil was above me, driven by
erupting gas domes far below.
Everyone else saw it coming,
and assumed that I would, too.
I passed seven gazelles as I ran!

265

Regardless of what they share while working together, or how easily each adjusts to the other's life, it is after their shifts change—when someone else probes the dunes, welds the pipe, controls the refinery, or just labors silently over accounts—that fundamental differences in Aramco-men show.

267

CHAPTER XV

Russians still call him "Kara Avni" Mizrak —Black Avni—because of the ferocity of his cavalry charges in the First World War. Today, high among the icy forests and rills of a land that has seen nine invasions come from the east, Black Avni's men ride out into blizzards which they welcome. Each storm reassures them of an ally long considered vital to the country's defense.

Erzurum, Turkey.
17 December, 1948

President Truman probably wrecked plans of the Soviet Union to dominate all of Europe, when he launched the Marshall Aid Plan for Turkey and Greece. It surely must give the other, war-ravaged lands cause for hope, too.

Here in Turkey, Harry Truman is teamed with President Inonu who rebuffed Churchill and Roosevelt during World War II, with a refusal to declare war against Germany or to send troops to the eastern front. He was sure the Red Army would have soon moved, as in the Balkans now, to occupy both the Dardanelles and Bosphorus—the historic dream of Russians for five hundred years.

This winter, as weapons of modern armies pour in, Black Avni's cavalry columns appear to be headed toward the pages of history— where they will probably feel more at home.

269

Any Renaissance
painter
would have shared
my surprise.

Kars, Turkey.
25 December, 1948

There was the child,
wrapped in swaddling clothes,
and his mother
in a veil of blue—
straining to see the way.
There was his father,
afoot,
leading cattle, the donkeys
having already passed.
There were his father's
friends, helping them
in their flight.
And, upon the road itself,
there were steel-chested
soldiers who,
in another time
would have been centurions
searching for one Child,
whose family
was seeking refuge
beyond the night.

Mercy dies, when *andartes*—rebels—hit a town.
Civil war, here, means guns spraying hospitals.
Tourists seldom come anymore to the Parthenon.
They *never* see Olympus, or Delphi, or Marathon.
Life ends, bleeding silently into the ground.

Athens, Greece.
8 April, 1948

Some Greeks are said to dislike a royal family,
being fiercely loyal only after they are gone.
Yet I have seen days when all Greeks loved the
King and Queen—all except the Communists who
base in mountains over Florina on the Yugoslav
frontier—who murder all who oppose them here.

King Paul and Queen Fredricka simply shook their heads, saying I was mad to have flown so low beside them and then ask the pilot to land on the road to Drama, just ahead. They, of course, were driving a jeep through Macedonia *unescorted*, immediately after rebels had butchered villagers nearby. In Florina, when the royal couple flew in to walk alone among the mourners toward the cemetery on the edge of town, rebel bodies were still being culled from those who fell defending the place, while the hospital was just a bullet- and flame-gutted ruin. This is war so cruel it sounds merciful when rebels stuff a man into the fire-box of his locomotive—where rebel dead are quickly searched, stacked, bulldozed from sight. After each battle, it is the King and Queen who first arrive; soothing, strengthening, sheltering (even those suspected of plans to kill them), hoping to ease the misery everywhere.

In Florina,
when a man is dead,
though killed by rebel fire,
there are few tears upon the faces
even of those who loved him best.
For these tears must be drawn
from wells now almost dry.
Fathers, uncles, brothers, sons,
mothers and daughters,
grandparents,
school children, too,
have fought the rebels
—or with them—
or been abducted over mountains
into Communist lands to the north.
Tears?
Like the villagers themselves,
very few are left.

Tragedy, and human weakness,
are qualities making the gods
of Greek antiquity
appear almost mortal.
They were carved
into the golden face of Artemis,
twenty-three hundred years ago.
Suffering, and human strength,
have also chiseled a face
—of a shepherd tortured by rebels—
whose eyes might have bridged
another millennium, even two,
had they only been sculpted in stone.

This is *another* India, a Kumbh Mela—Hindu festival—with a million pilgrims here. Some kiss the feet of holy men. Others close their eyes when meeting *sadhus*—stark-naked, bone-necklaced, ash-painted mystics—who have emerged from Himalayan eyries, and who are thought to kill with a glance. Wading into the Ganges where it first pours onto the Saharanpuri plains, the pilgrims anoint themselves with the sacred water then, looking into the sun, beg forgiveness of their sins.

Hardwar, Uttar Pradash.
13 April, 1950

No wonder pilgrims are awed by the holy men dominating Hardwar and its purifying "Brahma's Pool". The *sadhus* are all followers of deities from a pantheon of Hindu gods who determine a man's fate. Kali, goddess of death, roams the shrine with tongue dangling and glazed eyes in a murdered face. Vishnu the Preserver's deputy here is an unnerving sight, imperiously bedecked; ashes, rope and an elephant vertebrate necklace—holding court for Bairagis, wildest *sadhus* of all. In his mountains he is said to be the law itself, pronouncing judgement on local peasants, including death. Other *sadhus* are more benign; one even looked like a saintly man. Another, a Prince of Beggars, flashed smiles reincarnating movie Pirate, Douglas Fairbanks. Astrologers fix Kumbh Melas every twelve years. I'll be back—in 1962!

Drums throbbed in louder,
off-beat staccatos, while a
flat tenor wailing from
reed flutes cut into the
rumbling of the crowd.
A million pair of feet
went up on tiptoe
as the music drove a
wedge through them,
then the *sadhus* appeared.
Ecstasy,
shone in many eyes.
Men threw themselves into
the river gravel to stroke
the leaders' feet
in veneration,
then knelt, rubbing newly
sanctified hands upon
their chests, heads, and
across their eyes.
Others tossed coins;
later sifted by the poor.
Finally, almost running,
as though swept along by
the pilgrims' rising shouts
came the naked Bairagis,
beneath Medusa-manes
of ghastly hair.
Mingling hope with fear,
India's peasant masses
revere their *sadhus*, who
can twist stars from heaven,
hurl shadows across the sun,
and kindle life—or death—
in any heart.
They answer only to
Siva and Vishnu . . .
When they speak,
God Himself is near.

CHAPTER XVI

Poor old people!
It's war again and I'll bet
they don't even know.

Suwon, South Korea.
28 June, 1950

They probably think this
is just another summer day.
No baggage, no bedding,
no supper for along the way;
nothing but a son who pulls,
and a neighbor pushing them
on a journey from which
even the son will be lucky,
if he returns.

The North Koreans
are in Seoul,
seven miles up the road.

289

The author of *Ten Days That Shook the World* should
have been here this week, because now it's happened
in five! Sunday, before dawn, North Korea attacked
Seoul—first on the list. Monday and Tuesday, enemy
troopers swarmed south; nothing stood in their way.
Wednesday, a Security Council censure, then tough
old Harry Truman on MacArthur's phone, sent United
Nation troops on *their* way. Now, Friday: Yank jets
blast Red tanks; villages lie empty; every road is
full, except MacArthur's to Seoul. All flee—where?

Holy smoke, these RoKs fight on just their hearts!
No jets or bombers, or tanks, or even ammo much
of the time. Nothing but a few advisers to soldiers
like a kid colonel, a *child* private, and wounded
without morphine—only leaves soothe their eyes—
awaiting men without litters from "medics" below.
RoK? Republic of Korea. It means something, now.

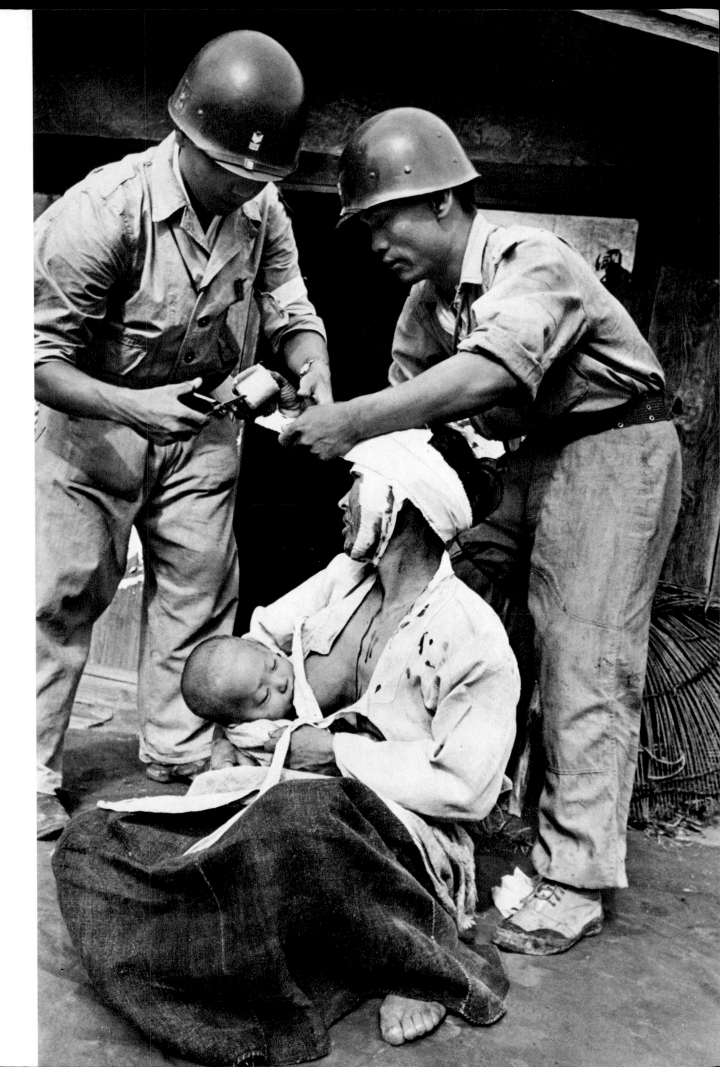

Each day,
while fighting
to hold the
river perimeter,
Marines
bless their luck
when seeing
the silent men
who simply appear,
half-smiling and
never in fear,
searching for the
fallen
whom they help
when they can.
If they find them
only wounded,
they lift each
like a child,
to carry him
from the hills
before going back
once again.

LIFE MAGAZINE   15 AUG 1950
NEWYORK   TOKYO

MANAGING EDITOR THOMPSON: I WOULD LIKE
RETURN KOREA FOR INDEFINITE PERIOD COMING
OUT ONLY AFTER HAVE MARINE COMBAT STORY
WHICH WONT REQUIRE ANY WORDS AFTER THE
INTRODUCTORY TEXTBLOCK. SEE IT AS LAYOUT
OF PICTURES WHICH SIMPLY SAY "THIS IS WAR".

It was impossible to reload cameras on the ambulance
jeep. As I leapt off an explosion scattered Marines
and bits of jeep all around. Its driver sat bawling
not from pain, but for his buddy who had offered to
carry wounded from the battlefield. He was instantly
killed when they struck the mine. Young Marines cry
rather often, when ammo's gone and they want to run;
when shot through both shoulders but then must walk
to where they can rest. I've seen captains cry when
seeing men falter. Probably all Marines cry sometime
before they grow old. It happens fast to them after
a few weeks under fire. Then they attack standing up,
ignoring what's ahead, *earning* their title: Marine.

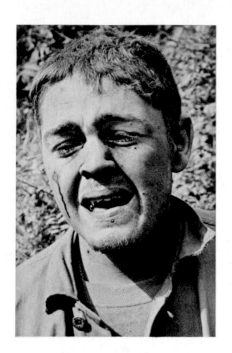

Three months to a day!
"Seoul is free."
MacArthur says so.
This place is liberated—except for an
enemy up many streets who disagrees.

Seoul, South Korea.
25 September, 1950

The Inchon landing was Mac's miracle—
putting us behind North Korean lines with
all of the strength in the world. Plenty of
them broke, probably heading for home.
But they left nests of gunners
holding every intersection in town.

Yesterday, the Marines were pinned for
hours by snipers and machine gunners
shooting from every window, from *under*
the streets. When a captain, Bob Barrow,
hit the edge of what lay ahead he dug in,
radioing for dive bombers to soften the way.
Despite heat from headquarters—who bore
the heat from MacArthur, who insisted
Seoul be delivered the 25th, today—Barrow
called again for the bombers, *and* artillery,
then watched the city's arsenals explode.

There may come a time when they will say
we weren't welcomed by Koreans today,
after the bombings and fires and the tanks
shooting point-blank through their streets;
today, when a girl and a young Marine
locked fingers for a moment after she
broke from the ruins, an instant before
she fled; today, when families ran straight
toward our tankmen who fought cannon
duels with other gunners barricaded beyond
the station; today, the day Seoul was freed.

301

. . . a million stars overhead—
. . . a hundred thousand Chinese out there in the snow.
I know, now, what to expect where it's forty below. I saw it
in the faces around me . . . just before dark
when the order came to go.

First Marine Division,
Kot'o-ri, North Korea.
9 December, 1950

Ten minutes more delay and I would have been too late.
They're pulling out. This afternoon planes and tanks
opened the way. Men share their fires; I'll have a chance to thaw a bit
before joining the column. What a change from vacationing
in New York last week, a billion lifetimes ago.

It's night. A Marine examines frost-bitten toes.
I've finished my notes. Now, I'll try to fix my cameras
hoping I can save a film that broke in the cold.

This was to have been their Thanksgiving
with every man headed for home,
war ended . . . wrong made right,
the Monster itself
at their feet—
Crusaders, welcomed home.
And yet,
each morning has been Thanksgiving
though it may not last until night—
or, if dark,
it may not last until dawn.
This is a world where
life is short
but it seems to be forever.
This is the world
where a Marine,
when asked what he wanted most
for Christmas,
reached for words
through his frozen lips,
then answered . . .
"Give me Tomorrow."

This week was *our* Dunkirk!

Hungnam, North Korea.
23 December, 1950

Marines, Army, Turks, RoKs, British Marines—and another ninety-three thousand North Korean civilians, wailing kids, tanks, trucks and ox-carts— everything! Everyone is going. The place is being left gutted, abandoned, stripped bare. Of course, there are those who are staying behind, no one yet knows how many—in the snow. The others, stumbling north? These we *will* see, someday.

Today, I wanted to shoot a sadist in American uniform. An artillery captain told a sergeant to bulldoze a path ahead of his guns. Koreans had ten minutes to take all they could from home. The sarge loved his orders, and did the job right. A general came in an hour, groaned in dismay, "I said *fire lanes!* Who needs kindling today."

We left a wilderness behind
in which Chinese are strewn
like coyotes after the hunt.
We left Hungnam shattered,
a hulk that once was a port.
We left our friends—hoping
to bring them home, someday.
We left mined wharfs, where
some pups and I stood alone.
Then they blew the place . . .
And now, it's Christmas Eve.

CHAPTER XVII

Japanese ghosts have no feet—as demons they are eternal. As earthen *haniwa* warriors they guard prehistoric tombs and, as masked Shinto priests, grimace before Ise's sacred Inner shrine. They prowl the night as Kabuki cats and float down from Kabuki lanterns, to make even a murdering *samauri* cringe. Here, fantasy and the supernatural create a world apart.

High on rainy Koya-san,
the medieval monastery of
Karukayado is one of
Buddhism's holiest shrines.
Faith, brought by pilgrim
hearts makes even grass divine.

Seventy-two years ago, when
twenty, Tokuju Taikju Mineo
renounced all possessions
to be a Zen monk of Hierinji,
a temple near Tokyo.
He worked in the fields,
made his clothing, learned
and administered discipline
—a stick upon the shoulders—
and became a master of scrolls.
Never again was he to leave
Hierinji's soil—where now,
he has carefully chosen a grave.

In Kyoto, as within all temples of Japan, Buddhas are named. The lotus, "Phoenix" Buddha of Byodoin meditates as it has for eight hundred years. Nearby, the "Thousand Buddhas of Sanju-Sangen-do" stand guard, life-size, in gilt array. Japanese pilgrims to China brought Buddhism home fifteen hundred years ago. Still, seeking solace today, a Buddhist often turns to the statueless cemetery on lofty Koya-san, the holy mountain, set in forest-twilight and soft rain. Emerald moss cushions all sound. A path winds among pilgrims, *samauri*, emperors. There, a deeper impression is pervasive— of walking to the horizons another way.

Tradition and color interweave Japanese life. Kabuki classics originated three hundred years ago. The Nakajimas, of Kyoto, have embroidered Noh costumes for five centuries. Tadafusa Fujiwara created his dance, *Butterfly Virgins of Ise*, in 1050. Sons of Mizaki watch a flower festival of lost origin. Artistic levels, here, are set by the Painter of the forests of Chuzenji.

When Yukichi Obata goes to his noodle factory in Tokyo's suburbs, Tomika, his wife, follows him to the gate. They bow good-bye. She then returns to a home where they enjoy lives rich in tranquility and austere beauty. He is seventy-two; she, sixty-five. On fine summer days, he lifts and removes *shoji* panels —sliding rice-paper walls— extending his view into the garden. Tomika meticulously arranges her flowers for the alcoved *tokonoma*, the family shrine and art repository, where hang *kakemono* scrolls. On rainy evenings, they practice for amateur Noh plays—she on the *tzuzumi*, or drum, he on his fué. Then they spread bedding upon *tatami* floors as gold as ripened wheat, and sleep.

When any of the five grandchildren visit the Obatas, life is keyed to the aging couple whose lives already seem somewhat foreign to the children. In their homes, few refinements of traditional Japanese houses survive. War and "Westernization" have now altered classical Japan beyond repair. When Ishinaka and her baby sister, Midori, get tucked in by their grandmother—while Yukichi Obata burns incense under his favorite *kakemono* before retiring—they are closing their eyes upon a world that will be gone, soon after they awaken.

Jiro Harada
was not offended—
we are good friends.
I had asked if Buddhas
of the National Museum
here in Tokyo
were ever sold,
or did he think one
might be sold?
My wizened friend
is lame. When I said
I spoke of *Miroku*, a
seventh-century bronze,
his smile deepened,
then he limped across
the entire museum
to see it again with me,
while telling a story:

"Last century,
during an epedemic,
our Crown Prince
was gravely ill.
All remedies were tried,
to no avail.
Then the Emperor—
when the end seemed
certain and near—
pledged a solemn oath:
if his son be granted
a miracle, and live,
he and the Empress
would acknowledge their
gratitude to God
and thanks to a nation
at prayer, by giving
Miroku to us all."

326

CHAPTER XVIII

Abadan, Iran.
7 December, 1951

In Malaya they're called bandits, in Burma, insurgents, in Iran, fanatics, in Indochina, rebels. In almost every land around the rim of Asia they are local men who have one thing in common—they are fighting against the last stand by white men upon their oil-rich deserts and rice-covered plains. They are fighting and winning, in some places with the direct support of the Communists, and the white man's Asian world is nothing much more than the ghost of what was once great empire.

Hong Kong is misleading, for there the ghost is incognito and its frenzied flapping can well be mistaken for vitality. The mammoth corporations which date back to the opium war days, like Jardine, Matheson & Co., are still listing their China coast affiliates and services. Although the United Nations embargo against Communist China has cut the registered tonnage this year at Hong Kong by one hundred thousand tons a month, the number of ships clearing the port has actually increased. Thus with the embargo it would seem that large ships stayed away, while smaller coastal vessels swarmed in and out of the port. In Hong Kong enormous tea-party fashion shows are crowded with civil servants, military personnel and their ladies. Few seem aware that theirs is the final stand on the mainland of China. The Hong Kong and Shanghai Bank, in the center of the city, is overshadowed by the towering new Bank of China, financed, owned and staffed by Communist Chinese.

The president of the Hong Kong stock exchange, whose hair turned even whiter during three and a half years in Japanese prison camps, chuckles and explains that British traders always have been involved in a risk business in faraway lands stirred by revolution, war lordism, brutal weather and cutthroat competition. Forty percent profits per year were commonplace—and it had been a good life. But then he represents that minority of men who helped create the British Empire, men who enjoyed the dangers as much as the profits and made no false representations about either.

The peoples of Indochina—Viet-Nam—are infected with revolt against the French and their weak emperor, Bao Dai. Only by the force of arms, many supplied by the U.S., an expenditure of wealth equal to the total granted France under the Marshall Plan, and a fearful loss of lives have the French been able to retain islands of barbed wire in what once was their most lucrative foreign property. Many French businessmen still try to convince themselves that Saigon, their biggest barbed-wire island, is the same "Paris of the Orient" that it was before the war. Each bed in the military hospitals holds a soldier who could tell them the truth. The Communists have exploited the fire lit by the Japanese— that Asia should be run by Asians. A Vietnamese bluntly pointed out that it was fear for our own American necks, not his, which made the United States support any force in the world that might be useful in keeping Communism from our own backyard.

Revolution in Malaya, just as in Indochina, has taken a terrible toll in property and lives. From the office of highest civil authority to the playpens of this generation's babies, death has reached into many homes. The British army, far bigger than their force in Korea, has been unable to defeat a band of only a few thousand men—men who attack from ambush and who have the sympathy of many of the peoples of the peninsula. Much of the guerrillas' armed strength is in weapons saved from World War II, when they fought the Japanese.

Chaos rules in Burma, a member of the British Commonwealth where the ghost of former empire sits at every table. Granted independence without even a preview of its responsibilities or difficulties, yet painfully reminded by the rows of decaying mansions of how life was before, the Burmese of Rangoon are living in a situation which reminded me of Tobacco Road at its worst. Warring factions have ripped the back country wide open, driving clouds of refugees into the city. Although the Burmese individually are warmly hospitable and good natured, their government views with apprehension and distrust the activities of all foreigners. They are so fearful of getting caught again in the meshes of economic and political empire that they have brought their land to the point of almost total disaster. Great fields lie empty where modern factories were to have been built by foreign capital. Roads and meadows are loaded with fortunes in scrap iron, a tragic resource left in the wake of the war. The Burmese, instead of shipping it out into the begging world market, are letting it rust away in their tropical climate—saving it for that vague day when they will have a steel mill. The refugees have swarmed into Rangoon's bomb-gutted and still unrepaired buildings. The only new construction to be seen in the city is a block of luxurious bungalows being built for the officials of the proud young Union of Burma navy. On Sundays some of the more fortunate Burmese crowd the clubhouse of the Turf Club, once restricted to the patronage of British colonials. Now they cheerily bite their cigars, wiggle their toes out of uncomfortable slippers and patiently wait for the winners and, optimistically, for better days for Burma.

India and Pakistan are different today too. It was a gentle little doctor working in a leprosarium, who boiled the difference down to a single sentence: "Although we expelled the system, the British as individuals are welcome to stay and live and work as long as they understand and respect one fact: we run things now." Except for those few Englishmen who

328

are living out their retirement or existing on menial jobs, not many others have stayed around to view the results of independence—or share its problems. Today, whether passing through customs or applying for import licenses, that handful of Britishers who have returned have done so just like all other foreigners. On the terrace of the ex-imperial Gymkhana Club in New Delhi, once one of the most exclusive spots in the entire British world, the few oldtimers who stayed behind now cling to the fringe of the social circle and watch, while turbaned waiters buzz around Hindu and Sikh members—who run things now. At Sunday morning services in St. John's Church of Meerut, where the bulk of the British Indian army was garrisoned, a single service is now performed before a half-dozen members sprinkled through pews built to seat a battalion. In the polished elegance of what was Durbar Hall in New Delhi, a magnificent Buddha now smiles serenely down from the niche where I saw Lord Mountbatten, the last viceroy, hand India to Prime Minister Nehru. The place has been dedicated to the public as the national museum of art.

Few events in Asia have shocked the Western world more than the Iranian nationalization of the Anglo-Iranian Oil Company, or made it more aware of the restless tides sweeping over many distant lands. Having visited the refinery during the years when it was run by the British company, it seemed fitting that I should wind up this journey through the wreck of Asian empires by another trip there. I went expecting to find Abadan looted bare of all movable parts, goats and donkeys in the gardens, and the desert sands drifting in. But the plant has been kept spotless. In place of the British general manager a four-man board of directors has been established, three of them engineers holding degrees from the finest European universities. The fourth man is a member of parliament who acts as liaison between the refinery and the government in Tehran. They insist that the least of their problems will be to refine the oil that comes into Abadan. They showed me many of the thirteen hundred applications already received from oil technicians in over twenty-five countries who want to fill the three hundred jobs necessary to run the plant at full capacity. Their major problem is to find ways to transport and sell their oil to the world market. One primary fact is very clear here in Iran, as in most of the other countries of Asia—they will never go back to the way things were, even though they commit national suicide. Iranians, Indians, Burmese and all the rest, want to run things from now on—for themselves.

329

. . . five stars and a fabled smile,
a stereo camera around his neck,
and the end of the world in each fist.
Ike is something new in diplomacy!

Athens, Greece.
11 March, 1952

For a week, General Eisenhower has been whirlwinding
across Turkey and Greece, welcoming them to NATO.
No similar American has ever been seen on these shores.
He represents total military power.
At the same time, and casually,
he represents himself—with exuberance.

In Istanbul, he was the thrilled tourist
with a camera in hand, shouting, "It's easy!"
when his picture seemed right.
Here in Athens, the warmth of his
salute to King Paul and his generals
filled the entire flag-bedecked garrison.

Today, with Britain's empire fading and that of France
soon to follow, one wonders just how well America
will play her role of leadership
with both nationalism and Communism
moving in to occupy those worlds now being abandoned.

Ike seemed perplexed when King Paul spun around. The voice of my old rapid-fire camera—like twin machine-gun bursts—reached across the steps where the NATO ceremony was to begin. Paul began telling of when he had heard the sound before—while we roamed much of Greece during the civil war. Ike's face remained furrowed. It seemed as though he was trying to place the staccato beat in his ears—despite it being there for a week. Now, I wonder about the many sides of a man who aspires to be President. I also wonder what became of the carefree man, at the beginning of this trip, whom I photographed in Istanbul.

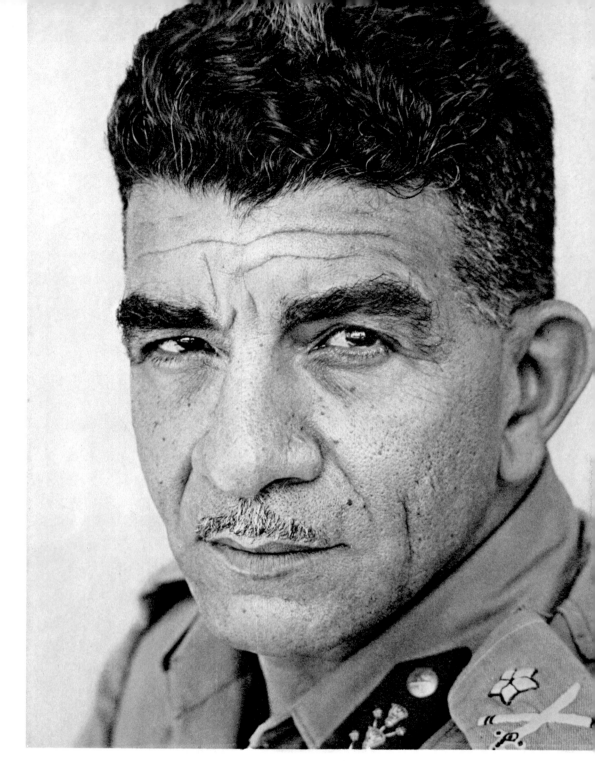

It's the year of
generals and kings,
and an ex-king!

"In our Koran,
it is written:
'Then the Word
went forth:
O Earth!
swallow up
Thy water
and O Sky!
withhold
Thy rain . . .
away with those
who do wrong.'"

Cairo, Egypt.
29 July, 1952

At precisely 1800 hours, July 26th, without apparent emotion, King Farouk looked up from his wristwatch—as a civilian. He stepped aboard the ex-royal yacht *Mahroussa* and sailed north, into exile. Throughout the Nile Valley he left palaces and treasure beyond the dreams of a dozen kings. He also left twenty million ex-subjects, many of them living under conditions unseen elsewhere on the face of the earth. Finally, he left a new-born infant—the first nationalistic revolution of Africa. It is led by a still anonymous Central Committee of nine young Egyptian Army officers, and godfathered by Major General Mohamed Naguib.

333

General Naguib straightened from his morning prayers.
Tea and toast were quickly finished. He scanned all of the
Egyptian newspapers; others of Paris, London, New York.
Sweepers with brush brooms began to clean the boulevard
outside his window in the Army headquarters, his home
since the coup. It was dawn. He wrote out recommendations
for immediate action regarding patients in the armed forces
hospital he had visited the day before. He knew many men
by their first names. His Arabic resembled musical notes
flowing across the plain military stationery. Then he spoke—
quietly and in great detail—of the corruption within palace
cliques and of his shame over appalling conditions at home,
and of his country's tarnished reputation abroad. He told of
The Plan . . . desert rendezvous . . . tanks, jet fighters and,
circling above them, the heavy bombers . . . of security so
complete that even he who was asked to lead the coup never
knew the identities of the nine junior officers of the Central
Committee until after he went aboard the *Mahroussa* to
salute and say, "Good-bye, Mr. Farouk."

CHAPTER XIX

King Farouk called the card himself
when he once joked,
"Someday,
there will remain only five kings—
Of England, and of
Clubs . . . Hearts . . . Diamonds, and Spades."

Alexandria, Egypt.
17 August, 1952

Probably not even Farouk knows, within a hundred million dollars, the value of the world he left behind. Pornographic trash is found everywhere in truckloads, and nudes—oil, bronze, marble and gold—by the ton. There are also superb collections of coins, Czech glass, Dresden china and Louis XIV furniture. The Pharaonic jewelry is priceless—looted from Egypt's museums. There is a sixteen-million-dollar stamp collection; a cache, estimated at one hundred million, is in gems. Here at Ras el Tin palace in Alexandria there is the throne of his dynasty, founded in 1811 by an Albanian terror, Mohammed Ali. His Queen's bed is at Abdin palace in Cairo. He will never see any of them again. They will become museums.

Farouk collected palaces: austere Kubbah, and Abdin with its phoney *Venus*, in Cairo; vast Ras el Tin and turreted Montazah in Alexandria, where *Mahroussa* anchored. "Rest houses" sit at the corner of Cheops' pyramid and on the Nile. He left mummy masks and portraits of Adolf Hitler—snapshot souvenirs of a man with everything except good sense.

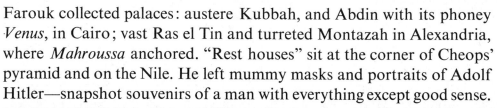

Eden had signed for Great Britain and Schuman for France; Acheson for the United States; Adenauer for the German Federal Republic. All of the Allies were in Bonn that 26th morning of May, to make peace with Germany—all except the Soviet Union. Stalin had said he would never sign until every Western soldier was out of Berlin, and the rest of Germany, too, Today, Kremlin agents are raising barbed-wire billboards— "No Eisenhower War Threat"—from Bavaria to the Baltic. They are splitting Germany. Before now, the "Iron Curtain" was only growled Churchillian thunder.

Lübeck, Germany.
20 September, 1952

Germany must be anesthetized! The Communists are ripping the heart from their land yet no one seems aware of it. When the East German People's Police, *Vopos*, appear along the edge of their newly proclaimed VERBOTEN frontier, vacationers look the opposite way, *laughing*. North Sea barge captains from Lübeck lean on the simple crossbar (erected postwar to mark occupation zones) watching havoc being done. Local *Vopos* take siestas while

a Mustin farmer carefully tends the wound gutting his fields. Deep in the forests which blanket the Bavarian-Czech border, American MPs of an anti-smuggling customs unit have only one real friend—Rolf, tracker dog of the *Vopos*. Even I—who had seen such a barricade long ago in Turkey—leapt a Trogen roadblock to shoot from their side in that minute before *Vopo* horsemen could arrive, dressed as if riding to hounds— which they were.

Once every month—never the same date twice—an aging political refugee comes to a remote path parallel to the Iron Curtain in Bavaria. His wife and daughter try to feign innocence while pursuing assigned chores of hauling wood for *Vopos* billeted in their home. It is not easy, especially for the child. They do not flee because of the other children now kept as hostages. After signalling another date, he hurries from sight. They share nothing more in life.

Albert Funk is a frontier patrolman who plants himself in the center of the tracks at Buchen waiting for the Hamburg–Berlin Express that passes twice daily—at dawn and at dusk. His is one of six similar posts spotted along the seven-hundred-mile Iron Curtain through which the West Germans maintain Berlin. Daily, when Albert Funk goes on duty—and at night— he is sure of the companionship of *Vopos* who will kill any German walking toward him.

LIFE MAGAZINE NEWYORK   29 SEPT 1952 BONN

THOMPSON: STILL NO MENTION KOREA BY EISENHOWER OR STEVENSON.
HOW ABOUT MY RETURNING FRONTLINES FOR SOLDIERS STORY ENTITLED
"WHAT ABOUT US?" MAYBE WE CAN FORCE ANSWER FROM CANDIDATES.

Korea went unvisited. Autumn became winter as I tracked Stalin's economic agents across Europe—multi-passport men who shipped embargoed Western war matériel to the Soviet Union. Then I returned to Cape Town, where I had first seen Table Mountain during the three hundredth anniversary of the city, nine months earlier. In South Africa, I found a land filled with desert splendour, vast mineral wealth and blacks battling whites for human rights. I felt at home.

What does one say when so much seems wrong
at the birthday party for a beautiful
and very old lady—three hundred years to the day;
a party where only babies were innocent of the rules.
Protest? Impossible!
The same ills exist at home.
Turn away and forget? Impossible!
That has never worked yet.
Take the camera and
shoot it straight? Okay!
But only with the prayer:
"Tonight, Lord, make it right: *First* at home, and then here."

CHAPTER XX

At noon today while walking near his home, three thousand miles south of Paris and four thousand northwest of Cape Town, unarmed Georges Ducrest was confronted by masked and drunken Africans, with whom he felt perfectly at ease.

Youkounkoun, French Guinea.
21 March, 1953

Bassari warriors of Negare then led him as their guest deeper into the forest to the chiefs who lay drinking millet ale in anticipation of dances to start with the rising full moon.

He was no ordinary guest of honor. Ducrest, without police other than a constable, or military other than his eight-man army of guardsmen, is the sole voice of France in the three thousand square miles of undulating forests and savannah of his realm. Here, May to September, six feet of rain flood the land where hippos, lions, partridge and gazelle abound.

Forty-two thousand tribesmen live here too—pastoral Moslems, and happy-go-lucky animists cultivating cocktail peanuts; seeing gods in rocks. Many experts are based nearby: Census Taker, Medical Director, Tribal Consultant, Game Warden, Fire Inspector, Official Host, Labor-Management Arbitrator, Judge and Commander-in-Chief of the Army. They are all M. Georges Ducrest.

No records of temperatures have ever been kept in Youkounkoun. Everyone knows it gets hot and it never is really cool, not even after the rains come. Until then, dust lays upon the land. There, it blends with morning mist to greet the Coniagui girls starting from home to harvest peanuts in nearby fields. The dust vanishes with the rain but it still is steam-hot—and the mud can swallow a man alive. Then, everyone dreams of the good dusty days in the sun.

When Bassari warriors dance to their full African moon, tribal virgins bind both arms in wire and bathe each other in peanut oil. Moments before the sun is gone they appear—dancing too.

351

Georges Ducrest's only contact with routine is Sunday when he hoists France's *Tricolore* atop Youkounkoun's flag pole and reviews the army. If the Bishop of Conakry dedicates a mission school, Ducrest attends—animist converts check their bows outside. He grades peanuts of Coniagui girls whose scarification marks them from the wire-braceleted Bassari. His Brigidier of Forests guides him for a kill, which he purposely alerts by coughing, never firing a shot. Bridges collapse; his houseboy knifes a pal; tribesmen by the thousands are tested for sleeping sickness (everyone has dormant malaria; malaria doesn't count), and one hundred thousand dollars in peanuts burn as their Lebanese owner escapes, then whispers of arson to the Administrator—who wonders, each night, what the next day will bring.

When Bassari and Coniagui fight they hit each other with sticks. When tired, they then go home. Besides good sense, they share common styles in *ipog*, "pants" woven of grass. As Youkounkoun's tribesmen emerge from their half-fiction lives and adjust to the world where few battle with sticks, they should thank M. Ducrest.

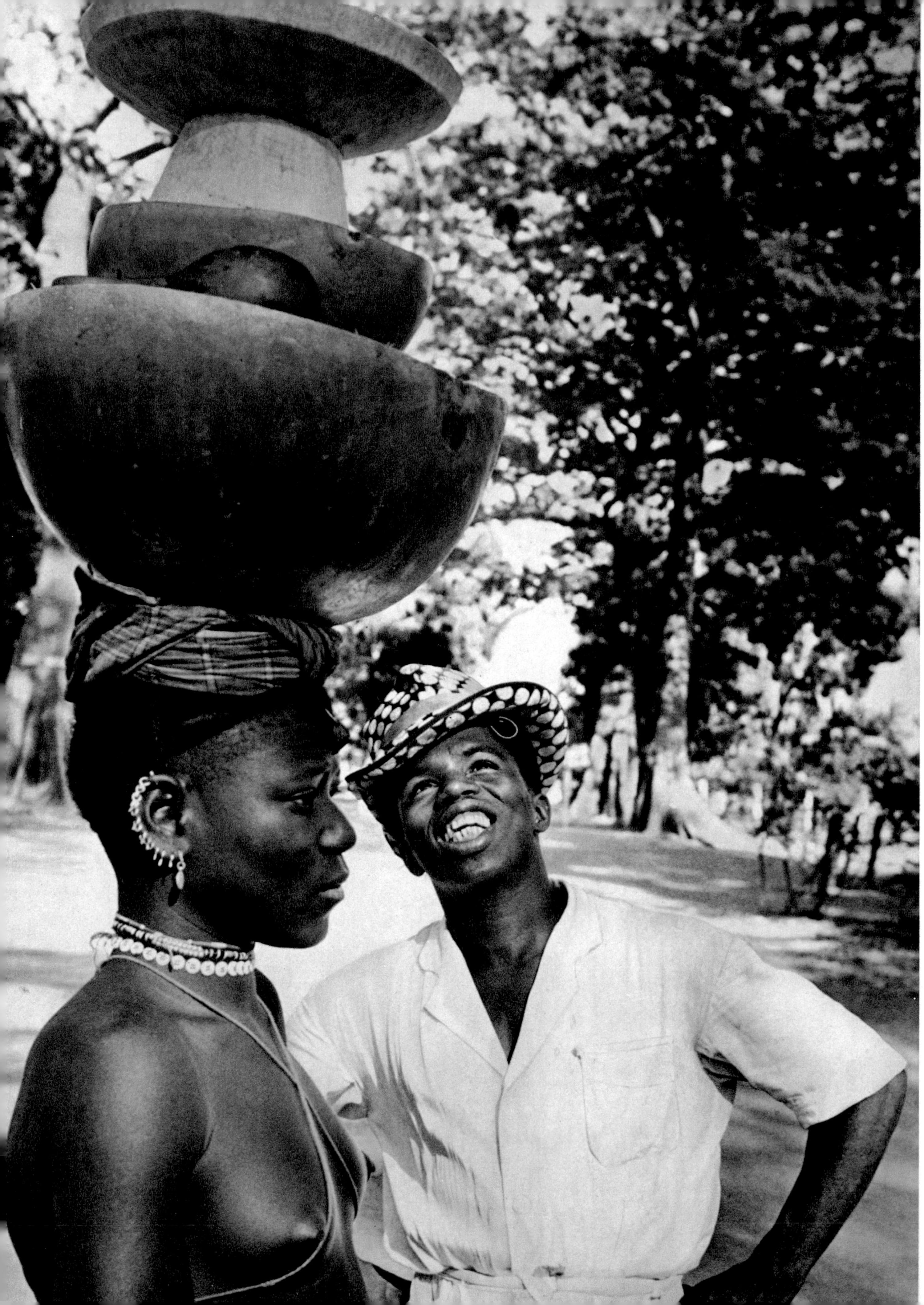

Their travel agents promised the spring vacation of a lifetime—for the lucky few—an expedition into the past—an honest-to-Allah camel caravan with Blue Men of the Sahara; silent, indigo-veiled Tuareg, whose world is one and a half million square miles of lore: their king, the grim Amenokal.

Tamanrasset, Algeria.
Lost in Time — maybe 1953

Local desert habitués—the two seen during our week on the trail—must have been shaken, when over their stark horizon there plodded a string of snowy camels upon whose humps were perched a Parisienne housewife, and an apertif distiller; a Belgian doctor, and a one-legged wartime pilot; a Swiss architect, his wife, and a wholesaler of paper; and a handful of saddle-battered-so-often-afoot others looking askance to God for survival, bypassing their siesta-prone Spanish-Algerian caravan director who had never before been on a camel. Leading the procession, was a six-foot-four Taureg nobleman. All were followed by a dehydrated photo-nomad from luxuriant Missouri, now walking through this deadly expanse of tortured earth to see more of the French Empire.

356

Arrived too late to rent my
camel—without any regrets,
they being the stubbornest,
most lurching tripods of all.
Did we find Taureg "lore"
in Ahaggar—the roughest—
emptiest—hottest by day—
coldest by night, and driest
of all the African deserts?
It was the most exciting long
walk yet taken in this life.

Here Lies
Pham-Ngoc-Linh
Partisan
3/6 R.I.C.
Died For France
20-6-50

French Military Cemetery,
Hanoi, Indochina.
22 May, 1953

Here, too, lies the heart
of the problem.
In the jungled mountains
to the north,
on the frontier of China,
an old man,
Ho Chi Minh,
speaks:
"*We* offer our lives, and
we die
for Viet-Nam!"

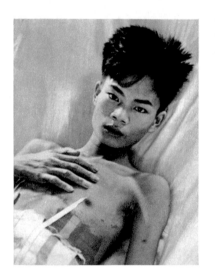

These Vietnamese troopers in Hanoi's streets look like I felt that first day they sent us on our way. We'd polished shoes and rifles since dawn; holding ranks—we'd drilled for three months; proud—the *Marine Corps Hymn* gagged in our throats and so sure all eyes were upon *us* some later claimed they made it the whole way looking at the ground. Then off we went—where friends fell, yet the *honor* of that first day followed them to their graves. This is the terrible failing here. Neither the official smokescreen or the dreams of Saigon's opium smokers will make it disappear. The truth is, when a Vietnamese soldier dies he is alone.

Senegalese sentries at the gates thought I was a French official (in my khaki clothes) when, at noon for three days, I walked into French General Headquarters here in Hanoi with an ultra-wide angle camera under my shirt, for panoramic pictures of the empty place during the hours that everyone takes for lunch and siesta. It seems wrong while others fight and die. One hundred seventy thousand French Union soldiers already are casualities; one-quarter *million* Vietnamese civilians have been slain, yet the end of it is nowhere in sight. Paris, fully aware that much is wrong, broke General Raoul Salan of the supreme command. His eyes betrayed his heart, as he stood taking his last salute.

367

Kipling would have felt at home here where wraith-like mountain men harass the French Army in nineteenth-century style forts. Some of the more rustic glower from behind hedge-rows of bamboo spikes. Others boast concrete-and-steel walls surrounded by earthen battlements, more effective than they appear. The Communist Viet-Minh are well supplied with mortars and bazookas—mostly captured American weapons—whose bombs are deflected by the mud to explode before burrowing through a fortress' walls. There is nothing secret about most forts' defenses since they are built, or reinforced, by lines of lithe peasant

women—whose Viet-Minh husbands often watch from nearby as every pannier of mud plops into place. Ho Chi Minh's guerrillas are rather particular about what they capture or steal from bourgeoning French supply dumps whose contents—tanks, bombs, jeeps, armored cars, bombers and fighters, ambulances and trucks of every description generally bear a stencil, "Made in U.S.A.". The Viet-Minh lean more to lighter loot—machine guns, grenade launchers and explosives of any type—lighter weapons to be used against their owners at night. Two wars are now being fought here. Kipling would have picked a winner.

Soldiers of France . . . Auvergnats, Bretons, Alsatians, Normans, Parisians—
Laotians, Annamese, Tonkinese, Senegalese, Congolese, Soudanese—
Moroccans, Mauritanians, Algerians, Guineans—
pilots, cooks, paratroopers, medics, tankmen, artillerymen, commando Legionnaires—
the wounded and the dead;
all are here—by the hundreds of thousands.
There will be no more . . . not Frenchmen.

It is nearly over and they are alone.
They are the tragedy—the cause was bankrupt from the start.
This evening, a single French soldier,
a Berber, prayed toward Mecca and home far beyond,
across the tops of mountain ranges
disappearing into the haze of the northwest . . .
the infinity of Communist China.

The story was called "Indochina All But Lost." It created a furor in Washington and Paris. Several men, who had helped me report the poverty and maldirection of American efforts to relocate Vietnamese civilians in shining "new style" villages, were fired by the American aid agency employing them. Another would have been fired except for direct intervention by Vice-President Richard Nixon, a friend since World War II when he was a Navy lieutenant who supplied me with new gear after I returned with the Fijian guerrillas from behind the Japanese lines on Bougainville. (Two years later Time *bureau chief for France, Frank White, was threatened with a duel, because of my story, by a staff officer of General Raoul Salan. Salan, later condemned to death for leading the Algerian rebellion against De Gaulle, then commanded all French forces in Morocco—his colonel had served in Indochina at the time my pictures were taken. White wisely declined the privilege of defending my honor, in absentia.)*

On 7 May, 1954, the French garrison at Dien Bien Phu—encircled by the Communist Viet-Minh who possessed massive artillery which obliterated any hope of either salvation or significant reinforcement—was overrun by the enemy.

In Washington, the White House was occupied by a five-star general who had led the Western Allies during their "Crusade in Europe" against totalitarian domination. His Secretary of State was to make the word "brinkmanship", and its implied threat to aggressors, known throughout the world. In the international waters of the South China Sea, squadrons of U.S. Seventh Fleet aircraft carriers were on patrol. Other squadrons cruised the Pacific Ocean and, in carrier time, the nearby Mediterranean and Atlantic. By May 7th, when the ten thousand French soldiers still alive at Dien Bien Phu lifted their arms to surrender, only Frenchmen had tried to send relief. America sent a telegram of encouragement. Our carriers stayed on stations in the China Sea, Pacific, Mediterranean and Atlantic, alert to any overt Communist threat.

At the Geneva Cease-Fire Conference of 21 July, 1954 (which the United States had pressed to convene, then refused to support as a fully participating member) a new premier, Pierre Mendès-France, accepted for France the articles whereby a Communist Viet-Minh state, the "Democratic People's Republic of Viet-Nam", came into being. Indochina was divided along the 17th parallel. Ho Chi Minh, one of the oldest and canniest of Asian Communists became the first president of his "People's Republic."

* * *

My story also triggered reaction at Life *magazine, which had required that a letter of clarification be sent to its managing editor, a tall, tough, blonde North Dakota Swede whose blue eyes —mirthful or baleful, pick your day—made him the greatest editor yet to work in the photographic news magazine world. Many times with deadline crises swirling around the edit-floor he could, and did, choose and lay out fast-breaking stories from wet negatives. Later, when prints had been pulled, no photographer ever complained that a major picture was overlooked.*

Mr. Edward K. Thompson
Managing Editor
Life Magazine   Rome, Italy.
New York, N.Y.   3 September, 1953

Dear Ed:

Last night, I had quite a conversation with Editor-in-Chief Henry Luce. It revolved around the Indochina story. Since the conversation also involved you I'd like to take this opportunity to write to you so you will know my feelings when he brings up the subject. The meeting lasted nearly two hours; I shall try to cover the highlights.

Mr. Luce was of the immediate opinion that my story was "defeatist" and therefore wrong. When I turned to pick up the magazine which I had brought with me, and started to say that there were some solid, constructive opinions about how the situation might be improved, he became quite indignant and said that I apparently had no desire to hear what he thought, as I, apparently, had no concern for any opinion other than my own. I told him I had the deepest interest in his opinions, and what he was saying about Indochina . . . but that as for the story being an irresponsible story based solely upon personal opinion I could not agree with him. I said that that story reflected the attitude of the majority of Americans in Indochina, under the level of aid administrator and ambassador.

Mr. Luce asked me whether I thought Jack Dowling (*Time-Life* correspondent based in Southeast Asia) would agree that the story was worthwhile, and whether he would agree with me. I said "Yes." Thereupon he handed me a cable from Jack, which said that the layout was fine, pictures fine and text accurate as far as it went, however it suffered by not telling all of the story . . . meaning, I presume, that we didn't say, again, as we did last year in Sochurek's picture story, that it is a dirty war and good Frenchmen are getting killed. I mentioned Howard's story, saying that that could be taken as incomplete, too, for it did not tell anything of what the Indochinese thought, or that the theater was being lost due to inertia. I did say that I felt fully qualified to judge, and report upon, the dirty side of the war, and that what I saw and reported from Indochina was weighed against all of the war experience I had ever had . . . and that I still didn't see how they will successfully win the war as long as present-day methods and mentalities are tolerated. Mr. Luce felt that great changes have been made in Indochina, and that my story told of a situation now dead. I did not agree, and said so.

While discussing other features of the story I pointed out that I had contacted every possible source in Indochina, and that our story reflected the opinion of the bulk of U.S. Mission personnel. He replied, saying that Acheson had been surrounded by defeatists, at the time China was lost. I answered that his suggestion that such was true today in Indochina did not seem to be the case, for most of the Americans I met were hopeful that some aggressive new strength might be injected into the French effort so that the war might be won. However, at the time I was there, most of them felt that no such energy was in sight, France had an on again-off again government, and that the Viet-Minh were winning by default more than any other reason. I again repeated that my sources were the most qualified men I could find, and I felt that the story was absolutely accurate.

376

Mr. Luce then pointed out that an entirely true story can be a wrong and malicious story . . . and drew a comparison between France's plight now and Britain's during 1940. He pointed out that it would have been wrong to point to the shortcomings of British colonialism at a time when the only country trying to stand against the Nazis was nearly on her knees. I did not say that I thought that the British effort under Churchill, at that time, was quite foreign to the French effort under migratory governments, today.

We then turned to discussion of how the story came into being in the first place. I referred to my Hong Kong cable to you, outlining the story, plus the comment that Hanoi odds were running 10-to-1 against our publishing such a story. I also told him you had replied that I had a hell of a nerve predicting what you would run until you saw it. Mr. Luce mentioned that that appeared to be one of my techniques . . . and I agreed, for then I was sure that you were well aware of the story in question, and followed it through the mill with even more than personal attention. I also added that I have really enjoyed tangling with you, and felt that you have too, for then each of us, in my opinion, got the maximum from the other's efforts. He then asked what I meant by that reference to the betting odds against *Life*'s publishing the story, and wanted to know whether I questioned your ability as a managing editor, or your desire to report stories fully. I answered that I never questioned your ability or intentions or methods as an editor. Mr. Luce then added that I must then have been referring to the policy of the magazine. I agreed. He then added that I must have been referring to him. I answered "Yes". I added that it was the opinion of many reporters, myself included, that a bare-knuckle story on Indochina would not be tolerated because of France's role as our ally, with all of its related problems. Mr. Luce leaned back into his garden chair, took off his glasses, and didn't say much for several minutes.

Mr. Luce handed me a translation from *Paris-Match*, which said that we had claimed that America was taking credit for paying for the war. I turned to the section on US military aid, where it clearly stated that our contribution was now climbing past 30%, and that in the future we may be called upon to carry more of the burden.

It was getting late, so we headed for the door. But just before getting up from the garden chairs Mr. Luce stated that I posed a real problem for you. I waited for clarification. None came by the time we got to the front driveway, so I asked him what he had meant. He answered that A must be in step with B, and that C must be in step with B. He said that you, as B must answer to him as A . . . and that I, as C, must answer to B, you. So I said that if my presence on the magazine was distasteful to him, and in any way made your job awkward, then the logical thing for him to do was to fire me. He said "No", that was not what he meant . . . that it all revolved around my getting along with you, and you finding a place for me. I left, but repeated that if I had become a source of trouble and embarrassment to you then the answer was really quite simple . . . I should be fired, and that would be that. He said again that that wasn't the answer, but that if only C (myself) is out of step then it poses a great problem for you, and your relationship with the staff.

This morning, I received a call from Mr. Luce's office asking that I be there at noon. He opened the conversation by saying that nothing much had been settled in the garden last night, and that he had had time to review much of what had been said. He wanted to make two points clear. The first was that my story was untimely. I added "true, but untimely?" and, I believe, his was an affirmative nod. The second was that I must get along with you. I replied that my prime responsibility was to report each story as I saw it, balanced against experience and knowledge and research . . . that preservation of magazine policy was the concern of the editors . . . that it was an every-man-for-himself fight until that particular issue closed and we all began planning for the next week's magazine . . . but until that final deadline had passed, my every effort would be spent fighting for that particular story being published exactly as I had seen and photographed it. He mentioned that it was, of course, the editor's problem, his problem, to establish and maintain top policy . . . such as during the Presidential election, despite feelings and efforts of those others within the magazine who were supporting Adlai Stevenson.

At the beginning of this conversation Mr. Luce referred, again, to a chewing-out he got, four years ago, from the Premier and Foreign Minister of France, all within one hour. I told him that I had wanted to ask him what he had done. He wanted to know what I meant. I said that I meant just that . . . "What did you do . . . with your understanding of what was right and wrong . . . with your dignity and pride in being Henry Luce . . . What did you do?" He replied that he listened . . . something that most correspondents have a difficult time doing, for we are usually talk, talk, talking. I asked him, again, what he had done . . . after listening. He answered that he had told them that they did not understand the problems or the role of journalism in America.

This second meeting soon ended. It did so, I believe, with fuller understanding having been reached between the two of us. I asked, as I had the night before, whether my story would be held against Assistant-Managing Editor Sid James, since he had edited it in your absence. Mr. Luce said that such was not the case, even though Sid would have done well to have checked more fully the implications of such a story, and the way it might be presented. He said that it is most difficult to measure the results of a story, and he still would not hazard a guess whether a "shock-treatment" story such as this might result in benefits. He then asked about my immediate plans so I told him of the upcoming vacation . . . to which he added that he hoped that I enjoyed it. And that was that.

In re-reading these pages, Ed, I realize that they might be taken as having been written in a light, almost trite frame of mind. Such is not the case. I simply want you to know how I view the entire episode, and that I mean what I told him . . . if I have fouled-up your operations at that end so as to make future operations difficult, where I am concerned, then drop me a line saying so. I'll fully understand, believe me, and shall write it off as the end of a great period of my activities, then turn to other things I've long had in mind.

CHAPTER XXI

No one has seen the Solar Boat of Cheops, although I photographed it today, stem to stern, with only my arm inside the vault. The old Pharaoh's secret, secure for five thousand years, will survive another weekend, until *Life's* editors get their hands on my roll of film.

Great Pyramid of Cheops
Giza, Egypt.
8 June, 1954

Imagine sprawling in the sand of the Egyptian Sahara Desert at noon in summertime without shade, trying to poke a camera through a ten-inch hole chipped in burning stone—to photograph a *boat* not seen since 3000 B.C.!

Today, I breathed incense from another world while firing my camera inside the vault below. Faint aromas of camphor, cedar, and time itself wafted from the hole, kept small until experts decide whether sunlight might endanger what is hidden. There sails the death bark of Cheops, launched by his priests with the Pharaoh's soul a lone passenger to the sun and his immortality. Tiny mirrors reveal the boat is here, although it is impossible to trace in the gloom. I too am waiting to see what lies beyond this stone porthole of the past.

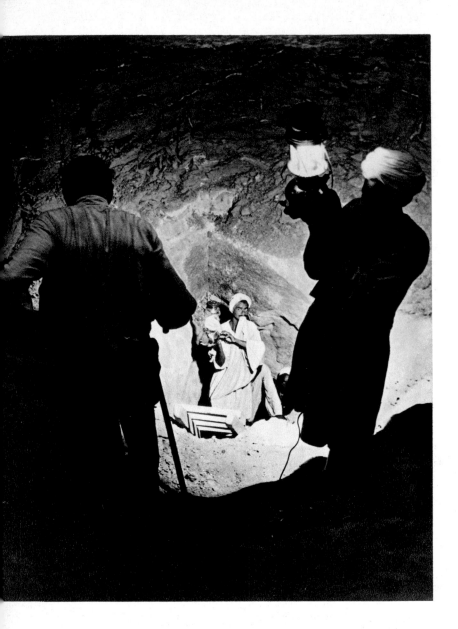

Pharaohs are bursting out all around! An archaeologist from the Cairo Museum just *fell* into the burial chamber of Sanakhet, the "lost" pharaoh who reigned a century before Cheops. His name appears in Third Dynasty hieroglyphs but no trace of him had ever been found, until now. Three years ago, Dr. Zakaria Ghoneim detected faint, curiously equilateral shadows etching all aerial photographs taken fifteen miles south of Cheops' Great Pyramid. Probing deep sand, he finally cut into a narrow tunnel, filled with stones, leading down. Today, as guest of Dr. Ghoneim and U.S. ambassador Jefferson Caffery (an ardent Egyptologist), I soon learned why many an Embassy Marine pales when seeing his old blue shirt and him swinging a cane as if on Park Avenue, heading for nearby dunes, wondering who wants to tag along.

"Lost" Pyramid of Sanakhet
Saqqara, Egypt.
11 June, 1954

. . . one hundred twenty feet under the Sahara; one hundred ten degrees and suffocating. Rocks fall, echoing everywhere. A man died earlier under crashing roof stones. It's a pagan tomb. The alabaster sarcophagus glows, pale peach. Upon its polished top someone placed a bouquet of perseus boughs, surely a gift to Sanakhet from his Queen. They may be the most ancient visible expression on earth today of a woman's love. My hand accidently brushed the leaves. It came away black, without sensation of it touching *anything*. I recall *She*, the eternal beauty who stepped into the flame of youth once too often—and ended like perseus ashes.

380

"There is no god
but Allah:
Mohammed is the Apostle
of Allah."

Absolute simplicity!
Allah *is* God
But there is more.

Djakarta, Indonesia.
5 November, 1954

This morning, Moslem hospitality opened even Hadji Selim's home—just after he had died. Here, Hadji Selim's family have made my story on the world of Islam complete by including me as another son during their day of grief. His daughter had answered my half-embarrassed request with a nod. "Yes. Father would have no objection, as he starts his last voyage. He loved your land, always wanting to return. Now, this is the best we can do." She made me think of my home where, at dawn one morning last year, I had told Mother that we had just lost Dad. She gazed up at me, then came to my side. "He always wanted to make a great journey—but I should have liked to go with him." This morning, in Hadji Selim's home, I wondered what Jean or my brothers or I would have replied had *his* son come to our door with a camera, to portray a Christian family waving a last good-bye to *their* father.

Purdahed Pakistani women; praying Egyptians during Ramadan; Jordanians on the Mount of Olives celebrating the circumcision of Mohammed el Riche's infant son . . . all has been opened in these lands where a desert code from their Prophet's time still prevails—the stranger is welcome, to grant his wish is a sacred law honored throughout the Moslem world.

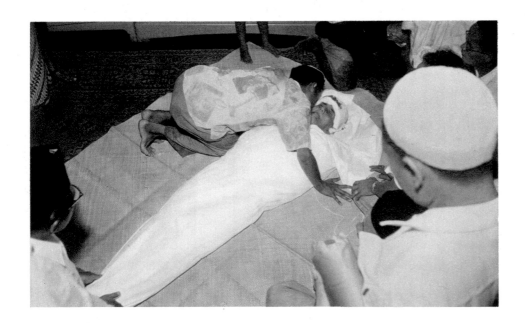

Fellah troubadors,
while zar dancing
amid Cairo minarets,
reveal the roots of
voodoo Africa
in earlier Egyptians,
whose zar dancers
exorcised devils
from even the insane.

In the lands of Allah,
the ninth month
of each Koranic year
is Ramadan, the fast.
From dawn to dark,
no water or food
touches the devout
Moslem's lips. It is
a fast of hardship,
for the Islamic world
is desert and tropics.

At dawn of
Ramadan,
Cairo women linger
a final moment
after their prayers,
before starting
the first and
most difficult day
of total fasting.

385

This valley
is Shangri-la!

Ait Mhand,
The Upper Dades,
Atlas Mountains,
Morocco.
15 April, 1955

James Milton must have come here to write *Lost Horizon*, then switched its locale to the Himalayas. I arrived last month—and want to stay forever. Ancient Romans called them *Numidea*, nomads—maybe that's where the affinity lies—though they are not wanderers, having always lived between the mountains of North Africa and the Mediterranean. Fifteen hundred years ago, Egyptian scribes carved them into hieroglyphs as *Barabara*, barbarians, which today they are not. Now, they are Berbers, who are still living in the Stone Age.

Here, every turreted village is an independent "state", yet each stands with the others on all questions regarding Berberland, especially where low-country Arabs are concerned. Conflict between them is unending. It began with the eighth-century Moslem conquests which carried Islam across Africa. Berber villages are now governed by the Jemáa, a council of men whose common qualifying characteristic is having passed that age when they received their first rifle, representing both manhood and sound judgement—sixteen years old.

This is a land where all grains are milled by hand between stones; where every weapon and tool of iron comes over the mountains from outside; a land where no wheel is ever used—and the girls look a stranger straight in the eye. This is a land where each Berber is a Moslem, who relishes wild boar steaks and relaxing under oak trees with a wooden goblet of fig wine; a place where the poorest and the rich gallop side by side to Jemáa councils, in which their voices are equal. This valley makes me wish that Ait Mhand could be my birthright, too.

No one knows when the first Berber shepherd followed his flock homeward to Ait Mhand. No one knows the origin of the sunburned men—whose written language is incomprehensible to almost everyone except Berbers—tribesmen who beneath burnoose and turban and beard are fair skinned, brown haired and grey or even blue eyed, unlike any other men of Africa. No one knows where Berber architects—every man is his own—learned to build their multi-storied village complexes of clay and straw and stone that defy the wildest storms of wind and rain, and winter's snow. No one has discovered the roots beneath countless superstitions which govern much of every Berber's life—fighters who dismiss death with a shrug and use the nearest convenient rock for a headstone, yet build their villages with the seemingly neglected cemeteries as an integral part. No one knows what motivates these diligent men who sometimes leave their mountains to serve in armies and the life of the outside world, yet who shed all foreign traits and affluence acquired during these journeys upon reentering the high passes guarding their homes.

Almost everything is mysterious about the Berber—except the Berbers themselves who are today among the happiest people on earth in *their* Shangri-la, making it better than Milton's. No one could leave his utopia. Here they always can go, but if they do, it is only to return.

Her name is Aicha; Aicha M'Bark—just like a Japanese-Scot! Sixteen, her hair is in bangs (denotes a virgin) and except for chin tatoo, she is without makeup. She watches from across the room. I have been photographing her mother and aunt behind their loom. Her sister, Itto, deeper in the gloom, has also stopped milling (the grinding stones rest silent between their knees); barley, maize and some rock salt are spread on an old burnoose ready for when they start. Strange, at first I saw nothing, it is that dark—only the smoke hole, probably thirty feet above, lets in a shaft of light. *Now,* I don't know where to look! Luckily, this is not Friday. The loom would have been completely dismantled and taken from the room, it being sacriligious to see it on a Sabbath. Aicha just burst into laughter and is back at work, as are her mother and aunt. And so is Moha ou Youssef, the ancient potter in the corner who turns his stone wheel with his foot. He is not of Berber origin—nor is his wheel—but from the Sahara. In this great Negro face there is love for his craft. If Rembrandt were only here today to paint what I see, Old Moha would live forever.

Childhood, like springtime, is fleeting in my hidden valley. Hard work and harsh seasons soon harvest crops that flower just once. A woman's summer quickly becomes winter. Every Berber works but only the men, almost war dancing, wash the burnoose. Tribal life is austere yet rich with compassion—seen as the Elders sit in judgement of an adultress.

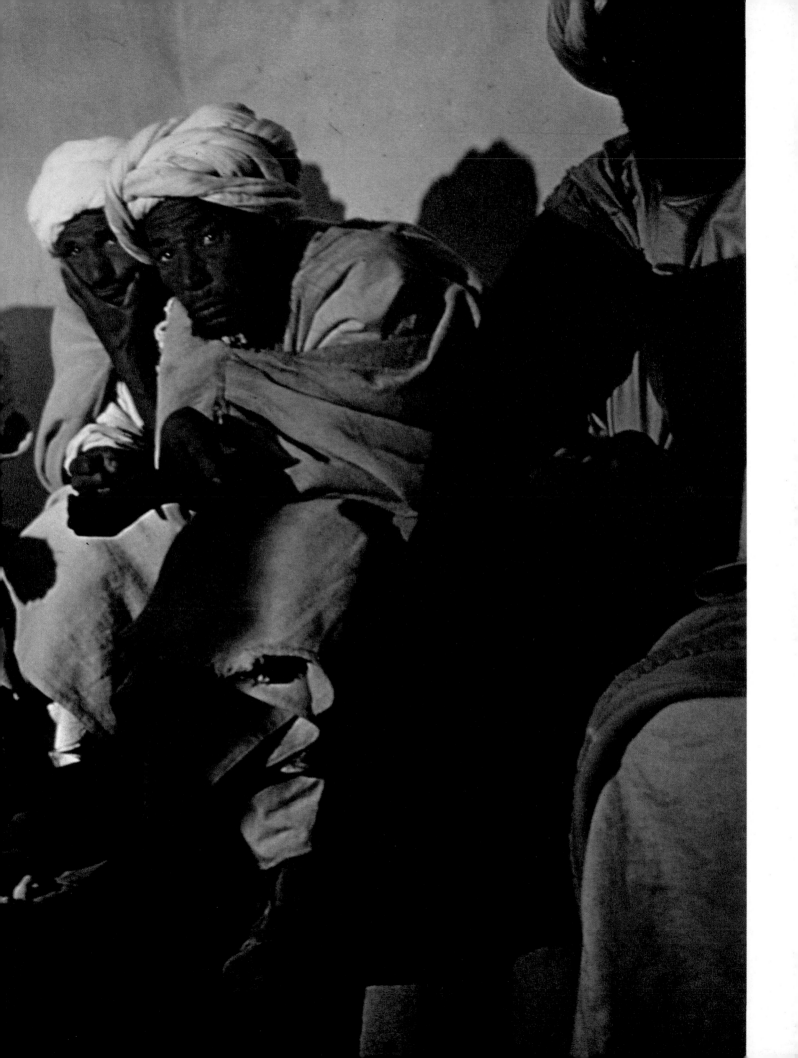

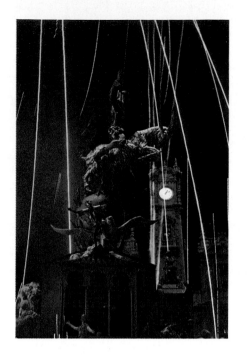

These Spanish carpenters
really celebrate their Saint's Day!

Valencia, Spain.
St. Joseph's Day, 1955

Earlier, neighborhood carpenters made annual bonfires of their shavings until one probably said, "We need *more* fire to show it's been a good year—and let's make figures of the saw-dust proving we're artists as well." Now, just before Easter, every square, crowned by the sombre Plaza del Caudillo, has its *fallas*, papier-mâché sculptures—some a hundred feet high—which cost an estimated hundred thousand dollars. Everyone contributes. At midnight, heralded by fireworks, all are burnt to the ground. Sometimes, of course, nearby buildings go too—barely noticed by artists planning next year's *fallas* to astonish the town.

Mano a mano . . . hand-to-hand!
Ordoñez—minueting his bull to its end.
Dominguin—a ballet, but for the blood smeared across his chest.
Each gauges his lifespan by inches
every Sunday they fight,
taunting death to come ever nearer,
without moving their feet.
Other matadors have styles which merit
their being in the same ring, the same afternoon,
but hearts stop when the feuding brothers-in-law meet.

We call them *Ghosts of Sindelfingen*.

Stuttgart, Germany.
21 June, 1955

Artur Keser thought I was quite mad.
I just strolled into his press office
at the giant Daimler-Benz autoworks
and casually told him I wanted their
fastest car—painted Mercedes red—
with their finest racing test-driver,
and the police to block the streets
of Sindelfingen while I shot pictures
to show *not* the car—but its spirit!

I also needed an engineer to calculate
the speed necessary for the driver to
flash across one hundred feet during
a half-second exposure, (he assigned
Wilfert, who designed the 300-SL); a
mechanic, (he assigned Hitzelberger,
who hand-makes the prototypes of all
their sportscars); and an interpreter
in case the cops worried, (he assigned
his colleague, Prince von Urach, who
handles cops, photographers and nine
languages with casual ease). And off
we went to the heart of Sindelfingen,
a nearby, sleepy village (past tense).

403

CHAPTER XXII

King Zahir Shah had nodded regretfully:
"Yes, I raised hounds which you call Afghans,
but no more. I really am sorry."
Today, a rug arrived from his home.

The Herat farmer had smiled: "My son dreams.
We grow not twenty-seven varieties of melons.
Only twenty-two. Come, you must taste them all."

The Maimaneh shepherd, braced against stinging
wind, had lifted empty hands—then reached
quickly to the ground, handing me a stone:
"Take this as my gift . . . I have nothing more."

Kabul, Afghanistan.
15 September, 1955

On the west is the Desert of Death, littered with cities destroyed by Tamerlane. In the north, Afghans are isolated from the Russians by the deep-flowing Oxus and badlands, where villagers endure arctic winters in adobe houses that are shaped like a girl's breasts. To the south rises the Khyber Pass, lair of Pathan tribesmen who now dance for their King but whose ancestors slaughtered invaders from India. China is beyond the roadless Himalayas to the east. Afghanistan's heart is the granite Hindu Kush—Hindu Killer. It balked Genghiz Khan's Golden Horde; their descendents are wrestlers. Alexander the Great also faltered at the barrier; he left Aegean ram fighting, now a national sport. At sunset, several days ago, an Afghan rested his horse—before galloping even deeper into the Hindu Kush, his home.

Someday I shall write a book, a true fable of these people whose origins are legendary, Moslems who may be Jews living isolated in a land once trodden by all the conquerors of Asia whose ruins, children, customs and symbols of faith are sown in the sands: Greek heroes, Mongol villains, Arab fanatics, Chinese gamblers, Buddhist priests, Hindu gods, Tartars-turned-threshers, and local mystics who paint faces on skulls and skulls on tombs.

CHAPTER XXIII

Everyone seems to have a word for it—the Afghans . . . *kuchi;*
the Japanese . . . *horosha;* in English—I've known it since childhood—*nomad!*
Am on the move again . . .

After Afghanistan, it got worse. I had to be more free to roam.
Returning to Egypt, I quit, cabling Life's editors it was time to break away.
No one was surprised; we've always known it would be like this, sometime.

Nor was President Nasser surprised when I went to say good-bye.
We've remained friends since his Revolution's first days. He just chuckled,
and said I couldn't leave Cairo empty-handed—it wasn't the Arab way.
He gave me Gaza Strip—always the Bible Land—now his buffer zone
between Israel and the Suez Canal; forbidden to all photographers.
Then he offered me another orange juice and wished me luck for New York
when I arrived with that first free-lance story in my pocket.

Connemara, Ireland.
3 October, 1956

This is a muted world, where shimmering fogs and mist drift over the lonely valleys and
hills of a land now being abandoned by many Irishmen.

Connemaramen believe that their glens of moss-encrusted beech trees, with trunks and
branches twisted into goblin shapes, are peopled by leprechauns, elves who reveal the hiding
place of treasure if caught. Rock-and-sod homes lie broken across the moors but they still
live in the hearts of those who moved away. Exotic anemones float upon an endless sea,
drifting ever nearer, then become clusters of wandering sheep painted for shepherds to see
among the wool-gray stones.

Shattered houses, tumbled walls, and the rib cages of sunken fishing boats are strewn as if
in the wake of war. Nature was victorious. Man has fled. An ivory stallion, carved by hilltop
wind, roams as a lord among the boulders—the only sovereign of the land.

Some families are still here; families big and poor—yet rich, in that there is little time for
temper or laziness but plenty for love and work, and even laughter. It's a place where a
child hunts blackberries, or wiggles his toes in the sea at low tide, or just watches seagulls
wheeling overhead—doing the many little-boy things that are so important—until suddenly
he is an Irishman, far away, dreaming of Connemara and the leprechauns near his home.

Tonight, outside my window, they celebrate the fall of the Romanov Tzars—and the Kremlin is dangling on searchlights as if on wires . . . the theater curtain of their Revolution.

Moscow.
7 November, 1956

Forget politics—it's a pageant place! The kids practiced their group formations for hours, then, as soon as today's parade was finished, they Indian wrestled, played tag and turned cartwheels all over Red Square. It looked just like Pieter Brueghel's light-hearted painting, *Children's Games*, with its background of sixteenth-century towers and walls; except for a squat red-and-black mausoleum, Lenin's tomb.

Muscovites offer lavish shows on their national holidays. Prancing Central Asian horsemen sweep in from the steppes. Fireworks and anti-aircraft searchlights ignite the skies. It is as though they hope to rival some of the flamboyant ways of their ousted tzars whose ornate lives are still clearly reflected in the gilt-and-frescoed Throne Room of the Palace of Facets, which once was the Kremlin's heart. Then there is St. Basil's, across Red Square—profiled now by fountains of fire—whose rock-candy cupolas twist into the night. What a stage! With another program and cast it might have been a part of *The Thousand and One Nights*.

428

Russian celebrations are visual festivals, but I came here to photograph the Volga. It's frozen. Now I want the Kremlin itself, where treasure reveals Russian history from the beginning. There are the jeweled thrones of every tzar and the Ivory Throne of Ivan the Terrible; crowns of diamonds, rubies, sapphires, emeralds, sable and filigreed gold; and the eleventh-century Cap of Monomakh, the first crown of all. The wedding gown of Catherine the Great is there. Medieval jewel-and-enamel Gospel covers line corridors and the richest ikons of Orthodoxy are counted by dozens. Among the patriarchal vestments is one with a Crucifixion on its breast that might have been woven by Giotto. The tzars' bedrooms serve today as models for the Bolshoi's stupendous production of *Boris Godunov*. The Great Hall of the Supreme Soviet is a converted Romanov chapel. The story of the Russian people is behind those Kremlin walls. If only I can work there unmolested, it could be magnificent.

My precautions were a waste of time! When *Collier's* editor sent me to join John Gunther for the Volga story and others on Russia today, I weeded from my gear those usual bits of a foreign correspondent's life that would make Soviet secret police certain I am a spy— *National Geographic* maps; binoculars; press passes to army bases everywhere.

But no one cares what I brought. Even at customs, nothing was examined. No one—that's sure—follows me through Moscow's freezing streets where I can see for blocks in all directions, as I walk all over this town photographing behind babushkas, snowy furs and drab doors—where another world is hidden.

Picasso's first Moscow show has outraged Party hacks who harangue the art students crowding his exhibit. Aram Khatchaturian appeared moody and miserable while struggling with *Spartacus*, a new work, yet he played an hour for me, including the *Gayneh Ballet*—known everywhere as *Saber Dance*. Puppeteer Serge Obraztsov, rated as world's best, writes scripts in which neither violence or sin, or political message appear: standing room only!

David Oistrakh sat listening. Among
the world's most gifted musicians,
he would not even consider lifting
his violin while his protegé played.

Ulanova hovered above the Bolshoi
stage, a hummingbird without wings.
Soon darting away in full flight,
she was everywhere—and all wings.

Galina Ulanova, already legendary in
Russian ballet, danced tonight for
probably the final time, her adieu.
Like Garbo, retiring while the queen.
Amber shadows veiled the stage, a
forest scene of *Giselle*. Then she
fell—streaking feathers shot down.
Wails broke the choked silence as
curtains crashed closed; then sighs.
It was only a sprain—not the end.

Khrushchev and Gomulka had just signed a
"Friendship Pact"—a Communist shotgun
wedding—so the Poles threw an enormous
reception to celebrate the vows. Firing
flash-pictures into Khrushchev's eyes,
I waited for the heavy police hand upon
my neck—tossing me out. It never came.

When Khrushchev raged, "We'll bury you!",
all Western ambassadors marched away but
hurried back when he stopped—the vodka
and smoked Polish ham were both superb.
During the tirade Premier Bulganin smiled
at the floor, then raised croupier eyes to
scan the envoys beyond the door. Old
Bolshevik Molotov seemed lost in thought;
President Voroshilov gazed piously aloft.
Finished, Khrushchev aimed a thumb at me,
"Who's he?", forgetting I had asked him
for the Kremlin story at a Turkish party.
"An American? Fine! We want to be friends
with you too. But it will have to wait—
we have time." Then they returned to the
Kremlin to crush a revolt, before too late.

John Gunther and I had crashed the Polish
Embassy—Moscow news is covered that way.

Andau, Austro-Hungarian frontier.
31 December, 1956 – midnight.

Oh, you heroic Hungarians—alone today,
against the Red Army—abandoned by us
who inferred every support if you would
only spark the rebellion. Now you freeze,
still coming to us. Happy New Year's Eve!

CHAPTER XXV

Where does one start, when trying to enframe a man
who has prowled through this life as if in a forest—
his only companions the creature-children of his imagination.
He has always been *with* someone . . . his wife . . . his sons or daughters . . .
his dealers or publishers or bullfighter pals . . . his greatest collectors,
who are sometimes favored with an audience . . . his admirers from around the world
bearing gifts to Cannes, like Gary Cooper with the war bonnet of
an Apache chief . . . or an artist from Montevideo who arrived at
the villa's gate, was admitted, then became so overwhelmed he cried,
"*¡ Es horrible . . . es horrible!*" When asked what was so terrible about being
inside the studio, he looked around: "It is horrible that *you* waste time
on *me* when I think of what you might have created in these minutes."
How does one start to tell a story of the challenge, and fun,
of following this other nomad's trail as though it were my own.

He's just *Picasso*
But were he not Picasso, born to paint—engrave—sculpt—etch,
and endure eighty-five years of his own rebel mind and eyes . . .
had he been born in a jungle hut or mountain cave, his tribe
would have seen he was marked to be their witch doctor—or king.

Pablo Picasso is Spanish and eighty-five; Jacqueline, his wife, is French and perhaps fifty years younger. Visitors to their Riviera home are struck by a shining fact—these two people are ideally matched. Lifelong friends swirl around Picasso, but only Jacqueline comes close to penetrating the artist's moods. When he questions someone with his eyes, her eyes search for answers. She is one of the very few with whom he will discuss art. She never poses for him yet is the model for many portraits. Her life is totally dedicated to him and his work.

One afternoon Picasso seemed despondent, unusual for him. Jacqueline and I gently joked with him; then I left. Returning at dusk, I found the two holding hands before a new painting. Later, he gave it to me. When Jacqueline sat near it, I saw the depth of reality captured in the canvas. It was my friend who, when I earlier projected my fish-eye portrait of Picasso against the studio wall, had switched from Spanish to English to murmur sweetly, "If you print *that* I weel keeeel you!" Picasso himself had enthused, "*Now*, you are a photographer!"

It started at the bathtub—on February 8th, '56 . . .
"This was an incredible day in a not-routine life.
I was greeted by the villa's gardener, a drowsy boxer
puppy—and the girl to whom I had explained I was a
friend of Bob Capa who'd promised to introduce us,
before he was killed in Indochina. The house has no
rugs or curtains, few chairs; but is full of crates and
ceramic fish and doves—and a live goat. And Picasso?
Picasso was in his bathtub waving good morning as
though I always stopped by en route to assignments
in Africa. She scrubbed his back as he examined the
carnelian rooster ring I'd brought from Afghanistan.
While he dressed, Jacqueline took me to the garden.
We laughed like kids at bronze owls stuck in trees.

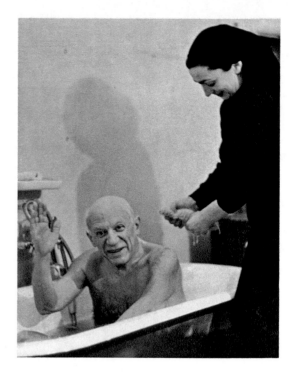

He then opened his studio—and I entered
another world, of cubist portraits, African
masks, canvases and ceramics wall-to-wall,
and a drawing of enormous depth based on
Rembrandt's *Warrior in a Golden Helmet*.
The boxer slept in sunlight among it all.
Picasso is . . . I don't know, really. Enjoy
his art or not, *he* is pure electricity on
two feet. It was a morning not to forget.
And I think he likes the ring. He called
to me, 'This is your home'—and meant it!"

After a short lament for the hours lost, when guests have stayed until dark, Picasso works most of the night. Paradoxically, he revels in visitors who enter his gate—through which he rarely ventures—as if absorbing the outside world from them. The system appears to refuel him forever. These visitors sometimes upset Picasso. They would never know it from his face.

The angriest I ever saw him was with me!

Daniel-Henri Kahnweiler, his veteran Paris dealer, brought *his* New York dealer in Picassos —the network is worldwide. Striving to project Picasso's Spain into the studio, she twisted through a flamenco that jolted the room. A Greek shipowner's wife soon followed. Upon seeing a regal canvas of Jacqueline as a Turkish bride, she tapped and arched into a peasant dance hoping Picasso might paint her as a Greek bride—then she offered to buy Jacqueline's portrait. Picasso wondered later whether anyone might like to buy his shirt or sandals, or his heart. He ate very little for two days. *The* parrakeet breeder of America arrived with his wife; he owning superb Picassos. Jacqueline showed the bird baron around while Picasso was an attentive host to the wife who—when he started to speak with Jacqueline—called after him, "Yuhoo, Mr. Chagall!" Picasso kept walking. The next day, as we headed toward lunch in the kitchen, he spun and slammed his fist into my chest: "Did you hear her? *Chagall!*" He ate three helpings of everything.

It was a hot summer night. *The Private World of Pablo Picasso* was finished. I had bought three Picasso posters as gifts for my publishers thinking I might violate The Code just this once: those closest to Picasso *never* ask him for anything more than his friendship—which is plenty. I took the chance. Posters, friends, family and ddd went flying. Months later, the posters were found where I left them, beautifully dedicated; dated the night I had asked.

440

Visitors to the UNESCO building in Paris may be mystified by
variations of brown seen in each figure of the Picasso mural.
So was the man who painted them. He kept sending Jacqueline
to the Cannes paint store for liter cans of identical brown.
Every can he opened was another shade. It was futile. Picasso
painted his giants with what he found in the can of that day.
When I suggested a seemingly logical solution—that he buy a
five-gallon can for the job, he turned his own chestnut eyes
upon me astonished: "What would I do with the paint left over?"

After publishing *Picasso's Picassos*, a book of his own unknown
paintings, I estimated what half of its earnings would be and
sent him a bank draft for ten thousand dollars. Weeks later,
I returned to his Riviera villa. He stalked toward me holding
my letter—like a skunk by the tail. Without a word, he opened
it, took his crayons, the check, slashed across its face, then
flipped it over. There he drew an applauding faun, and handed
it to me—punching my chest: "He likes *Picasso's Picassos!*"

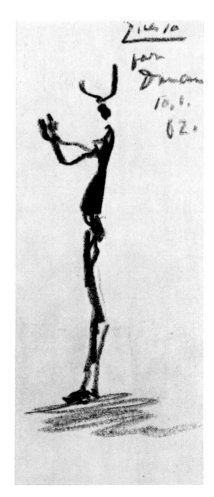

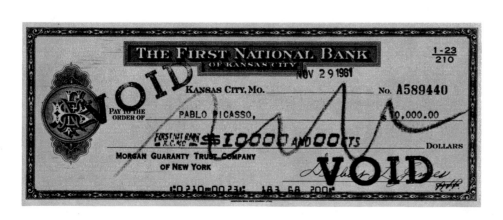

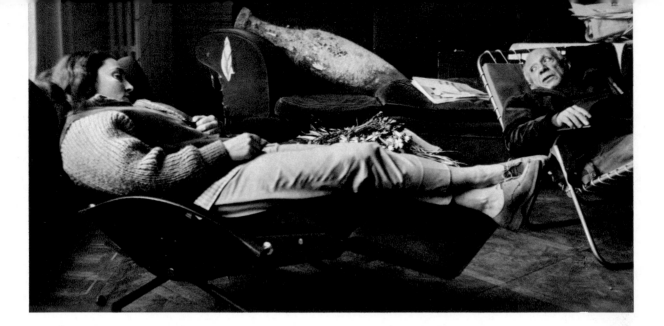

Welded warriors,
a pregnant bronze goat,
The Dancers—sold later for
a quarter-million dollars—
everything of value . . .
all were going.
Villa *La Californie's* khan
easily abandoned his
clothes, the fortress-studio,
even his easel,
while he migrated
to another camp, the
Château de Vauvenargues.
This is a true nomad—
but what a tent!

Luck always followed me with Picasso from the start, good luck . . . except just once, then it was a disaster!

My first visit occurred shortly after Piccasso met his Jacqueline, the most loving person to enter his life. They live an almost frugal existence together, usually eating in the kitchen which Picasso says is the heart of a home. Competition has been keen between the dogs for scraps handed from the table. A bright green frog sits in his jar near the stove hopefully peering with bulging golden eyes at the man and girl who take turns catching flies for his dinner. Friends, renowned in their own arts, mill constantly around Picasso. It is, perhaps, a house unique on earth. Picasso's magic has made it possible, but Jacqueline's love has added its final wondrous glow. It was into this world that I first stepped—to stay for years, and write two books.

The first was a story of the happy world I discovered behind their gate. It took a year. One day, I made a closeup of his eyes. When he saw the print, he tore a sheet from his sketch pad, cut two holes, charcoaled a silhouette, and handed me back himself—as an owl.

The second book took a year and a half, after copying five hundred works that told of each turn in his life. Many canvases were shrouded in subject-deadening dust. A feather broom freed pigments unseen for fifty years. I also found a Picasso self-portrait, nearly life-size and of total purity. It was drawn in austere charcoal. Every inflection of Picasso's hand showed. I ruined it. One sweep of the turkey duster—and my heart exploded. The charcoal had never been fixed! Dust and charcoal were about all that remained of Pablo Picasso's face.

It was after midday. He stood in the studio—and must have seen the anguish in my eyes. After hearing what had just happened, he asked at what time I started to work that morning. Learning that it had been shortly after dawn, he shouted to Jacqueline to hurry in the kitchen, that she had two starving men on her hands— and we walked in, without another word, to have lunch.

One evening in the last week of April, of 1959, I stopped by for supper with Picasso and Jacqueline at their villa, *La Californie*, in Cannes. They had just returned from his huge *Château de Vauvenargues*, ten miles northeast of Aix-en-Provence. He bought the fifteenth-century estate during the summer of '58 but still had not left *La Californie* for more than a few days at a time. Friends said he would never abandon Cannes for Vauvenargues. All of his paintings and sculptures and ceramics and engravings, and all of the seemingly unrelated mountains of hats, masks, pets, primitive statues, books, cow skulls, rhino horns, hippo jaws, Renoirs, Rousseaus, Matisses, Modiglianis and Cézannes—all of the nearly endless list of objects that his imagination had magnetized and pulled into *La Californie*, lay strewn around the villa. It appeared most unlikely he could ever again break free. Yet once, during another visit to Vauvenargues, in the winter of 1958 when Picasso wanted to check on the installation of heat, lights and waterpipes, I had mentioned how exciting it would be to see all of the contents of *La Californie* in the château. Picasso had turned and looked back down at me—we had been climbing its monumental staircase. "When I come here it will be with my hat and shoes, nothing more! Otherwise, why move?"

Months passed. The château acquired its heat, lights and waterpipes. Picasso and Jacqueline made several more inspection trips but the *Château de Vauvenargues* remained empty.

That night at *La Californie*, the conversation dealt mostly with the bullfights which Picasso and Jacqueline had seen the previous Sunday in Nimes. They also mentioned that two trucks were due at the villa the following morning to haul paintings to exhibitions in Paris and Marseille. They asked about my work on a book of treasure in the Moscow Kremlin, about the blizzard I had just driven through in the Alps, and wondered how many hours I needed in my racing Mercedes to reach Paris, my next stop. It was at this moment that Picasso suggested we all go to Vauvenargues, the next morning. I explained again my plan of driving through the night to reach Paris for a meeting with a publisher the following day. I saw just a shadow in Picasso's eyes—something I could not interpret. At midnight, leaving the villa, I wondered again about his expression—and decided to overnight in Cannes, hoping I might help load his paintings in the morning.

When I arrived, truckers were packing Picasso's recent canvases, his 1957 variations on Velásquez' *Las Meninas*. Jacqueline watched the movers. Picasso was in bed, as is his habit —he often works until nearly dawn. He also hates seeing his pictures leave for their first exhibition. One of the *Meninas* was slightly torn—it fell months earlier while we were looking at the entire series—so I carried the canvas to Picasso to remind him that it was not the truckers who had damaged it. He brushed it aside, asking only how long it would be before everything was aboard. He came down as the last painting was being stowed away, peered into the truck—then asked the movers to follow him to the garden. Pointing to the bronze, seven-foot sculpture of his famed *Man With a Sheep*, he asked whether they could lift it. Three of them did. Picasso told them to put it in their truck too . . . and I ran for my cameras. The statue had dominated the garden for years, something akin to the personal standard of a medieval knight—wherever planted, there was the home of its owner. With the *Man With a Sheep* leaving, *La Californie* was apparently finished.

Picasso was migrating to his *Château de Vauvenargues.*

In the world of art, Picasso's moves are almost legendary. He simply walks out, locks the doors and leaves everything behind—as he did from his Paris studio on Rue des Grands Augustins, his Vallauris pottery, the Grimaldi Palace at Cap d'Antibes. Thus he left *La Californie*. His dozens of pigeons, *never* before inside the villa, paraded into the heart of the studio itself as though to say good-bye in that lost moment when Picasso drifted aimlessly— waiting to be caught again in the swirling currents of his own artistic fervor which would engulf him in his new home.

The *Château de Vauvenargues* is as vast and, for the moment, as bare as a subterranean grotto. Picasso's hand is unmistakeably imprinted only in the bathroom. There a faun plays his flutes on the wall. There, too, I once asked the artist if he had taken up housekeeping— his head was almost out of sight—I thought he was washing the tub. A muffled snort, "I have a *corrida* with a scorpion—and he may win!" Nearly three thousand acres of scrub pine and rocks climb from the château to the peak of Ste. Victoire, the mountain immortalized by Cézanne. All three thousand acres belong to the estate and its new master. The land looks as though it is part of the Spanish *cordillera* north of Málaga, Picasso's birthplace.

The excitement of the move; the château with its massive unpainted walls; the scrub land and the mountain and the region's striking resemblance to Spain—together with those other impressions of which only the artist himself is aware—perhaps are keys that will open more sources of youthfulness and imagination for Picasso, qualities that have made his work the dominating influence in twentieth-century painting. Taken together, they may also provide him with the strength needed to bend much of the world around him into new expressions of his own artistic language, to which he adds an even richer meaning almost every day.

444

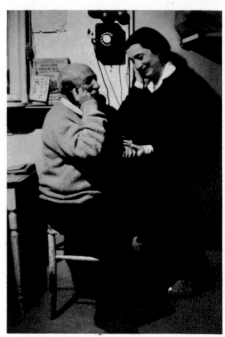

At dusk, March 13, 1961, I returned to *La Californie* from America. Picasso had migrated back from Vauvenargues. He was speaking with Paolo, his forty-year-old son by an early marriage to ballerina Olga Koklova, now dead. Paolo had arrived from Paris, where he lives. He went to answer the telephone while his father told me of recent work. Paolo burst back into the studio, with an enormous grin, "Papa, they say you're married!" Jacqueline, the artist's companion, confidante, hostess and shield for seven years came downstairs; friends were asking from everywhere. Picasso stomped to the wall-phone—bellowed "Oui!" They had been married eleven days earlier in nearby Vallauris.

Calling for champagne, Cathy (Jacqueline's daughter by an earlier marriage), Marcelle and Lourdes and Janot (housekeeper, maid and chauffeur) the Pablo Picassos celebrated their wedding announcement quietly at home. Then Cathy was sent to bed, Paolo headed for Vallauris, Marcelle and Lourdes and Janot said "Good Night"; Lump, the dachshund, and Perro, the dalmatian were in their blankets; the parrot and love birds were asleep—and we went to the kitchen where the wedding-announcement banquet was spread . . . unseasoned vegetable soup, grilled cheese-and-ham sandwiches, lettuce salad, fruit and coffee. The green frog was given his last fly, and I drove off into the night leaving the newlyweds alone.

Picasso often told me photography never challenged him—too mechanical.
"Long ago, I pointed to the lens and said the trouble was *here!*"
Maybe so, Maestro . . . but then again—maybe not.
Anyway, here is your friend Maurice Chevalier, and Paris—*my way!*

Place de la Concorde

Le Pont Neuf
on the Seine

Arc de Triomphe

Les Invalides,
Napoleon's Tomb . . .

Tour Eiffel

Cathédrale
Notre-Dame

Le Lido . . .

*Venus
de
Milo*

Maria

Maria . . . daughter of a cowboy named Cooper,
radiates an aura of times long lost;
of wisps of lace dropped from turret windows to Crusader knights . . .
of the wide-eyed gaze that challenged the best of men from
Botticelli to Gainsborough to Goya.
For from her bower
of Côte d'Azur blossoms there effuses a simple truth—
here is the flame that is woman, the most elusive subject of all.

McCALL CORPORATION
230 Park Avenue, New York, N.Y.

Herbert R. Mayes
    President

Mr. David Douglas Duncan   November 7, 1963
Plaza Hotel
5th Avenue & 59th Street
New York, New York

Dear David:

Yesterday some of my associates here were going over with me, again, the pictures that
you took of Paris and I think I ought to be on record, also again, as saying that they are
purely fantastic. To me they represent a new dimension in photography and I couldn't
be more pleased than to have them in the magazine. Though several of my people feel
that the agreed on price of $50,000 is on the spectacular side, I've never been one to
quibble about price when convinced that full value has been received.

We've received full value.

                                                                 Sincerely,
                                                                 Herb

One autumn morning, I received this letter which, in a single area alone, seemed to justify
all that I once had hoped "photo-journalism" might provide for me as a way of life. It also
made me wish that my old friend Harry Cooling, Sunday editor of the *Baltimore Sun*, might
see it for perhaps it would help him to recall those other days—a quarter-century before—
when he had strained his budget to buy my work at three dollars a print, for the best I had.
It might not have been worth more, of course, but he would have been glad to have made
me think so, of this, I am sure: Cooling, Thompson, Mayes—they represent a breed apart.

That's just the way it was,
until now . . .

Castellaras,   *Easter Sunday,*
Mouans-Sartoux,   *10 April, 1966*
France

"With Regret"

Mrs. John F. Kennedy
The White House
Washington, D.C.

Palais Miramar,
Cannes, France.
4 February, 1962

Dear Mrs. Kennedy:

Judging by the letters and cables that have caught up with me here, it would seem that the entire publishing world hopes to look over your shoulder when you finish decorating your home. For good reason—it'll be a truly great subject, so should make a magnificent book. My own interest in it is still intense. I have thought about little else since you so graciously escorted me through some of the most beautiful rooms. The theme, as I see it, would be to tie the rooms to the great Americans who lived in them and who left symbols of themselves, and their tastes, in the White House. But this is not enough—at least for a book such as I envision. I'd like to seek out key words from the most important utterances made by these same men while they were President. Their words would fill-in a bit more of their character, and would give the illustrations a deeper significance. It seems to me that each President's words should constitute the bulk of the text. There should be an appendix of historical data regarding each illustration, much as I used in *The Kremlin*—text which would have destroyed the picture subject if played next to the illustration. I feel that you should write an Introduction. After all, the White House is now your home. It is you who have launched the drive to make it a place of national beauty, as well as giving to it a far deeper sense of shrine to most Americans. The Introduction should be supported by a color chapter of family photographs such as I employed in presenting Picasso in his home. Then the pictures of the White House will stand alone, exactly as Picasso's paintings stood alone.

Now, we come to an entirely different side of the project: public domain. To me, this book belongs to all Americans, as does the White House itself. Naturally, the work should never be offered as charity. However, it seems to me that there should be no profit involved. Therefore, I'd like to make a suggestion . . . an offer. I will shoot, write, design and produce *The White House* as a public service, on a "no-profit" basis. Since seeing you I have been consulting with my friends in Switzerland, with whom I made both *The Kremlin* and *Picasso's Picassos*. They also, both printer Ami Guichard, of Lausanne, and etcher Jan Schwitter, of Basel, will offer their services on a "no-profit" basis, as a gesture of friendship for the American people. This leaves only the question of finding an American publisher-distributor who, also, will contribute all profits to the White House Historical Fund (if there isn't one there will be) for adding to and paying for new works, and extra care in the future. Possibly some sort of control committee could be organized among the First Ladies (Roosevelt-Truman-Eisenhower) with you as Chairwoman. Anyway, by removing the normal profits as each stage of the book it can be sold to readers with average incomes, and still be a terrific color production. All color! I'll be in the States in a couple of weeks so hope to call and get the word regarding your reaction to the project. Wish your husband Good Luck.

Saludos,
David Douglas Duncan

Mrs. John F. Kennedy
The White House
Washington, D.C.

Palais Miramar,
Cannes, France.
24 February, 1962

Dear Mrs. Kennedy:

Apparently your mail goes astray, too! While in Rome, this last week, I received a couple of frantic cables from Cass Canfield of Harper & Brothers, informing me that you never received the original of the letter enclosed, regarding the White House book. Not having a carbon copy in Rome, I hopped a plane back here this afternoon to get one for you—and to bring Picasso some new fangled lights so that he can work better at night.

The original letter still states my feelings fairly clearly. However, since writing it, I have read reviews of your White House TV tour. Your narrative brought the house to life. This is what the book *must* have . . . some great, deeply human people have lived in that house—so why not project your TV narrative right into the design of the book. Naturally, when the time finally comes to edit the overall package—pictures, layout, text—you will have had a hundred new ideas about what you might want to say. Regardless, it would be a dreadful waste to ignore what you already have given to the White House story. So, I'd like to suggest that we do it together, and still bring in key quotes from those speeches that I refer to in my first letter. Because I shall be near, I shall try to call when you pass through Rome, next week, both to welcome you to Italy and to get the word regarding the book project. Incidently, during your tour of India and Pakistan, I understand NBC's Gene Jones will be shooting a TV movie. He's lucky to have drawn the assignment, and he must be delighted for I know that he was praying it would work out. Gene's an old friend from the worst of the Korean War—where he was terribly wounded—and one of the great talents in TV today. So, you're lucky, too, that he will be directing the camera units . . . his film will be *the* most beautiful yet made of you, I assure you, even before he starts. Give him my regards—and make him jump!

You and the President will be interested, I think, to know Picasso's reaction to Colonel Glenn's space flight. The night of the cancelled flight, after Glenn had been cooped up in the capsule for five hours, then released, someone had taken a photo of that haggard face, with its sunken eyes turned into the sky. The shot was carried on French TV. Picasso turned to me and said, "There's a man—just like St. Francis!" The night of the orbit Picasso phoned me in Rome. I've rarely heard him more jubilant . . ." I'm as proud of him as if he were my brother." Coming from a man who was of military age during the Spanish-American War, and who should be an atheist if he *really* is a communist, these two expressions of feelings are most revealing . . . they portray the Pablo Picasso whom I know so well.

Have a marvelous Eastern trip. Come home.

Saludos,
David Douglas Duncan

BASIC POLICY GUIDANCE FOR THE WHITE HOUSE BOOK BY
DAVID DOUGLAS DUNCAN

1) David Douglas Duncan will be given access to the White House during the years 1962 and 1963 for any period of time he deems necessary to obtain necessary photographs.

2) The book to be published will be a completely non-profit venture.

    a) Mr. Duncan will be entitled to recover expenses plus a sum to compensate for the time involved in preparing the book at a figure to be agreed to between Mr. Duncan and the White House.

    b) The book will be distributed at no profit; the distributor will be allowed to collect sums of money of remuneration for the cost of advertising, promotion, book selling expenses and certain agreed to office expenses in connection with the distribution of the book. The choice of the distributor will be made by Mr. Duncan but the distributor must agree to meet the terms of this agreement. The publisher and the author will further agree that all publicity and promotional material in the sale of the book will require prior approval of the White House.

    c) Printers of the book will work at no profit. They will be reimbursed for printing expenses, cost of engraving, and salaries and incidental expenses of those involved in the production of the book.

    d) Any sums over and above those especially enumerated above will be turned over to the White House Historical Association as a contribution toward furthering the historical work of the White House.

3) While the rights to the photographs remain in the possession of Mr. Duncan he agrees that any other project evolving from the production of this book, such as subsequent

books, magazine articles, television, radio and movie projects, will be subject to separate discussion and subject to prior approval of the White House except as outlined in paragraph 7.

4) Mr. Duncan and no one else connected with the production of the book is to offer for sale or to write and/or broadcast information obtained during the writing of the book which is not directly concerned with or contained in the book.

5) The concept of production and execution of the book will be in the hands of Mr. Duncan and not subject to review. Mr. Duncan will, however, submit all written copy to be carried in the book for clearance by the White House. The White House will have the right to object to the use of any particular photo(s) but Mr. Duncan will reserve the right to make the final judgement.

6) During the time Mr. Duncan is working on this book the White House will not cooperate on any similar venture through the publication date. Mr. Duncan agrees, however, to bring the book out prior to September 1st, 1964.

7) The transparencies will remain the property of Mr. Duncan but future use of the transparancies will be governed by paragraph 3 above. The restrictions of paragraph 3 will become non-operative on January 20th, 1969.

8) The contents of this agreement or any parts of this agreement shall not be released to the press without prior approval of the White House.

Pierre Salinger
(for the White House)

David Douglas Duncan
April 3, 1962

Mrs. John F. Kennedy   Hotel Lafayette
The White House   Washington, D.C.
Washington, D.C.   11 December, 1962

Dear Mrs. Kennedy:

Yesterday, as I am sure you now know, I came to the reluctant decision to abandon our project for the White House book, a decision arrived at after the most careful weighing of all factors involved in making the book. It was a personally painful way of killing the dream of what I had hoped our book would be, for I have done little else but think of its construction and execution since we first met, just over a year ago. Since I am sure that you shared many of my hopes of creating something truly beautiful, a book worthy of all the work and affection which you and your committee have lavished upon the White House, I should like to explain to you exactly why I have deserted you in what you possibly may feel is midstream.

The obstacle is the National Geographic produced "guidebook". The problem it raises is purely economic. Let me explain: On the credit page of the guidebook one reads "Photography and production by the National Geographic Society as a public service." This means—and is a fact—that the guidebook was produced at *no cost* to the White House Historical Association. It means that all photographic, editorial, etching and proofing costs were absorbed by the National Geographic Society. This is marvelous for the White House Historical Association, which gets the book for nothing, for the public, who get the book at an incredibly low price, and vital to the very structure of the National Geographic Society for it helps to preserve its image as a public service institution. Of course, the price and the actual guidebook are unrelated; on the open market (had it been produced even on a "no-profit" basis) it would have been necessary to sell it for somewhere around $12.50, for the color alone pushes it into the deluxe field. Now, I have been told, there are plans to offer it in a hard-cover edition for only a slightly increased price, and also to keep it updated with new color as other rooms are redecorated. All of these plans are exciting and worthwhile, and I certainly agree that they should be supported. But, in the overall, they make my position, as producer of another book in color, both difficult and hazardous, for my book must pay its own way, since neither Harper and Brothers nor I can do it as a public service.

When I returned to Washington this time, I brought a contract signed by Harpers whereby they were obligated to take 30,000 books, to be sold at $25 a copy. These books

472

were to contain at least 100 full pages of color, the size of the book to be based upon my *Picasso's Picassos*. Because of our earlier books, and their success in the market, Harpers left everything else to me; format, design, schedule. By signing a contract with me, with every clause wide open, they made me responsible for something approaching one-quarter million dollars of their capital.

Had Harpers and I made our book it would have carried the notice that it was done on a "non-profit" basis, meaning that we still would have deducted from the book's income our overhead costs, both as publishers and producer. It would have been larger than the page format of the guidebook, yet the *number* of color pages would have been about equal to the guidebook. I am convinced that few potential customers would have stopped to weigh the difference between "public service" and "non-profit". They would have been struck by the difference in prices—one twenty-five times higher than the other—and would have howled bloody murder. To sell 30,000 deluxe books in the United States is not easy. The books *had* to sell before Harpers or I got back basic costs. With all of the subject material already photographed in color, by professionals, I could have brought only my own point of view to the subject. It would have been far more dramatic and passionate than that of the guidebook, of course, yet the pictures would have been of subjects now well known. *The Kremlin* was the first-ever book of the treasures by a Westerner, and the first by anyone in color. In *Picasso's Picassos* I revealed the artist's personal collection, with the man himself at my shoulder guiding me through them. Both books were considered successes, and each sold fewer copies in the U.S. than our estimated break-even figure for our White House book. Thus, with regret, my decision to reconsider the project was made after I saw that the guidebook had become a far handsomer work than anyone earlier imagined; because it will also be in hard-cover; and because I feel deeply responsible in protecting Harpers from the economic consequences of a personal decision regarding a venture which I would have undertaken—just to prove it had merit and beauty—if I could have done it alone.

I hope you will understand.

David Douglas Duncan

Miss Maria Cooper
700 Park Avenue
New York, New York
U.S.A.

Castellaras
Mouans-Sartoux,
France.
3 December, 1963

Maria—

Months pass, the seasons run almost full cycle and letters go unwritten—it will be like this, or worse, for the next two years.

These last several months have been spent mostly in the 300-SL pounding around Switzerland, Germany and Holland, contacting printers who will perhaps be the ones I shall work with when I go into production on the new book. It will be twice the size—in pictures and content—of either *The Kremlin* or *Picasso's Picassos*. Just slam-bang adventure with a camera. At the International Book Fair in Frankfurt, in October, with nothing more than an outline of the material and a blank dummy to show for approximate bulk, enough interest was aroused among the various "foreign" language publishers for them to give verbal orders for 60,000 books. Naturally, the joker is that word "verbal", yet at this stage it does indicate massive interest in the effort. With luck, and work, I'll have the pictures edited and text written by this time next year, then shall actually print the book during the spring of '65. It will be one that you will like, I think . . . one that your Dad would have agreed with me as being worth my spending three years in the doing. Its title you know already, for I'm sure I tried it out on you very early, years ago—
Yankee Nomad.

Today, it seems like a stranger's life . . .

On the 25th of November, '62, after another leisurely walk through the White House, the sound of children's songs came through a nearby door, which I opened. John John was having his second birthday party, surrounded by his screeching pals and Caroline's quieter friends. A three-piece Marine Corps band had been called to duty, for which they certainly must have been kidded later. From among the horde, Mrs. Kennedy looked up and called a casual welcome. I pointed to the burnished light slanting into the room from a setting, late autumn sun which illuminated the brooding profile of a massive copy of Borglum's head of Abraham Lincoln—looking down upon the party—a year to the day before I stood, at home here in France, listening to the sound of Taps over Arlington's rolling hillsides, and to an old friend, Bill Downes of CBS, choke up and lose his voice—a man with whom I came off the Hungnam beach of North Korea, in 1950.

Dave

474

The Editor
The New York Times
New York, New York
USA

Castellaras,
Mouans-Sartoux,
France.
5 December, 1963

Sir:

Now, nearly two weeks after President Kennedy's assassination, the work of the world resumes, other nations' leaders have returned to their capitols, our new President has moved effectively into command in Washington—and global homage and tributes have emblazoned the name and memory of John Fitzgerald Kennedy. But, something else remains to be done—the United States of America's formal acknowledgement of the incredible role filled by Jacqueline Kennedy during the shooting. Let there be no misunderstanding. She, as much as any man who ever wore a uniform and faced enemy fire during wartime, was representing every other American in a field of combat. However, unlike a man during warfare—for which he has been trained and conditioned—there was one thing about Jacqueline Kennedy that made her conduct unique and even more heroic. Within the fraction of the second that the assassin's first bullet was fired and had struck the President, Jacqueline Kennedy was thrown from joyous civilian life into the face of point-blank enemy fire. She never wavered. She sought no protection within the bulletproof body of the Presidential limousine . . . she ignored it. She attempted to shield and comfort the President of the United States, who happened to be her husband. She climbed out over the rear of the car to drag in a Secret Service agent, exposing herself to even more fire from the hidden gunman, then crawled back to cover the stricken President with her own body—all within seconds. She never stampeded. There, is an honest-to-God heroine for all of us!

Only one means is available for every American to express the country's respect for what she did on November 22, 1963, which was unprecedented in our nation's history. Our salute to her heroism must be equally unprecedented. Jacqueline Kennedy should be awarded the Congressional Medal of Honor. It is the least, though the most, that we can do. Unlike other awards of the Medal of Honor made during wartime, when the accompanying citations are based upon reports of a few eye witnesses who were present during the action, Jacqueline Kennedy's heroism has been documented in the film of Mr. Abraham Zapruder, for us all to see. Finally, Jacqueline Kennedy's citation for "valor" and "courage above and beyond the call of duty" can be affirmed and dignified by the signature of the highest authority in the land, the President of the United States. He was there.

Respectfully,
David Douglas Duncan
Lt. Col., USMCR (Ret.)

475

Postscript

Yankee Nomad was conceived in the summer of 1951, which probably rivals the incubation period of the great dinosaur, *Brachiosaurus.* The world around us all was *Nomad's* mother. There are three godfathers: an almost-rabbi turned publisher, in New York (Arthur A. Cohen, of Holt, Rinehart and Winston, who switched from theology to editing, and who bought *Nomad* within two hours of seeing its dummy—it had been rejected as impractical by nearly every other major publisher in America); an almost-Guardsman turned book binder, in The Hague (Herman Friedhoff, of Van Rijmenam, who fought with Dutch underground forces during the war, escaped to England where he continued until the end, then came home to make books and greet me for eight years at the Frankfurt, Germany, International Book Fair with introductions to everyone he knew in his specialized craft) one of them an almost-Santa Claus turned printer, in Haarlem, William Bitter, of Joh. Enschedé en Zonen. This ruddy, white-haired, blue-eyed Dutchman saved *Nomad* when it was sinking, as a book project, for the third and last time. He offered to print the first American edition at a six thousand dollar *loss* for Enschedé, because he was convinced *Nomad* could be produced within the minimum cost factors I had to guarantee, while still keeping quality as high as his press masters could deliver. The English language edition would then give me the foundation from which I could solicit and build an international, multi-language first printing of fifty thousand copies—at which point Enschedé would recoup its loss and the project would become practicable. Now, *Nomad* is a fact. Now that it is over—where to start in telling the background story of finally trapping it between Herman Friedhoff's binding, part of which he gave me in a final effort to help deliver the baby within my production budget—and on time.

An earlier book, *This Is War!*, appeared in the summer of '51 on the first anniversary of the Korean conflict. It attempted to tell, in photo-narrative form, something of the ordeal suffered by infantrymen in battle. It also led to the dream of reassembling every photograph taken in my life, which could then be edited into a book-size, cycloramic tale of our times—of my time, anyway, which has spanned the mid-twentieth century generation . . . wild, rough, wonderful years.

There were many interruptions—five more years as a *Life* photographer; two books on Pablo Picasso; one on the Kremlin treasures; three cancelled contracts when my publishers decided I was going too far, this time, in proposing the most ambitious and costly adventure book ever made, a photographic story that would have to be priced at the level of an "art" book. There was the entire year spent tracking down, then getting again into my possession all of my old negatives and color films. For the first time in their publishing history, the editors of *Life* magazine returned to one of their photographers every picture taken while he was on staff. Editorial Chairman, Henry Luce; Chairman of the Executive Committee, Roy Larsen; President, Jim Linen; Chairman of the Board, Andy Heiskell; Publisher, Jerry

476

Hardy; Editor, Ed Thompson; Managing Editor, George Hunt and Lawyer, Jack Dowd—I thank all of you, for those years with you are the heart of my story.

Mr. and Mrs. Michael Lerner simply tossed me the keys to their Fifth Avenue penthouse nature-museum library, returning all of the thousands of negatives I made while on Lerner-American Museum of Natural History expeditions off the west coast of South America. Dr. Melville Bell Grosvenor, President and Editor of the *National Geographic* magazine sent back *pounds* of our pre-war and wartime correspondence—every word—and all of my earlier color work, still safely filed in their photographic vaults. Roger Wolin, press director of Pan American Airways' Latin American Division, discovered my "lost" West Indies negatives in an unnumbered box; they were on the next plane coming my way. Pan Am's Dick Barkle, in New York, made special arrangements—when I was flying back to France with all of the *Life* films—for my almost unliftable suitcases to be strapped to the floor in mid-plane, so that I could make an attempt to grab them and hoist them into a life raft, in case the plane went down.

Everyone had said it would be "impossible" to get negatives back from the Marine Corps. They don't know the Marines—when the request comes from an old Marine. A long-unseen, football-playing high school buddy, Brigidier General Bill Jones, explained my search to another Marine, General Wallace M. Greene, Jr., Commandant of the United States Marine Corps. The guys and girls in the Headquarters' photo-lab ripped the place apart for two days—and I flew back to Europe with every wartime shot in a box under my feet. How many pictures have been edited for *Nomad*? Who knows! There are ten thousand on just the Kremlin—and probably thirty thousand of Picasso. But let's guess . . . one-half million.

That search covers only photographs. Background captions, press files and earlier articles are something else. Stacked around me on three great French farm tables—one is ten feet long and a yard wide—is all of the important mail I ever received in my life, every Marine Corps order, flight logs of every plane trip (date, type of aircraft, times of takeoff and landing at each field), all telegrams and cables, piles of expired passports (some so filled with extra pages they are telephone-book thick—New York telephone book) . . . everything is here that a human packrat could save from a lifetime of wandering everywhere, that would later provide the vehicle for journeying again over every trail when the day came to pause for a moment, before starting anew on different ground. There is also the legacy of my father. When we lost him, I found that he had saved and chronologically filed every letter I had sent home since my first camping trip through the American west, after graduating from high school. They really aren't letters, but stories, sharing as best I could the adventure and romance found along the way with a man who was, at heart, the greatest wanderer of all—but his family trapped him before he could start. These envelopes are filled with my best research, written under the impact of those now-fading times.

There was a year when *Nomad* was basically text, with only a handful of illustrations. That manuscript, half-finished, totalled nearly two hundred thousand words. I left it with a publisher while tracking final negatives of early stories, then called again at his office. He was speechless—and *slate gray*. His housekeeper had just burned the entire manuscript. It had been left among the New York Sunday papers—which still leaves me wondering how anyone could have carried that armload to the incinerator. It was the best thing that ever happened to *Nomad*! I started again—this time as it should have been from the beginning— as a photo-narrative, like *This Is War*! . . . but on a wider screen.

Actual production of *Nomad* began in 1960 while I was still working on *Picasso's Picassos* at his villa *La Californie* in Cannes, just over the hill, here on the French Riviera. I needed a base near an international airport (Nice: twenty minutes); printers and binders (Holland: two hours); special photo-paper supplier (Paris: one hour); isolation, at the same time (Maritime Alps, olive groves, pine woods, Mediterranean, and the golden mimosa of Grasse *parfumeurs* are spread for hundreds of square kilometers beyond my studio window). I built a house in which to produce *Nomad*. There may have been another way—but this has worked. With these pages, all text will be finished. Tomorrow is my final deadline.

One technical aspect of making this book is unique among all illustrated books of which I have ever heard, either those published by my photographer-colleagues, or manufactured anywhere. Every enlargement in *Nomad* was developed in an automatic "rapid processor". I first saw the device in Cologne, Germany, at the International Foto-Kina of 1963. I recognized it as the answer to enlarging and developing problems awaiting me when I started into darkroom production of the hundreds of monochrome illustrations for *Nomad*; that many more negatives were printed, then discarded.

The machine is simple, consisting of two trays of chemicals (one an activator, the other a stabilizer) into which are fitted pressure rollers, all turned by a motor operating at a never-varying speed. I convinced the manufacturers, Fotorite of Chicago, that I would steal their display model if they didn't sell it to me. They helped squeeze it into the back of my old black Mercedes 300-SL. Even they had never heard of anyone attempting to process, with their machine, enlargements of the size and quality I required. Yet with it, I was freed of developer, hypo and washing trays in my tiny (six-by-eight feet) darkroom, which also holds an oversize Omega Variable-D enlarger, wash basin and safelight—there is space for nothing more. With this combination, I was able to print, develop and layout every page of *Nomad* without leaving the darkroom. Many layouts were altered, printed, developed and fitted into the book within minutes after seeing what I felt was a better idea evolve while changing negatives in the Omega.

All enlargements were printed on a revolutionary and, I believe, beautiful paper made by Mimosa of Kiel, West Germany—it being perfected as the companion for rapid processing machines. The paper contains developing agents as integral elements in its emulsion; the first bath in the rapid processor only activates them. The stabilizer bath does just that—the

478

image will not fade for years. If one desires a permanently "fixed" print, it is only a matter of running it through conventional hypo, wash and dryer. Dr. Werner Berthold, Mimosa's chief of research at Kiel, briefed me on their paper's special characteristics, the basic one of which is fabulous.

Unlike conventional photographic projection papers, which take about an hour from initial exposure under the enlarger (then through developer, fix, hypo, wash and dryer) to arrive at a workable print, Mimosa Two Bath Rapid Process paper gives me an eighty-five percent dry, fully developed and stabilized print—in thirteen seconds! I could not have hit deadlines for *Nomad* without it.

As is true of so many great things, there is one shortcoming with rapid processors—and it is enormous. There is no possible way to dominate the print in the activator, either to drag the developing time or to shorten it, if one sees a good print coming up too fast that could have been saved if thrown into the fixative bath. There, also, is no way to control local areas of the print during development, although shadows can be opened with a reducing solution later. The rapid processor is king for those thirteen seconds your masterpiece is rolling around through its innards. One must be—or soon become—a master print dodger, for that is your only real control. Even so, if aiming at uniform, photo-etchers' quality, the wastage in lost prints can be considerable. There are other hazards, unknown in conventional darkrooms. No water should fall upon a print—it will spot. The rapid processor must be *absolutely* level and the solution trays kept brimming, otherwise the rollers will produce streaks. Few rapid processors other than Fotorite's are built sturdily enough or big enough for steady work handling double-weight enlargements wider than fourteen inches, without showing blemishes. For the moment, I feel, Mimosa's paper is superior to most available rapid processors, yet the day will soon come when they balance. However even now, once you learn the rules, the rapid processor is a blessing—almost miraculous—and it opens new horizons in the darkroom to photographers like myself who do everything alone.

The cameras represented in *Nomad* include just about all of them, from that first Bakelite, thirty-nine cent Univex given to me by my sister, to the "bazooka" with which I photographed Paris and Picasso, and which is worth a couple of thousand dollars—at the source. Its elements were made for me by Fritz Joachim Otto's optical engineers, at Astro-Gesellschaft Bielicke & Co., in West Berlin. Other cameras have been Leicas, Speed Graphics and Graphlex-Ds, used during the Lerner-American Museum of Natural History expeditions to Chile and Peru; Rolleiflexes, Super Ikonta-Bs and Leicas, carried while a Marine in Pacific Oceania during World War II; Linhofs and Meridians, when on assignments like those in the Saudi Arabian oilfields during the *Life* magazine years; then —Korea, and Nikon lenses made by Masao Nagaoka's and Hiroshi Shirahama's men at Nippon Kogaku, in Tokyo. When Horace Bristol and I switched to Nikons, in the spring of 1950, we had no idea it was marking the watershed of post-war miniature photography. Today, of course, optical products of Nippon Kogaku have revolutionized 35 mm photography—ultra-high speed lenses, faster wide angle lenses, fish-eye lenses, zoom lenses and probably others, now, with which I am unfamiliar, having been so long out of circulation while producing *Nomad*.

Ludwig Leitz, of Ernst Leitz, at Wetzlar, made my double-winder Leica M3Ds, which I still consider the best field camera in the world and the camera I would use again, were I to return to places like Viet-Nam—leaving the single lens reflexes at home. But, since all stories are not of violence—where two Leica M3Ds fitted with 28mm and 50 mm Nikons are impossible to beat—we then come to the Nikon-F and, finally, for me at least, to my "bazooka". It is a flared barrel, the narrowest end of which fits over the nose of a Nikon-F, both mounted in tandem on an aluminum track-bracket. Interchangeable, multi-faceted prisms sleeve into the barrel; exotic, four-inch wide lenses lock onto the barrel's flared snout; Nikon lenses zoom and double-action gears rotate prisms and lenses simultaneously clockwise and counter-clockwise—you get the idea . . . it's a seventeen-ring circus, with only aerialists performing in those rings. And one helluva lot of fun! It also gives me a medium with which to fragment a subject, then reassemble the whole, or a portion of its parts, into an entirely new interpretation of that subject or mixture of subjects—chosen, re-designed and branded by *me*. The result is not a montage, but a single transparency. And I still have my Leica M3Ds with Nikons . . . so when *Nomad* is finally off the presses I'll be ready for anything.

DDD
11 April 1966

Here it is . . . the final page.
There were months, while trying to meet deadlines
during this final year of producing Nomad,
when average work days climbed
from sixteen to eighteen hours, and stayed there;
times when this page seemed
a hopeless target . . .
which it would have been,
without my wife Sheila.

Thank you, Zeke.